AF686221

Personal Finance Bundle

Dividend Investing During Inflation

How to Set-Up a World-Class Dividend Portfolio

Disclaimer

While the author has taken the utmost effort to ensure the accuracy of the written content, all readers are advised to follow the information mentioned herein at their own risk. The author cannot be held responsible for any personal or commercial damage caused by the information. All readers are encouraged to seek professional advice when needed.

Investing is a risk, and you can lose money during times of high market volatility or bad individual company performance. No investment is guaranteed to make you money. And the best investments are generally personalized based on your individual cash flow and net worth. Ensure you consult a qualified financial advisor to ensure that you are adequately diversified and pick the investments that work for you.

Table of Contents

Book 1:

Book 3:

Introduction

“Do you know the only thing that gives me pleasure? It's to see my dividends coming in.”

This is amazing proverb, and guess who said this? Someone just as great... John D. Rockefeller.

Dividend investing has been an overlooked term in an age of booming tech startups, mega FAANG overreach and cryptos exploding to the moon.

Have you heard anyone say the following? **Dividends are booring man. I’m going to the moon. Have fun staying poor.**

Well, Dividend Investing is not for everyone. It’s for those with patience. It’s for those who love passive income. Dividend investing is one of the simplest investment strategies to understand and is a great way for beginners to start investing. It is a low-risk way of investing, ideal for risk-averse investors. This investment strategy focuses on maximizing the benefits of dividends, whether they are reinvested or used otherwise.

So why dividend stocks during inflation? Investing during inflation is a treacherous pursuit. People, families, small business, large business, everything and everyone is fighting against rising expenses. At the same time, everyone is reducing their spending. Businesses are losing revenue. People are getting unemployed. Margins getting crushed.

There's one thing that can help people stay above ground in such a situation. **Income!!!**

Income from your job, income from investments, royalty income, business income.

Income can be increased with increase in inflation.

Income that keeps pace with inflation is like oxygen on the moon. It needs to be treasured, studied and replicated.

Dividend income is one such income. It is one of the simplest forms of income that you control, and that can increase with inflation. If you follow the advice in this book, and buy the right stocks at the right time, it is one way to protect yourself.

The best protection is a job whose income increases with inflation. The second best is dividend income.

It's like the shield that will protect you and your family while the inflation dragon is breathing down on you.

Once the inflation dragon runs out of fire and collapses, you can resume your journey to stronger financial times.

Bitcoin, Google, Amazon stock..... There's a lot of hype there, but they pay no dividend. The bigger they are, the harder they can fall during an inflationary collapse.

The tortoise will beat the hair.

Get ready to jump on the dividend tortoise.

This book contains an introduction to inflation investing and then nine chapters after that. Each chapter is dedicated to a significant aspect of dividend investing, with detailed descriptions and examples. At the end of each chapter is a quiz that acts as a summary of the chapter. The questions are designed to check if you understood the concepts in the chapter. If you are able to answer all the questions in the chapter, then you have a strong understanding of the concept and are able to move ahead.

What is Inflation?

So, what is inflation?

Inflation is when you paid $15 for a $10 haircut you used to get for $5 when you had hair. This hilarious quote, by former baseball star Sam Ewing, summarizes inflation better than the Harvard economists who always fail to predict inflation.

The inflation crisis of 2021-2022 is similar to a lot of previous inflation crises that have plagued the world. It starts with excessive government printing of money in response to an external crisis like a war, famine or pandemic. Or maybe sometimes just a lazy unproductive population.

Inflation is defined as the general rise in the prices of goods and services in an economy. The inflation rate is, therefore, the rate at which that change happens. When inflation goes up, it implies that whatever you are buying has become more expensive. This reduces the buyer's purchasing power, and they can buy less. This is a huge problem for many investors, and many are left wondering how to fight this. Here's how you can go about it.

You must fight inflation head-on if you intend to safeguard your long-term investments. Inflation is a long-term problem, and it will always be there.

On the other hand, inflation is an opportunity. There are ways to take advantage of inflation to benefit from inflation.

While detailed methods to fight inflation are beyond the scope of this book, we will mention some of these principles in this chapter.

There is nothing better than an investment strategy that helps make inflation work for you. The inflation mechanism that increases the prices of goods and services is the same mechanism through which company profits increase. There is a hidden advantage to inflation proofed investing. This is the advantage of pricing power. Most world-class companies have pricing power which allows them to sell more products to more people at high prices. If certain companies were to hike their prices the same way, they would witness a great decline in sales because they do not have the same pricing power.

The demand for the goods and services of companies with pricing power does not decline with increases in prices. People will not be prompted to let go of their favorite product because of a slight increase in price. Great businesses that have durable competitive advantages like intellectual property and brand recognition have pricing power. The durability of the advantages that these companies have make dividend investing a long-term solution for inflation. A rising tide lifts all boats. Inflation-proof investments are like a rising tide on which all lifeboats float, but for you to survive, you must be on a lifeboat.

The lifeboat in this book is dividend investing. Other strategies you can use involve investing in previous metals, commodities, currency diversification, real estate with fixed long-term debt, investing in high cash flow businesses, REITS etc.

If you're interested in a book focused on a broader approach to inflation investing, you can check out my book on Inflation Investing here.

https://www.amazon.com/gp/product/B08WJZCTPV/

But now, let's get back to Dividend Investing....

Pros/Cons of Dividend Stocks During Inflation

Dividend investing has its fair share of advantages and disadvantages. It's best to have a strong understanding of both, before you dive in.

Advantages

- Dividend investing makes it possible to invest passive income and to increase share ownership. The reinvestment of funds means that each time there is reinvestment, the number of shares held also increases. If paid out in cash, the dividends can also be collected as supplementary income.
- Dividend investing helps you gain capital without using your savings or getting into debt. You can grow your portfolio without having to worry about borrowing from brokers whose rates are very high. You also do not need to make any out-of-pocket expenses to buy shares to increase your holdings. The system is self-propagating.

- Your portfolio is less subject to volatility and is very stable. Most people invest in dividend-paying companies for the long term. So, they are unlikely to sell into volatility, like growth stocks. You will have less sleepless nights worrying about your portfolio. Low volatility also directly translates to lower risk.

- Stockowners are rewarded for their long-term holdings because dividend investing holds the prospect of rising dividends.

- Dividend investors pay fewer taxes in comparison to investors who engage in frequent trading. Dividend payments are taxed as regular income in most countries instead of capital gains. In certain countries, tax free dividends are common.

- Dividend investments are a good hedge against inflation because they are very stable. Inflation can drive the stock market down, but dividend investments, in most cases, stand the test of time (Faulkenberry, 2018).

- High-yield dividend investors have the advantage of profiting from their investments in bear markets. If the dividends payouts are not cut, they continue to receive income.

Disadvantages

- Dividend stocks have lower growth potential. Their level of appreciation is, therefore, lower than that of inflation. They then can get engulfed by the prices soaring higher at a faster rate.
- Dividend investing requires you to set aside some of the money you receive to pay taxes. These investments are taxed at the long capital gains rate. In the case that you hold your stocks in an account that is tax-deferred, you will not have to pay taxes in the year the dividends are received.
- A long-time horizon is required for a dividend investing strategy. It is not ideal for investors who start investing later in life. They may outlive their investments and will not be able to maximize their returns.
- When you sell a dividend investing stock, you cut off the income that you were receiving from that stock.

Historically, dividends of high-quality companies have been known to outgrow inflation, and investors that hold them have always survived periods of high inflation. Because of their ability to increase when price levels are increasing, dividends are an excellent protection against inflation, especially in the long run. For instance, if you hold 2,000 shares of a certain company for $2 a share, which pays an annual dividend of $0.05 per share, you are entitled to collect **$100** in dividend income per annum. If, in the following year, there is 3% inflation, the company increases dividend to $0.1. So, the person receives a dividend of **$200**. The growth in dividends that comes with the right companies helps investors to outpace inflation.

As the years have gone by, the shares of companies that initiate and grow their dividends have done better than the shares of companies that have kept their dividend the same or have not paid dividends at all. **Dividend growth stocks are less sensitive to rising rates as compared to other instruments like bonds.** Looking at history proves that in the United States, dividends have done well during periods of high inflation and even during stagflation. During the key inflation periods of 1940s and the 1970s, there was dividend income growth of over 10%. This shows that dividends are, indeed, a hedge against inflation.

Chapter Quiz/Summary

1. What are a few good investments that can carry you through inflation?
2. Company profits always go down during inflation (True/False)
3. Inflation means that your salary will definitely go up. (True/False)
4. What is the most important way to fight inflation?
5. Company X is at $2 per share. It pays an annual dividend of $0.1. If you own 100 shares, what is your annual dividend income from company X?
6. Company Y is at $20 per share. It pays an annual dividend of $2. If you own 1000 shares, what is your annual dividend income from company Y?

Answers...

1. Gold, Commodities, Real Estate, REITs etc
2. False.
3. False
4. Increased Income
5. $2000 per year

What is Dividend Investing?

Dividend investing is a style of investing where you invest in companies for the main purpose of receiving a passive source of income. You may receive growth in the asset value as well, but the main investing goal is income. This is one of the best ways to invest, considering that most companies that pay dividends are fully grown and very stable. This provides some form of assurance to the investor that the investments will do well. Dividend investing does not usually yield disposable income quickly. In most cases, it requires a long-time horizon for it to fully play out. In the early years of the investment, the dividends received are usually reinvested to compound the income.

Dividend investing is sometimes considered boring by some people. This is because the investment is for slow and steady payments from companies. Steady returns are not boring if you are the investor who understands the essence of long-term investing. Most present-day investors are interested in high yields, unlike the earlier generations of investors who were interested in dividend investing. When investors buy shares in companies, they are paid dividends at the end of a defined period. This may be quarterly, annually, and in some cases, monthly.

What Are Dividends?

Publicly traded companies that generate cash flow and net profit have four ways to deploy the cash. They can invest the money back in the company in the form of research and development. Secondly, they can save the money for a rainy day. They can also buy back shares of the company to support the share price. This is a common American practice known as a stock buyback. And finally, they can pay the money back to shareholders. This payback is known as a dividend. To simplify the understanding of dividends, they can be viewed more like the interest that is earned for keeping money in savings accounts.

The dividend is the amount paid by the company to a shareholder; while the dividend yield is the % yield of the share price paid to the shareholder.

Dividend Yield = (Dividend/Price per share) X 100

The Dividend yield is an indication of your return on investment. For example, if the dividend yield is 5% per year; and you invest $1000; you get $50 per year.

Let's take another example.

For example, if you hold a share whose value is $50, a 5% annual yield will see you earning $2.50 per year per share. The total dividend payout depends on the number and types of shares that you hold.

How Often Are Dividends Paid?

Every company pays dividends at different intervals.

Company dividends are either paid annually (once a year), semi-annually (once every 6 months) or quarterly (once every 3 months).

Who Decides the Dividend Amount?

The Board of Directors of the company decides the dividend to be paid to investors.

What Are Dividend Dates?

Dividend dates for a stock are important dates that all dividend investors need to keep a track of.

There are 4 key dividend dates to keep track of for each dividend payment:

Declaration Date: This is the date on which the board of directors of the company declares the dividend amount.

Ex-Dividend Date: This is the cut-off date for investors to buy the stock to be eligible to receive the dividend. So, investors need to buy the stock before this date to be eligible for the dividend.

Record Date: This is a date when the company makes a list of all shareholders that will receive the dividend on the payment date. So, investors need to buy before the ex-dividend date and sell after the record date to be eligible for the dividend payment.

Payment Date: This is the date when the company pays out the dividend to the shareholders.

Now, let's look at an example of the important dividend dates for company X:

Declaration Date	Ex-Dividend Date	Record Date	Payable Date
June 1st	June 14th	June 15th	July 1st

Company X declares a dividend for its shareholders on June 1st. The company's board of directors then announces a record date of June 15th. Investors who are shareholders on June 15th will be eligible to receive the dividend. Typically, the ex-dividend date would be 1 business day before the record date. In this case it is on June 15th. An investor who purchases shares on or before June 13th and is a shareholder of record on June 15th and will receive the dividend on July 1st.

An investor who purchases shares on or after June 14th will not be entitled to the dividend.

So, the investor who purchases on June 13th or before; and sells on June 16th or after is entitled to the dividend.

Where Can I Get Dividend Information?

Dividendhistory.org is a good spot to get all the dividend information you need. It gives you the ex-dividend date and payment dates of a large number of companies for decades.

You can just search for the company on the search box area on the website:

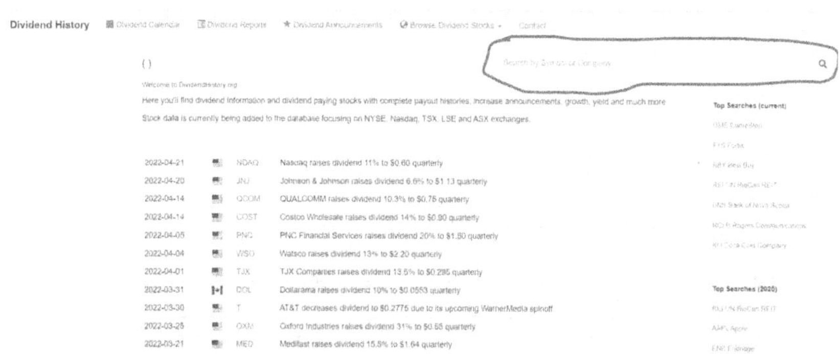

Types of Dividends

As mentioned in the introduction, there are some companies that offer dividends and others that do not. The main reason for the difference lies with the cash flow. Companies that have stable cash flows usually offer dividends. This is done to raise the confidence of the investors. There are three major types of dividends that can be offered.

Cash

This is the most common dividend type. When a company earns profits, they payout cash as dividends to their investors. These are paid out directly to the investor through their brokerage account. Investors who receive cash dividends in their early years of investing usually reinvest the dividends by buying more shares and growing their portfolios. Only in later years do some investors treat the dividends as disposable income.

Stock

Another name for this is dividend automatic reinvestment. Some companies issue common stocks to shareholders as dividends.

The general agreement is usually that when this common stock is issued, it should not exceed 25% of the current shares. If it does, it will be considered to be a stock split. Some investors prefer to receive stock dividends over cash as this helps them to save better. Some find it difficult to reinvest manually, so with stock dividends, the process takes place automatically.

Property

This is another alternative to cash or stock dividends. It is less common than the previous types. In this case, the company issues a tangible asset—products that are sent to shareholders in lieu of cash. Companies that issue dividends are usually those that have a good track record of solid cash flows. The balance sheets of these companies are usually very healthy, and their returns are very high (there are exceptions which we will cover later). There are cases where a company may issue what is known as scrip dividends. This is a promissory note that is issued to the shareholder in the event the company is unable to pay dividends on time.

Investors should know that dividend payments are not always guaranteed. Companies can pay out dividends if they have good cash flows. In times of hardship, these dividends can be cut. When a company cuts its dividends, this is a sign that it is struggling on the financial side. If the dividends continue to be paid on time, it means the company is financially healthy. In most cases, dividends are, therefore, a good measure of the well-being of a company.

Chapter Quiz/Summary

1. Dividends are paid by governments to people (True/False)
2. Dividends are paid by a company to shareholders annually, semi-annually or quarterly (True/False)
3. Dividends are decided by the CEO of the company (True/False).
4. Apple declares a dividend of $0.05 per share to be paid quarterly. If Sam owns 100 shares...
    a. How much dividend income does Sam get per quarter?
    b. How much dividend income does Sam get per year?
5. It's March 5. The Microsoft Board of directors declares a dividend of $2 per share to be paid on April 2nd. All investors who own the stock on March 19th are eligible. The company makes a list of eligible shareholders on March 20th.
    a. What is the announcement date?
    b. What is the ex-dividend date?
    c. What is the record date?
    d. What is the payment date?

Answers:

1. False
2. True
3. False, decided by Board of Directors
4. $5 per quarter; $20 per year
5. March 5th is the announcement date; March 19th is the ex-dividend; March 20th the record date and April 2nd is the payment date.

Getting Started

Dividend investing is one of the best ways to develop a fixed income stream. Many companies pay out dividends, and obviously, some are better than others. You cannot invest in just any dividend stock. Understanding how dividends work is very important. You should know the differences before you jump in. **This chapter will help you to understand how the concept of dividend investing works, and then break down all the steps you need to get started.**

As you know by now, a dividend is a payment that is made to qualified shareholders out of the profits of a company. In most cases, they are paid in the form of cash, although there can be other forms of dividends, as explained in the previous chapter. Dividends are one of the ways that companies offer returns to their shareholders in addition to increasing share prices. The company's board determines the rate at which dividends are paid out and the amounts. This information is readily available before you invest. Sometimes one-off dividend payments are made, for example, if it has been a profitable year.

Step 1: Get a Brokerage Account

You need an online brokerage to trade dividend stocks. It's best to get an international brokerage account so you have access to stocks both in your home country and outside, and you are able to access a wide variety of stocks. Here are the list of brokerages that you can use:

US Brokers

Charles Schwab

Interactive Brokers

FirstTrades

UK Brokers

IG

Interactive Brokers

Australia Brokers

Stake Brokerage

Step 2: Get a List of Dividend Stocks in Your Brokerage Account

Contact your broker or go into the Research section in your online brokerage account and find a list of dividend stocks.

Step 3: Get Dividend Yields for Each Stock

Create an excel sheet that can store relevant data for your research. The first thing you should include for each dividend stock, is the current dividend yield.

Step 4: Get Dividend History for Each Stock

Go to Dividendhistory.com and make a note of the 10-year dividend growth for the stock.

A good place to do this is on dividendhistory.org. It has a good list of dividend stocks all across the world.

Step 5: Get Payout Ratio for Each Stock

Go to finance.yahoo.com and get the payout ratio of the stock. It is located in the Statistics section of the Individual stock in Yahoo finance as shown below for Apple stock:

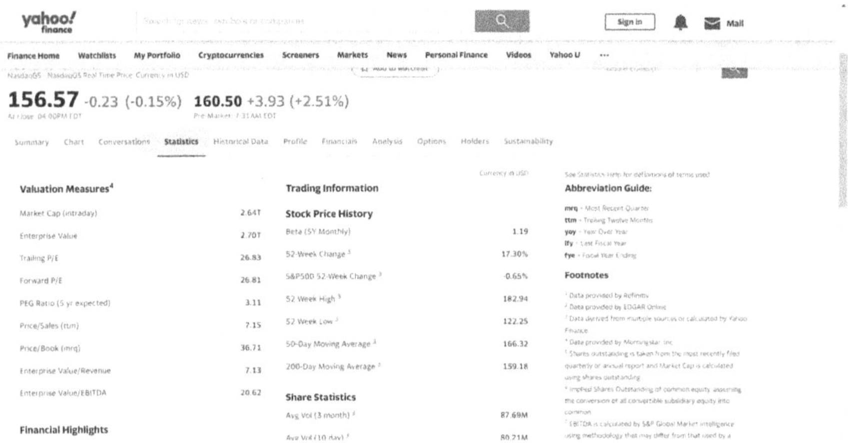

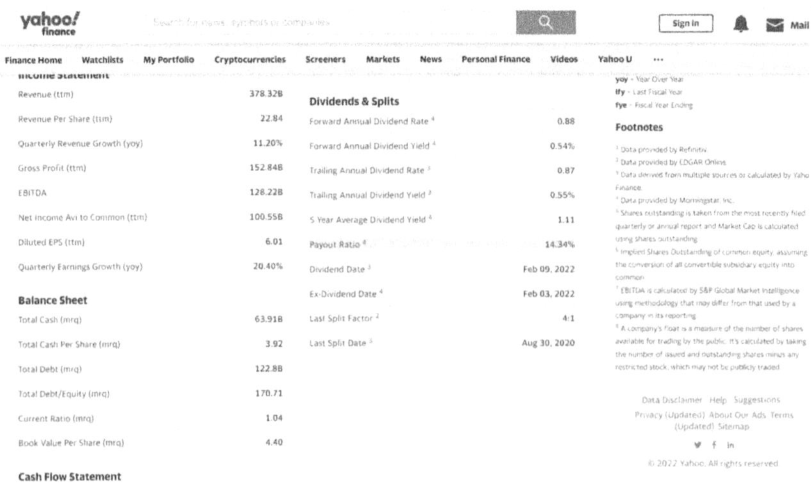

Step 6: Get Intrinsic Value for Each Stock

Use the techniques in the next chapter to get the intrinsic value for each stock. Make a note of it in your excel sheet

Step 7: Get Discount for Each Stock

How far below the intrinsic value is the current value of the stock? Let's say you calculate an intrinsic value of $100 for Microsoft stock. If the stock is at $70, the discount rate is 30%.

Step 8: Document all info in an excel sheet for top 10 dividend stocks

Document all the above information for the top 10 stocks that you have picked.

Here's look at a hypothetical scenario example below if Stock MSFT was at $160.

We like the Dividend history growth of 10% and payout ratio of 20%; but we're not too happy with the Discount and Dividend Yield.

It's only 12.5% below Intrinsic Value

So, if you want to get a 30-50% margin of safety, you want to wait for the stock to drop more before buying.

Stock Ticker	Dividend Yield (%)	Dividend History (Growth %)	Payout Ratio (%	Current Valu	Intrinsic Value	Discount (%)
MSFT	1.2	10	20	160	140	12.5

Do the same for 9 more stocks.

Step 9: Construct a Diversified Portfolio of Stocks

Use the techniques in Chapter on "Setting Up a Diversified Dividend Portfolio" to ensure that the top 10 stocks represent a properly diversified portfolio.

Buy these stocks when they discounted below intrinsic value. It's preferable to buy stocks at 50% discount; but a 30% discount is acceptable as well.

Also, ensure that they have a low debt to asset value.

I know that these steps could seem a little confusing right now, especially for new investors, but it'll make a whole lot of sense once you go through the different chapters in this book.

Chapter Quiz/Summary

1. The first step to getting started with investing is to get a brokerage account (True / False)
2. What is another name for the real value of a stock?
3. What type of discount below intrinsic value should we buy the stock?
4. How many stocks should be document in the excel sheet?
5. Where should I get the dividend history for the stock?

Answers:

1. True
2. Intrinsic Value
3. 30% or more
4. 10
5. Dividendhistory.org

Dividend Investing for Value Stocks

Dividends are a value investor's best friend. Value investing is a strategy that is employed by investors to discover and validate publicly listed companies before investing in them. The investors do so to find stocks that they believe are undervalued. They compare the share price of the stock to its true value. Value investors thrive on finding and taking advantage of that gap between a stock's intrinsic value and its listed price.

Dividend Investing is a subset of value investing, and we will focus on this subniche in this chapter.

Value Stocks or Growth Stocks?

Growth stocks are the stocks from companies that have the potential to outperform the market in the future. Value stocks are the companies that currently trade below their real value and are expected to appreciate in the future. The major question that most investors have is which one is better: value stocks or growth stocks?

The concept of comparing value stocks and growth stocks generally comes from fundamental stock analysis. Over time, growth stocks are expected to outperform the market. Growth stocks are found in all sectors, that is, small, mid, and large-cap. They keep their growth status until they have achieved their expected potential. These stocks have a very good chance for expansion. The potential comes from the fact that they might have product lines that are expected to sell well in the future. Perhaps they have a competitive advantage that gives them an edge in the market.

Value stocks are those from larger and more established companies that are trading below their actual worth.

There are several reasons for the undervaluing of stocks. In some cases, the price has to do with the general perception of the market. For example, if a company is caught up in a major scandal, people begin to see the company differently and will value it less. This may drive down the stock value. If, however, the company has solid financials, this presents an ideal entry point for investors: the public will eventually forget about what happened with the company and the prices will rise again.

The question is, therefore, which one benefits an investor better. Neither of the two is always correct. Sometimes the stocks may behave adversely. Stocks are usually a blend of these two different categories. This means that they might be undervalued and at the same time have the potential to go above and beyond the current price. When comparing these two factors, it is always important to ascertain the time horizon and the amount of volatility. Value stocks are considered to have a lower risk because they are found in large and established companies. Even if the stock doesn't get to the price that was predicted, they may still offer considerable capital gains.

Growth stocks usually do not pay out dividends directly to the investor. Instead, they reinvest the profits into the company. Growth stocks present a greater probability of loss to the investor, especially if the company cannot keep up with growth expectations. Growth stocks have the highest potential reward, but they come with the highest risk as well. The battle between growth and value stocks has always been complicated. Because of the risks and uncertainty, there cannot be surety over which of the two is the best.

The decision over which stocks to invest in is better left to the investor because it depends on their investment goals and levels of risk tolerance. If the time horizon is a little shorter for both growth and value stocks, their performance will largely depend on the point of the economic cycle that the market is in. If the market is still expanding, the stocks will expand. If it is declining, it is probable that the stocks may also decline. Value stocks tend to outperform during recessions and bear markets, and growth stocks excel in bull markets and economic expansions. Short-term investors and market timers should take this into consideration.

For dividend investing, we prefer value stocks as they are more stable and provide consistent dividends even during times of recession and economic uncertainty.

Why Value Investing?

Value investing is just as easy as described above, but sometimes you need to make careful considerations before you invest in a stock that you perceive to be undervalued.

Value Investing Anchors the Stock Value

The typical value investor studies and goes into minute detail to discover stocks that are being underpriced. Investing in such stocks will see your income increase by a great margin. Dividends are extremely important in value investing, and this is why the company you invest in should have a history of at least 10 years of consistent dividend payments.

They Indicate Quality

It may seem like you are narrowing your scope too much if you insist on something like 10 years of dividend history. However, it is the greatest guarantee you can have because it is impossible to fake 10 years of dividend payments. A smaller number of years is not a very solid foundation. It can be faked.

Sometimes, troubled companies pay out a high dividend for a quarter of two to lure investors in before they go bankrupt. Learn more about this in our chapter on Dividend Investment Traps.

What may eventually happen is not what you expect to happen. You can also look into good corporate governance. Did you know that there are some companies that pay dividends out of borrowed money? The only reason they pay dividends is to safeguard their reputation—a missed dividend could negatively affect their share prices. Be sure that the company's dividends come from profits, not borrowed funds. A good way to check this is to ensure that the company has a low Payout Ratio (<70%); a good Debt to Asset Ratio (<0.5) and a good Debt to Free Cash Flow ratio (<5)

They Contribute Greatly to Your Income

The importance of dividends in an investor's overall return cannot be underestimated. An investor who ignores stocks from dividend-paying companies is not making use of their full earning potential. Dividends offer regular income, and value investing can really be worthwhile. When a stock is undervalued, and you buy it, it may take several years before the market catches up to prove that your perception was correct. This is why I overemphasize the value of patience in dividend investing. The wait is not that difficult, considering that you will be receiving dividend income all the way.

An Extra String to the Bow

Value investing and dividend investing do not need to exist separately. They can go hand in hand. Dividends are very important because they increase returns, and they mitigate risk. Combining dividend investing and value investing will help you to do better with your investing.

Determining the Intrinsic Value of a Stock

Every asset has some sort of intrinsic value that is not influenced by external factors. In most cases there are external factors that influence the value of stocks. There can be other factors like unemployment, politics, inflation, and Gross Domestic Product (GDP) figures. When determining the intrinsic value of a stock, boil down the external factors so that you come up with the value of a stock based on its own merits. The intrinsic value is influenced by internal factors like the quality of management of a firm, the products, the brand strength, and the market strength.

When it comes to stock market investing, investors are interested in the cash that is available to stockholders. The internal factors listed here are a determinant of the cash that a company is likely to generate. There are methods that are used in calculating the intrinsic worth of a stock on the basis of the cash generated as well as the expectations for growth in the future.

One of the main reasons why investors are interested in intrinsic value is because it helps them to spot stocks that are underpriced. When a stock is priced lower than its calculated intrinsic value, it means the current market price is a bargain and a good investment. The different methods of calculating the intrinsic value are the price to book value, dividend discount method and the discounted cash flow method.

Method 1: Using the Price to Book Value

There are some key things that you can look out for in a company's balance sheet. These things will help you to determine the intrinsic value of a company. It is very important to know what the company can earn from the assets that are on the balance sheet. The term "balance sheet" describes a document that reflects the assets, liabilities, and equity of a company. It shows the assets that the company owns and how it is financed, that is, debt and liabilities.

The book value is an important indicator of a company's current valuation, that is based on formula below:

Book Value per Share = Equity / Number of Shares

Equity is also known as the value or the shareholders' equity. If you divide the equity by the number of outstanding shares, you will come up with the book price per share.

Price to book value is calculated using the formula below:

Price to Book Value = Price per Share/Book Value per Share

Now, let's look at an example...

Consider the following information for ABC company:

	2014	2015
Equity	210,185.00	221,857.00
Common Stock Outstanding Numbers	3083.037	3099.48

ABC's book value (2014) = 210,185/3083.037

= 68.174

ABC'S Book Value (2015) = 221,857/3099.48

= 71.57

If the price of ABC in March 2016 was $42.83, then we calculate the price to book value based on 2014/2015 book value below (as we do not have equity information for 2016 till the end of the year):

2014: $42.83/68.174 = 0.6268x

2015: $42.83/71.57 = 0.5983x

A low price to book value, especially below 1, is often a signal to investors that a stock is undervalued. If it is greater than 1, the best possible interpretation is that the stock is trading at a premium.

There is some risk on the rate of return on investment, as anything can happen in the global economy. So, we want to add a factor of safety of 50%.

So, we want to see a book value of below 0.5 before we invest, to account for the 50% Margin of Safety.

Let's look at a second example. Let's look at Amazon stock. It's trading at $2485.93 in 2022, as shown on Yahoo Finance below.

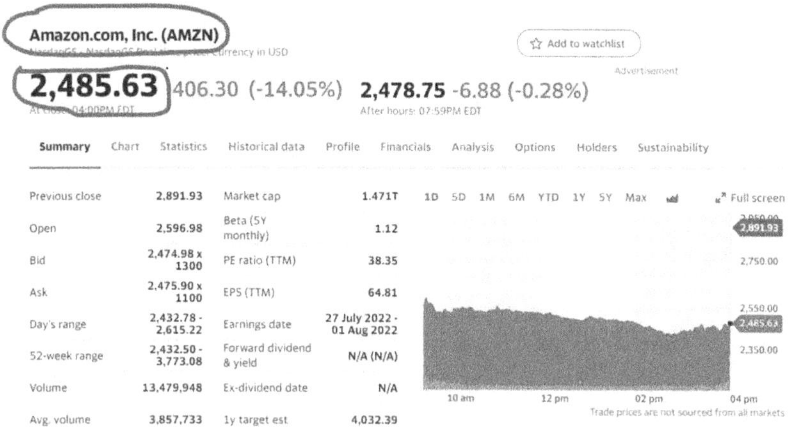

Let's have a look at last year's equity. We go to the Financials tab and look at Balance sheet to get the Equity and Number of shares.

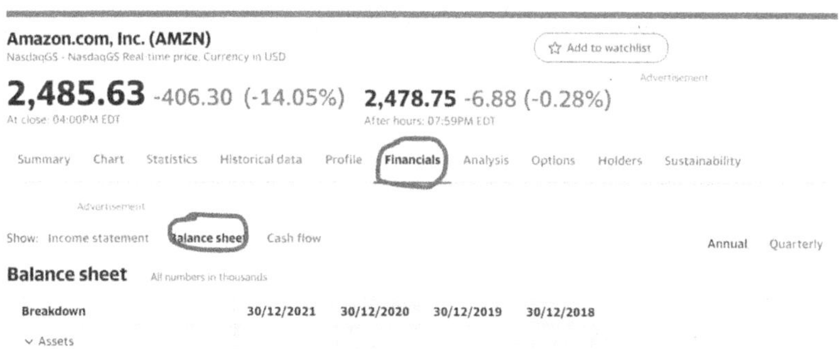

Accounts payable	78,664,000	72,539,000	47,183,000	38,192,000
Accrued liabilities	51,775,000	44,138,000	32,439,000	23,663,000
Deferred revenues	11,827,000	9,708,000	8,190,000	6,536,000
Total current liabilities	142,266,000	126,385,000	87,812,000	68,391,000
Non-current liabilities				
Long-term debt	48,744,000	31,816,000	23,414,000	23,495,000
Deferred tax liabilities	-	-	-	2,386,000
Other long-term liabilities	23,643,000	17,017,000	12,171,000	8,535,000
Total non-current liabilities	140,038,000	101,406,000	75,376,000	50,708,000
Total liabilities	282,304,000	227,791,000	163,188,000	119,099,000
Stockholders' equity				
Common stock	5,000	5,000	5,000	5,000
Retained earnings	85,915,000	52,551,000	31,220,000	19,625,000
Accumulated other comprehe...	-1,376,000	-180,000	-986,000	-1,035,000
Total stockholders' equity	138,245,000	93,404,000	62,060,000	43,549,000
Total liabilities and stockholde...	420,549,000	321,195,000	225,248,000	162,648,000

So, Amazon Equity = 138,245,000*1000 = 138000 million = 138 billion

We can find the number of shares in the Statistics tab of Yahoo Finance.

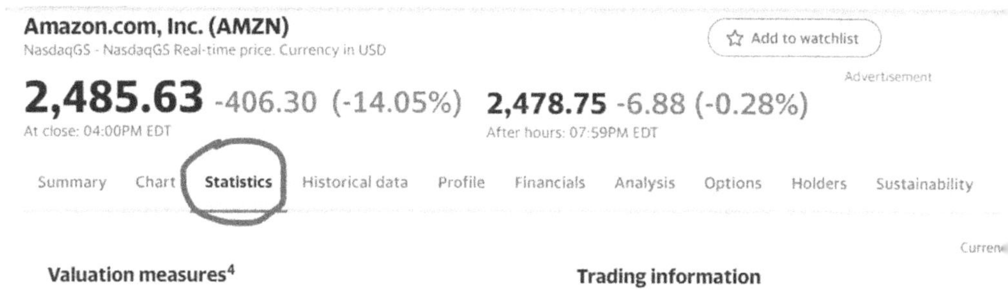

Amazon.com, Inc. (AMZN)
NasdaqGS - NasdaqGS Real-time price. Currency in USD

☆ Add to watchlist

Advertisement

2,485.63 -406.30 (-14.05%) **2,478.75** -6.88 (-0.28%)
At close: 04:00PM EDT After hours: 07:59PM EDT

Summary Chart **Statistics** Historical data Profile Financials Analysis Options Holders Sustainability

Curren

Valuation measures[4] **Trading information**

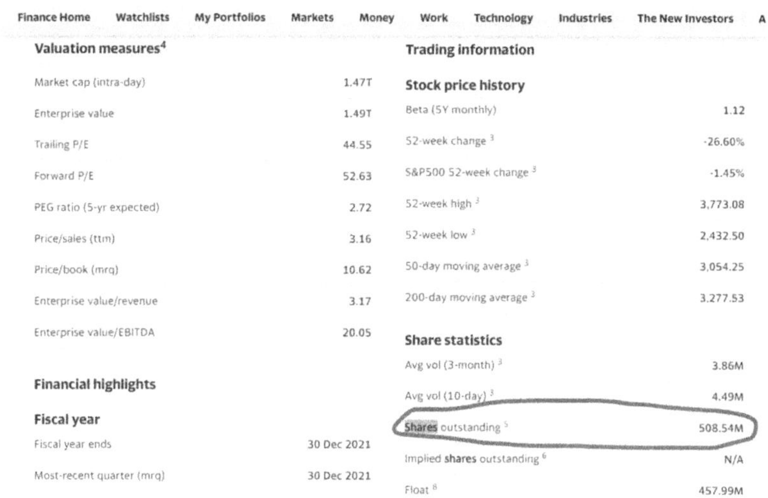

Finance Home Watchlists My Portfolios Markets Money Work Technology Industries The New Investors A

Valuation measures[4]

Market cap (intra-day)	1.47T
Enterprise value	1.49T
Trailing P/E	44.55
Forward P/E	52.63
PEG ratio (5-yr expected)	2.72
Price/sales (ttm)	3.16
Price/book (mrq)	10.62
Enterprise value/revenue	3.17
Enterprise value/EBITDA	20.05

Financial highlights

Fiscal year

Fiscal year ends	30 Dec 2021
Most-recent quarter (mrq)	30 Dec 2021

Trading information

Stock price history

Beta (5Y monthly)	1.12
52-week change [3]	-26.60%
S&P500 52-week change [3]	-1.45%
52-week high [3]	3,773.08
52-week low [3]	2,432.50
50-day moving average [3]	3,054.25
200-day moving average [3]	3,277.53

Share statistics

Avg vol (3-month) [3]	3.86M
Avg vol (10-day) [3]	4.49M
Shares outstanding [5]	508.54M
Implied shares outstanding [6]	N/A
Float [8]	457.99M

Amazon Shares Outstanding = 508.54 million

Amazon Book Value (2021) = $138000 / 508.54 = $2710

Amazon Current Share Price = $2485.63

Book Value Per Share = $2485.63/$2710 = 0.92

The Book Value per share price is 0.92.

If you are looking for a margin of safety of 50%, you want to wait for the share price to fall more to Buy. This is assuming that we've already done homework on the balance sheet of the stock to make sure that all is good there.

Stock ABC is priced at **$500**. The stock is expected to generate income over the next five years. In the first two years, it is expected to generate a cash flow of $8, and in the third year, $14. It is also expected to generate $28 in the fourth year and $90 in the fifth year. Suppose the expected growth rate of the cash is 7%, then calculating the DCF is done as shown below:

$$DCF = \$8/(1+7\%)^1 + \$8/(1+7\%)^2 + \$14/(1+7\%)^3 + \$28/(1+7\%)^4 + \$90/(1+7\%)^5$$

$$DCF = \$8/(1.07)^1 + \$8/(1.07)^2 + \$14/(1.07)^3 + \$28/(1.07)^4 + \$90/(1.07)^5$$

DCF = **$111.42**

At the end of 5 years, you can also sell the company at 5 times the cash flow. So,

Year 5 Adjust Cash flow = \$90/1.07^5=\$64

Total Intrinsic Value = \$111.42+\$64*5=**\$431.42**

\$431.42 is the intrinsic value of the cash flows done by the company.

So, the company is considered overvalued unless it falls below \$431.

So, it is not a good idea to buy the company at a price of \$500.

I would personally not buy this stock unless it falls below \$215 (50% discount).

Method 3: The Dividend Discount Method

Better known as the DDM, the dividend discount method is a quick and easy method to determine the intrinsic value of a stock. It is mostly used by large, stable companies. This method utilizes a formula that is based on dividends, giving much consideration to their value in the present as well as projected growth as time progresses (Alvarez, 2022). The formula is as follows:

Intrinsic stock price = $DPS_1/(r-g)$, where:

DPS_1 = Expected dividends in a year

r = the discount rate or simply the expected rate of return on investment

g = the growth rate of dividends per annum in perpetuity

For instance, a company that has a large and stable customer base may expect to pay $20 on every share in a year when there has been a stable 4% growth rate. This means that the g in the formula is 4%. If the required rate of return is 8%, it represents the r in the formula. The calculation of the intrinsic value of the share would look like this:

Intrinsic price = $20/ (.08-.04) =**$500**

So, I would not invest in the company if it is at or below $250 (50% Margin of Safety) based on the dividend discount method.

Dividend Discount Model

The Dividend Discount model can be calculated using two different methods.

Zero Discount Model

The zero-discount model formula assumes a zero growth rate for the company stock price. It is as follows:

$\mathbf{P_0 = Div/r}$ where:

$\mathbf{P_0}$ = price at time zero, with no dividend growth

Div = future dividend payments

r = discount rate / expected growth rate

This model works if there is no assumption of company growth. For example, for a company that has a required rate of return of 9% and pays dividends of $1.50 per year, the intrinsic value is calculated as follows:

Intrinsic value = Annual Dividend/Expected Rate of Return

=$1.50/0.09

=$16.66

So, after considering factor of safety, I would invest if it was below $8.33

Constant Dividend Growth Model

If a stock is paying a $6 dividend, with a steady growth of 8% per year, and assuming that the expected rate of return is **10%**:

Intrinsic Value **=D*((1+g)/(r-g))**

where D is the dividend; r the growth rate and g is the growth rate

= 6 (1+0.08)/(0.10-0.08)

Intrinsic Value = **$324.00**

So, after taking into account factor of safety, I would invest if it was below $162.

Return on Invested Capital (ROIC)

The Return on Invested Capital or ROIC is a simple method of estimating the value provided by a company. It tells you what percentage of amount invested in a company is returned to shareholders.

A company with a growing ROIC and a ROIC of 10% or more is considered good value for investors.

The ROIC history chart is available at https://roic.ai/company/ as shown below. It has a 15 year ROIC history for a wide range of companies.

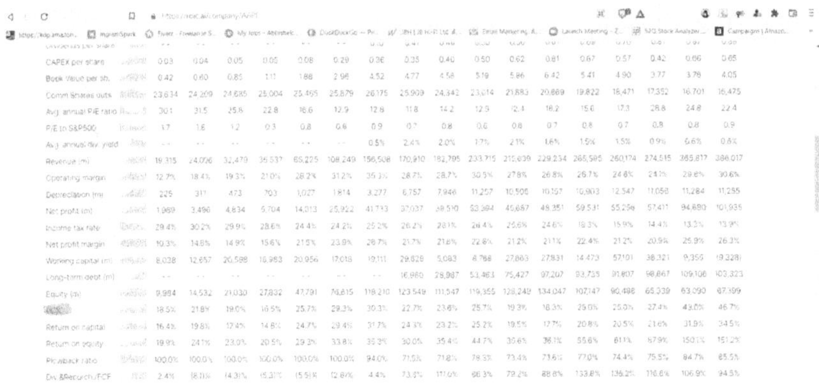

CAPEX per share	0.03	0.04	0.05	0.05	0.08	0.29	0.36	0.35	0.40	0.50	0.62	0.81	0.67	0.57	0.42	0.66	0.65
Book Value per sh.	0.42	0.60	0.85	1.11	1.88	2.98	4.52	4.77	4.58	5.19	5.86	6.42	5.41	4.90	3.77	3.78	4.05
Comm Shares outs.	23,634	24,209	24,685	25,004	25,465	25,879	26,175	25,909	24,342	23,014	21,883	20,869	19,822	18,471	17,352	16,701	16,475
Avg. annual P/E ratio	30.1	31.5	25.8	22.8	16.6	12.9	12.8	11.8	14.2	12.9	12.4	18.2	15.6	17.3	28.8	24.8	22.4
P/E to S&P500	1.7	1.6	1.2	0.3	0.8	0.6	0.9	0.7	0.8	0.6	0.8	0.7	0.8	0.7	0.8	0.8	0.9
Avg. annual div. yield	--	--	--	--	--	--	0.5%	2.4%	2.0%	1.7%	2.1%	1.6%	1.5%	1.5%	0.9%	0.6%	0.6%
Revenue (m)	19,315	24,006	32,479	35,537	65,225	108,249	156,508	170,910	182,795	233,715	215,639	229,234	265,595	260,174	274,515	365,817	386,017
Operating margin	12.7%	18.4%	19.3%	21.0%	28.2%	31.2%	35.3%	28.7%	28.7%	30.5%	27.8%	26.8%	26.7%	24.6%	24.1%	29.8%	30.6%
Depreciation (m)	225	317	473	703	1,027	1,814	3,277	6,757	7,946	11,257	10,505	10,157	10,903	12,547	11,056	11,284	11,255
Net profit (m)	1,989	3,496	4,834	5,704	14,013	25,922	41,733	37,037	39,510	53,394	45,687	48,351	59,531	55,256	57,411	94,680	101,935
Income tax rate	29.4%	30.2%	29.9%	28.6%	24.4%	24.2%	25.2%	26.2%	26.1%	26.4%	25.6%	24.6%	18.3%	15.9%	14.4%	13.3%	13.9%
Net profit margin	10.3%	14.8%	14.9%	15.6%	21.5%	23.9%	26.7%	21.7%	21.6%	22.8%	21.2%	21.1%	22.4%	21.2%	20.9%	25.9%	26.3%
Working capital (m)	8,038	12,657	20,598	16,983	20,956	17,018	19,111	29,628	5,083	8,768	27,863	27,831	14,473	57,101	38,321	9,355	(9,328)
Long-term debt (m)	--	--	--	--	--	--	--	16,960	28,987	53,463	75,427	97,207	93,735	91,807	98,667	109,106	103,323
Equity (m)	9,984	14,532	21,030	27,832	47,791	76,615	118,210	123,549	111,547	119,355	128,249	134,047	107,147	90,488	65,339	63,090	67,399
[illegible]	18.5%	21.8%	19.0%	16.5%	25.7%	29.3%	30.3%	22.7%	23.6%	25.7%	19.3%	18.3%	25.0%	25.0%	27.4%	43.0%	46.7%
Return on capital	16.4%	19.8%	17.4%	14.8%	24.7%	29.4%	31.7%	24.3%	23.2%	25.2%	19.5%	17.7%	20.8%	20.5%	21.6%	31.9%	34.5%
Return on equity	19.9%	24.1%	23.0%	20.5%	29.3%	33.8%	35.3%	30.0%	35.4%	44.7%	35.6%	36.1%	55.6%	61.1%	87.9%	150.1%	151.2%
Plowback ratio	100.0%	100.0%	100.0%	100.0%	100.0%	100.0%	94.0%	71.5%	71.8%	78.3%	73.4%	73.6%	77.0%	74.4%	75.5%	84.7%	85.5%
Div.&Repurch./FCF	2.4%	(8.1)%	(4.3)%	(5.3)%	(5.5)%	(2.8)%	4.4%	73.6%	111.6%	86.3%	79.2%	88.6%	133.8%	136.2%	116.6%	106.9%	94.5%

Which Method to Use?

Using any of these methods, you can come up with the intrinsic value of stocks. I am sure by now you have realized that to calculate the intrinsic value of a smaller company, the discounted cash flows are more ideal.

For larger and stable companies, which are not subject to as much volatility, the dividend discount method is ideal. Besides, you cannot use the dividend discount method on a company that does not even pay dividends.

The simplest method to calculate the intrinsic value is the **Price to Book Value** method, combined with the ROIC check; and this is a good method for beginners.

For those who have the ability and patience, it's best to use all of the methods, and then using the lowest intrinsic value found as your base value. This gives you the maximum possible margin of safety. Buying quality stocks at 50% margin of safety gives you a huge advantage.

Chapter Quiz/Summary

1. Are value or growth stocks better for dividend investors?
2. What is the best method to calculate intrinsic value for beginners?
3. Which is the best method to calculate intrinsic value for dividend stocks with zero growth?
4. Which is the best method to calculate intrinsic value for dividend stocks with growing dividends?
5. Which is the most accurate and most widely used method to calculate intrinsic value?

Answers:

1. Value Stocks
2. Price to Book Value
3. Dividend Discount Model – Zero Growth
4. Dividend Discount Model – Constand Dividend Growth
5. Discounted Cash Flow Model

A Short message from the Author:

Hey, are you enjoying the book? I'd love to hear your thoughts!

Many readers do not know how hard reviews are to come by, and how much they help an author.

I would be incredibly thankful if you could take just 60 seconds to write a brief review on Amazon, even if it's just a few sentences!

Thank you for taking the time to share your thoughts!

Your review will genuinely make a difference for me and help gain exposure for my work.

Dividend Investing for Commodity Stocks

Commodity stocks are stocks that are backed by valuable resources that are essential. Investing in commodity stocks gives you a certain level of confidence, since they have daily consumption characteristics. One example is stocks that are issued by steel companies. There may be great fluctuations in the price of iron ore, but the risk of it becoming obsolete is very low. The general implication is that there is always some value in commodity stocks, and this provides a margin of guarantee that investors want.

Commodity stocks, at most times, issue dividends to investors. This is good for investors because, besides enjoying the safety of commodity stocks, they also get regular income payments from them. The main reason why investors love commodity stocks is because of the dividend payments which are guaranteed. The fluctuation in the price of the stock does not really matter to the investors. The strategy of investing in commodity stocks is solid because it does not depend on stock market appreciation for its success.

Why do Commodity Stocks Have High Dividends?

Investments in commodity stocks are growing very fast. As explained above, there are advantages that investors love, and this is why the sector is growing rapidly. One of the reasons why investors love these stocks is because the dividends are almost always high. Here are some of the reasons why commodity stocks yield high dividends.

Minimal Outside Influences

The stock market in general is often bombarded by several outside influences. This is not the case with commodity stocks. They have this unreal security against external factors. This is because when investing in commodity stocks, you are not just investing in a piece of a company that is co-owned by a few individuals. The fact is that you are investing in the physical products and raw materials that are needed for everyday survival. It is unlikely that the commodity prices completely sink to zero. Some of the commodities that usually back commodity stocks include natural gas, minerals like silver and copper, sugar, and coffee. These commodities have designated exchanges that they trade on throughout the United States. Most of these exchanges are found in New York, London and Chicago.

Commodity Price Changes Are Predictable

Upward or downward price movements in commodity stocks is easier to predict and are quite methodical. This is because investors are better able to get a handle on the movements since there are not as many sources of commodity data that may give out conflicting facts. Of late, there have been large hedge funds that have invested in commodities, but these do not have much of a directional impact on the behavior of the stocks. There may be resultant upward movements, but they are temporary; the commodity markets are so large that they do not take much time to get back to themselves again.

Because commodity markets are large, they are able to accommodate different players with their diversities without much of a hitch. The chart analysis, inventory, and growing cycle data in the commodities market make way for more predictable movements. This is very important for investors because there are not as many surprises in the market. They almost always know what follows and what to expect in the coming months. Wouldn't we say that knowledge brings a lot of peace of mind?

The dividends are not very much affected at any time because of this.

Commodities Offer a Better Tax Break Due to Dividend

Commodities often receive favorable tax treatment in the US, as compared to stocks and stock options. Most investors operate on a short-term basis that could span less than a year. The short-term gains on commodities and commodity options are usually split on a 60/40 basis. This implies that 60% of the short-term gains are taxed at the lower, long-term rate, and 40% of the gains are taxed higher. It is always advisable that before jumping headlong into commodities, you consult with a tax professional to be sure of your options; as tax options will differ based on region.

For the reasons listed and explained here, commodity stocks often pay high dividends to investors. They have turned out to be a lifesaver in the investment world because they make investing so much easier. Commodity investing can be viewed as ideal for new investors who may not yet have mastered the art of predicting market behavior.

Commodity Cycles

What are Commodity Cycles? How do they work?

It is very important for investors who buy in commodity stocks to understand the commodity cycle. The cycle is important because it helps investors to determine future direction. Every commodity goes through the commodity cycle, which is mostly driven by the investment behavior of producers.

A commodity cycle usually begins with a huge increase in prices of the commodity due to undersupply. This leads to a commodity boom, and a lot of producers start getting into the market.

The producers compete, leading to oversupply and a crash in commodity prices. Other factors like recessions lead to an even lower demand in oil supply and leads to lower prices. This leads to a lot of businesses going bust; and producers are hesitant to start more supply.

Over time, this leads to another period of undersupply, and the cycle repeats.

If you intend to invest in commodities successfully, you should be able to identify where a commodity is relative to its cycle. It would be ideal to get in at the start and go along with the cycle.

Let's look at a 20-year price chart of oil. Commodity price history charts are found easily at Macrotrends.com and you can easily zoom into any period of time. Make sure that you remove the log scale and set it to Inflation-Adjusted values. Now, let's have a look at the oil commodity chart.

Link: https://www.macrotrends.net/1369/crude-oil-price-history-chart

You see the part that is highlighted in red is an oil cycle between 2000-2008. Oil prices started increasing in 2000. Between 2000-2008 there was a was a decreasing supply of oil, which led to an increase in prices. In 2006-2008, there was a huge increase in oil producers looking to take advantage of high oil prices. There was also a decrease in demand from the Great Recession.

This led to a huge crash in the price of oil in 2008.

That was the point when a lot of oil producers went out of business.

And then, we had a similar cycle play out between 2008-2015.

So, we recommend buying high quality, high dividend stocks when oil is below **$60 per barrel (inflation-adjusted price)**, as seen in chart below.

Keep reinvesting the dividends till you reach the other end of the oil cycle, and then you can start taking profits.

Make Commodity Cycles Work for You

All commodities, whether it be copper, iron, wheat, corn, have a cycle that is based on the supply demand curve. You can find these charts at Macrotrends. Make sure you look at inflation adjusted returns over 50 years, and start buying high dividend, high quality stocks at the bottom of the commodity cycle.

If you own the stock and the stock is at the top of the commodity chart, you should consider taking profits.

Remember, you want to make sure that no stock is more than 5% of your portfolio. So, if you bought oil stocks in 2009 and it has doubled; you might want to sell a portion of your stock so that it gets back to 5% of your portfolio,

How to Choose Commodity Stocks

Step 1: Choose your commodity

Use the commodity cycle charts as described above to pick the best commodity for your portfolio.

Step 2: Get a List of 10 Large Cap Commodity Stocks

Start looking through your brokerage for global commodity stocks. It's important for your brokerage to be able to trade globally. A lot of the best commodity stocks are outside the United States. Your brokerage should have a research section to pick out top quality commodity stocks. If you cannot find the section, call your brokerage to find out. Make sure that that you pick 20 large cap stocks. These stocks have a market cap of at least 10 billion. These stocks are more stable, and more likely to pay dividends.

Step 3: Filter out high debt companies

You want to filter out companies that have a lot of debt. The debt to asset ratio should be less than 0.5; ideally below 0.3. We will show you an example of how to do this in the next section.

Step 4: Check the dividend history

Check the dividend history of the stocks in dividendhistory.org. Make sure you check that the company does not cut dividend payment during down cycles for the commodity. Filter out any companies that don't have a consistent dividend history.

Step 6: Check the payout ratio

The payout ratio tells you what percentage of the company's profits are used to pay out dividends. If a company is paying out too much of its profits to pay dividends, it is very unhealthy and could be a dividend trap. We want to invest in companies with payout ratios below 50%. Filter out companies with payout ratios above 50%.

We will show you an example of how to do this in the next section.

Step 6: Buy the high dividend companies

Buy the top 5 companies by dividend yield. Make sure that no single stock is more than 5% of your portfolio.

Debt – Asset Ratio

The debt to Asset Ratio is a good indicator of the financial health of a commodity producer. Cash flows may not be a good indicator as these go up and down with the commodity cycle. A company with a high debt to asset ratio will have lower dividend yields and is more likely to go bankrupt during a down cycle.

So, how do we check this? We look at Yahoo Finance Balance sheet tab under Financials.

Let's look at the example of Chevron.

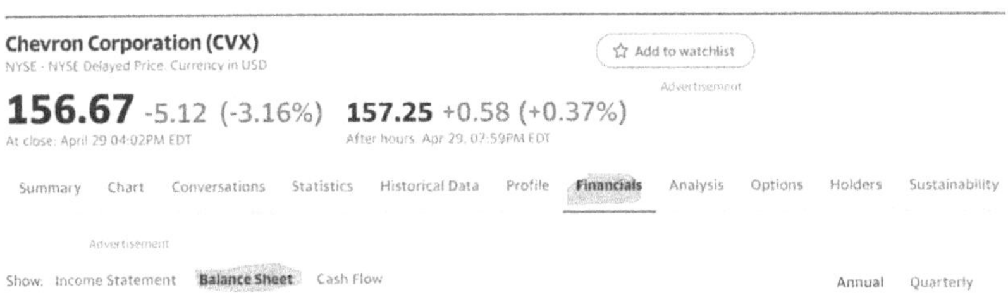

Finance Home Watchlists My Portfolio Cryptocurrencies Screeners Markets News

Breakdown	12/30/2021	12/30/2020	12/30/2019	12/30/2018
> Total Assets	239,535,000	239,790,000	237,428,000	253,863,000
> Total Liabilities Net Minority Int...	99,595,000	107,064,000	92,220,000	98,221,000
⌄ Total Equity Gross Minority Inte...	139,940,000	132,726,000	145,208,000	155,642,000
> Stockholders' Equity	139,067,000	131,688,000	144,213,000	154,554,000
Minority Interest	873,000	1,038,000	995,000	1,088,000
Total Capitalization	169,731,000	174,008,000	167,622,000	183,287,000
Common Stock Equity	139,067,000	131,688,000	144,213,000	154,554,000
Capital Lease Obligations	449,000	447,000	282,000	-
Net Tangible Assets	134,682,000	127,286,000	139,750,000	150,036,000
Working Capital	6,947,000	3,895,000	1,799,000	6,850,000
Invested Capital	169,987,000	175,556,000	170,904,000	189,013,000
Tangible Book Value	134,682,000	127,286,000	139,750,000	150,036,000
Total Debt	31,369,000	44,315,000	26,973,000	34,459,000
Net Debt	25,280,000	38,272,000	21,005,000	25,117,000
Share Issued	2,442,677	2,442,677	2,442,677	2,442,677
Ordinary Shares Number	1,929,806	1,925,186	1,882,168	1,902,838
Treasury Shares Number	512,871	517,490	560,508	539,839

It has a debt of 31,369,000 and total assets of 239,535,000. So, it has a debt to asset ratio of **0.13**, which is amazing. We like all stocks with a debt to asset ratio below 0.5.

Now, let's look at the payout ratio. It's under Yahoo Finance Statistics tab.

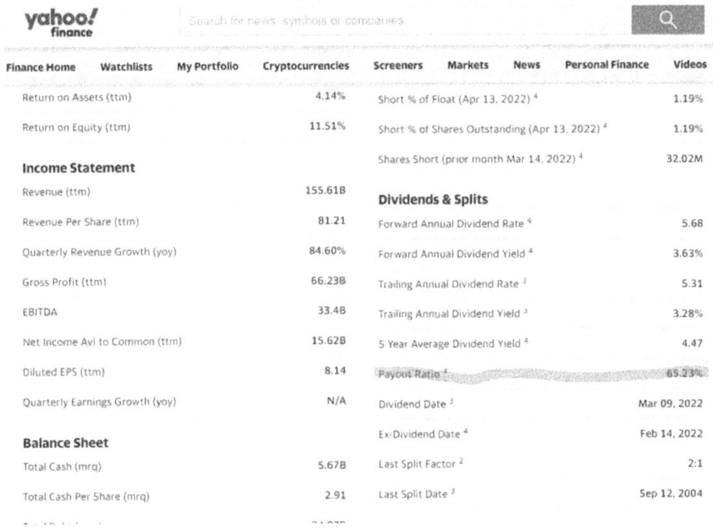

Return on Assets (ttm)	4.14%
Return on Equity (ttm)	11.51%
Income Statement	
Revenue (ttm)	155.61B
Revenue Per Share (ttm)	81.21
Quarterly Revenue Growth (yoy)	84.60%
Gross Profit (ttm)	66.23B
EBITDA	33.4B
Net Income Avi to Common (ttm)	15.62B
Diluted EPS (ttm)	8.14
Quarterly Earnings Growth (yoy)	N/A
Balance Sheet	
Total Cash (mrq)	5.67B
Total Cash Per Share (mrq)	2.91

Short % of Float (Apr 13, 2022) [4]	1.19%
Short % of Shares Outstanding (Apr 13, 2022) [4]	1.19%
Shares Short (prior month Mar 14, 2022) [4]	32.02M
Dividends & Splits	
Forward Annual Dividend Rate [4]	5.68
Forward Annual Dividend Yield [4]	3.63%
Trailing Annual Dividend Rate [3]	5.31
Trailing Annual Dividend Yield [3]	3.28%
5 Year Average Dividend Yield [4]	4.47
Payout Ratio [4]	65.23%
Dividend Date [3]	Mar 09, 2022
Ex-Dividend Date [4]	Feb 14, 2022
Last Split Factor [2]	2:1
Last Split Date [3]	Sep 12, 2004

We see that Chevron has a payout ratio of **65.23%**, which is acceptable. We prefer payout ratios below 50%, so we would wait for Chevron to get a better payout ratio.

Chapter Quiz/Summary

1. What is the most important part about choosing a commodity to trade?
2. A commodity stock has a debt to asset ratio of 1.3 with a high dividend. Should we buy this stock?
3. A commodity stock has a payout ratio of 90% with a high dividend. Should we buy this stock?
4. How large should a commodity dividend stock market cap be?
5. At what part of the commodity cycle should we buy?

Answers:

1. The commodity cycles.
2. No, it has too much debt. It should be below 0.5
3. No, the dividend is unsustainable. The payout ratio should be below 70%.
4. 10 billion or more
5. At the bottom of the commodity cycle.

Dividend Growth Investing

There is nothing that excites people more than earning income while sitting at the beach. This is what companies discovered a long time ago when dividends were first created; dividends are the investor's path to passive income. When an investor holds enough stocks that pay dividends, they receive a regular paycheck through the dividends. This is fantastic for many investors. But for it to come to fruition, you must invest a substantial amount of money. You cannot expect much out of a small investment.

The dividend growth strategy works if you have a lot of money invested in companies that have hefty growing dividend yields. This helps you to earn the most out of your investment. This may sound easy, but you must never forget that your investment can be affected adversely, which may see you lose your money. This is exactly what happened to investors who had invested their money right before the COVID-19 pandemic. They found themselves losing more than 30% of their earnings. The pandemic caused multiple stocks to plunge. Some stocks did so by more than 85%. Millions of dollars were lost.

The general idea behind avoiding losing your money is to choose high quality stocks. When you find good stocks, you must be informed about what to do with them, and at the same time, you should know the pitfalls to avoid. Many investors have fallen into an expensive pit, making it difficult for them to ever rise again. Many investors are blinded by their love for passive income. This is why this section has been specifically designed to help you to understand how to invest in dividend growth stocks and how to stay afloat while doing so.

What are Dividend Growth Stocks?

Dividend growth stocks are those stocks that have **a consistent record of increasing their dividends over time**. But unlike other dividend stocks, they also invest a part of their cash flow into growth and expansion of their company.

Dividend growth not only consistently increase their dividends; they also increase their stock value, cash flows and equity at a consistent value.

With the dividend growth investing strategy, the investor chooses and invests in stocks that have a growing dividend yield. The investor is actively involved in the market to identify such stocks and invest in them. The main reason why investors employ this strategy is to maximize their chances of earning passive income. Dividend growth investing is considered to be more stable than other forms of investment. Investors from different walks of life flock to this strategy because it works in almost any sector. Many people place their savings—for example, retirement savings—into dividend growth stocks. This is done in an attempt to grow their earnings significantly.

How Does the Strategy Work?

Put simply, dividend growth investing is quite easy when compared to other forms of investing. The investor must make selections of stocks that pay investors high dividends and place their money in them. The best stocks to go for are those that have a long-standing track record of having paid dividends to investors.

There is, however, more to this strategy than there is on paper. There are several aspects to be considered before investing using this strategy. For example, you must probe into the quality of the dividends that have been paid to investors over the years. Consistent growth for several years is more favorable than growth over one or two years followed by much lower growth. Consistency in quality is key.

Once an investor has selected stocks and begun to invest, the dividends should then start to come in. It is up to the investor to figure out what to do with their dividends. They can live off them or spend them in any way they might please. However, for dividend growth investing to fully work, there is a need to reinvest the dividends to set up higher earnings. When you reinvest, the next time the dividends come in, they will be higher, and so on when you reinvest yet again. The cycle continues.

As a dividend investor, you must ensure that your portfolio grows over time. To some investors, it may sound too good to be true. Of course, there are risks involved when it comes to dividend growth investing, and the investor should be aware of them. Try to educate yourself as much as possible about dividend growth investing, so that when you set up your investment, you factor in every possible factor. The health of your investments depends on how carefully set up your portfolio is.

How to Spot Quality Growth Stocks?

Finding the best company to invest in is critical when it comes to dividend growth investing. It is important to select companies that have been paying high dividends for a long time, but there is more to the selection process than that. There are other aspects of the company that you must look into. All these aspects, put together, add up to quality growth stocks. So, you should remember that it is not only dividends that you should look for, but there are also other important factors to be considered, which include consistent cash flows, company size, and potential for growth.

Frequency: Quarterly

Dividend History (adjusted for splits)

Ex-Dividend Date	Payout Date	Cash Amount	% Change
2011-08-16	2011-09-08	$0.16	
2011-05-17	2011-06-09	$0.16	
2011-02-15	2011-03-10	$0.16	
2010-11-16	2010-12-09	$0.16	23.08%
2010-08-17	2010-09-09	$0.13	
2010-05-18	2010-06-10	$0.13	
2010-02-16	2010-03-11	$0.13	
2009-11-17	2009-12-10	$0.13	
2009-08-18	2009-09-10	$0.13	
2009-05-19	2009-06-18	$0.13	
2009-02-17	2009-03-12	$0.13	
2008-11-18	2008-12-11	$0.13	18.18%
2008-08-19	2008-09-11	$0.11	
2008-05-13	2008-06-12	$0.11	
2008-02-19	2008-03-13	$0.11	

Previous Next

Above is a dividend history chart of Microsoft (MSFT). Here you see that the dividends paid during the 2007-2008 recession. Not only were the dividends paid during this period, but they also actually increased by 18%. This is an indicator of a strong recession proof dividend stock.

Another company, Ford cut its dividend during the 2008 and 2020 recessions temporarily. Thus, Microsoft is a better dividend growth company than Ford; even though Ford offers high dividends.

Many companies know that many investors only look at dividends and can easily be fooled. For this reason, companies engage in practices that deceive investors. Did you know that borrowed money can be used to pay dividends and maintain consistency when in fact the company is not doing well?

Therefore, it is vital to make a close analysis of the performance of the company to be sure of its actual position. Here are some points to note in spotting good dividend growth stocks.

The Divided Yields Must Be Much Higher than Bank Interest Rates; and Preferably Beat Inflation

The dividend yields out of the investment must be significant. If you look at the dividend yield plus annual growth rate without factoring in inflation, you may think that you are making money, yet you are not. You should therefore ensure that when you invest, the dividends are above the inflation rate to allow for accumulation and growth. Specifically searching for stocks that beat the inflation rate is very difficult because the rates of inflation change on a constant basis. However, this consideration still has to be made time and again.

The Company Should Have Low Debt

The only reason companies with debt may offer high dividends is because they want to encourage investors to invest their money to boost cash flows. This is quite worrying because the payment of dividends by the company is dependent on debt and sales. It is only a matter of time before schemes like those fall apart and the investors lose out. Things may turn sour if the company does not get as many investors as may have been expected. An ideal stock to invest in is one that has a debt-to-equity ratio of 0.5 or lower; preferably below 0.3.

Now, let's have a look at an example of a company with a good and bad debt profile.

Let's look at AMC stock on Yahoo Finance Statistics tab.

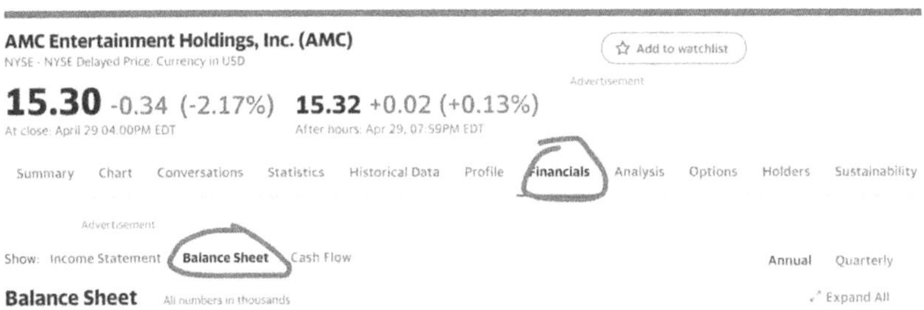

yahoo! finance

Search for news, symbols or companies

Finance Home | Watchlists | My Portfolio | Cryptocurrencies | Screeners | Markets | News

Balance Sheet All numbers in thousands

Breakdown	12/30/2021	12/30/2020	12/30/2019	12/30/2018
> Total Assets	10,821,500	10,276,400	13,675,800	9,495,800
> Total Liabilities Net Minority Int...	12,611,000	13,134,600	12,461,600	8,097,800
> Total Equity Gross Minority Inte...	-1,789,500	-2,858,200	1,214,200	1,398,000
Total Capitalization	3,618,500	2,810,700	5,947,600	6,105,800
Common Stock Equity	-1,789,500	-2,885,100	1,214,200	1,398,000
Capital Lease Obligations	5,323,400	5,667,600	5,599,500	669,800
Net Tangible Assets	-4,372,700	-5,595,600	-3,770,200	-3,742,800
Working Capital	82,400	-1,091,500	-1,260,100	-546,800
Invested Capital	3,638,500	2,830,700	5,967,600	6,188,000
Tangible Book Value	-4,372,700	-5,595,600	-3,770,200	-3,742,800
Total Debt	10,751,400	11,383,400	10,352,900	5,459,800
Net Debt	3,835,500	5,407,500	4,488,400	4,476,700
Share Issued	513,979	228,066	107,582	107,208
Ordinary Shares Number	513,979	224,333	103,850	103,475
Treasury Shares Number	-	3,733	3,733	3,733

It has a total debt of 10,751,400 and total assets of 10,821,500. So, the debt to asset ratio is 0.99 (10,751,400/10,821,500). So, AMC is a company we want to avoid investing in as it has a debt to asset ratio way above 0.5.

Now, let's look at Apple stock (AAPL).

From Yahoo finance again, it has a debt of 124,719,000 and total assets of 351,002,000. The debt to asset ratio is 0.36. This is within our acceptable range of 0-0.5. So, we consider Apple to be in a good financial position.

The Company Should Have Enough Cash on Hand

Companies with cash on hand are good to invest in. Sometimes a company may not have debt but may still be unable to pay dividends that are as high as you might expect. Most companies make dividend promises out of the revenue that they are currently earning. Imagine what would happen if that revenue fell. The company would be forced to borrow or to employ strategies that allow it to sell more shares in order to pay dividends. As long as a company borrows money to keep its investors happy, it is not operating on the healthy side. Cash on hand is an indication that the company can honor its obligations and still have money to spare. This implies that the stocks of such a company are good, and growth can be guaranteed.

The cash ratio is a good way to measure the strength of a company's cash position.

Cash ratio is measured as:

Cash ratio = Cash available/Total liabilities

We want the company to have a cash ratio of 0.5 or above; ideally above 1.

Now, let's have a look at Apple's cash ratio. Apple has an available cash of 63.91 billion and total liabilities of 28.79 billion. Apple has a cash ratio of 2.21, which is incredibly good.

Companies With Long Term Growth Expectations

Continuity in the growth of a company is something you should look for. A company may have done well in the several years that you review, but things may turn for the worse and it may not perform as well anymore. There are cases where, because of technological advancements, some companies that used to do well are being forced out of business. The expectation should be that the company will continue to grow in the foreseeable future. This may be difficult to ascertain but, at the least, most factors should be pointing toward that. If a company does not look like it will grow in the long term, investing in it may not be a very good idea.

Over the years, companies whose stocks grow consistently have outperformed the market. Dividend growth stocks do that well. It is true that, by steering away from low-growth stocks, you will be doing yourself a great favor. Stocks that pay growing dividends have also outperformed those that do not. Dividend growth investing has become the order of the day. This is not a bad thing because, if the dividends don't grow, your earnings will be stunted.

The Power of the Dividend Snowball

A dividend snowball refers to a progressive cycle where dividend income continues to grow, mainly as the result of a dividend reinvestment strategies. To kickstart the dividend snowball, you should make an investment in high quality **dividend growth stock** shares. Your investment will generate income and, to increase it, you should continue to add more funds either by reinvesting dividends or adding an investment. The more you do this, the more you earn from your investments. The earnings that started small will begin to grow, which is why it is referred to as the dividend snowball. This chapter will help you to create your own dividend snowball. Let's get started!

Regularly Inject Money into Your Investments

As is often said, it takes money to make more money. The biggest financial task that you may be faced with is to make more money. You can increase your chances of making more money to inject into your investments by improving your skills, creating more value in your business, and working hard at a side hustle that generates more income for you. Having earned the money, you should be able to save more for the creation of your snowball.

You can ensure this by cutting down on your spending and having more leftover income.

Reinvest All the Dividends That You Receive

When you receive dividends, you can choose to invest them again to increase your future dividends. There are two options for the reinvestments process.

Automatic Dividend Reinvestment

Reinvesting can be automated through your brokerage firm and reinvest the dividends paid by buying more shares in the same company. The advantage of this option is that once you set things up, you can forget about reinvesting and just watch your portfolio grow. What you do when reinvesting automatically is that you give a standing instruction on the account into which your dividends are paid. Once the dividends are paid into that account, they are automatically used to buy back stock. It becomes one less worry. The disadvantage, however, is that you lose control over the investment decisions.

Just keep in mind that a lot of countries don't allow dividend reinvestments, while the US does. So, if you're investing in a country like Australia or Brazil, they might not have this option. In this case, you should use the lump sum dividend reinvestment method.

Lump-Sum Manual Dividend Reinvestment

The second reinvestment option is where your dividends accumulate in cash. The dividends that you accumulate are added to your monthly savings, and that money is invested in dividend stocks that you choose.

As is the case with automatic dividend reinvestment, with manual reinvestment, you receive your dividend and direct it back to your investment so that it grows. However, in this case, the reinvestment is a large amount paid at once. Let's say your dividends accumulate into $10,000 cash. In lump-sum manual dividend reinvestment, you don't reinvest the money in dividend stocks as small amounts over time. Rather, you invest the whole $10,000 at once.

Be Patient and Give Your Snowball Strategy Time to Play Out

If you are the type of investor who wants to get rich quickly, you may find it very difficult to create a dividend snowball. It takes time for dividend compounding to play out. When creating a snowball, think long-term. See into the future, set out a solid plan, and forget about it. Being calm and patient is the best way to go about it.

Keep At It Until You Reach Your Dividend Crossover Point

Your dividend crossover point is that point where you reach the monthly or annual dividend income that you were targeting. You set up the crossover point as part of your snowball strategy. You should constantly check your position in relation to the crossover point that you set for yourself. You should do whatever it takes to make sure you achieve it. Achieving your crossover point usually shows that your portfolio is doing very well.

I hope this chapter has been an eye-opener to you. Many investors are taking advantage of dividend investing and making good money in the long term. If you are not the type of investor that wants instant results, you can try out dividend investing. As has been mentioned, patience is one of the most important virtues a dividend investor should possess. Dividend investing is also a good way to save up for your retirement, so if you are a future-oriented investor, you should start now.

Chapter Quiz/Summary

1. Dividend growth stocks have growing stock prices with same dividends. (True/False)
2. Dividend growth stocks have same stock prices with growing dividends (True/False)
3. Dividend growth stocks have growing stock prices with growing dividends (True/False)
4. Where do I check dividend history of a stock?
5. A company has a debt to asset ratio of 1.2. Is that good?
6. A company has a cash ratio of 0.4. Can I invest in this?
7. The dividend snowball strategy works if you keep selling your stocks (True/False).
8. The Automatic Dividend Reinvestment strategy means your dividends are automatically reinvested back into the stock (True/False).
9. Patience is the key to Dividend Investing (True/False).

Answers:

1. False
2. False
3. True
4. Dividendhistory.org
5. No. You should invest in stocks with debt to asset ratios below 0.5; preferably below 0.3
6. No. You should invest in stocks with cash ratios above 0.5; preferably above 1
7. False, the strategy relies on holding your stocks and reinvesting your dividends back into the stock.
8. True
9. True

Dividend Safety Stocks During a Market Crash

Stock market crashes are a difficult time to endure. Investors can cushion themselves from the hard effects of a crash by owning stocks of high quality and keeping a strong reserve of cash. Even during the economic downturn, these good companies will still be doing well, and they will still give their investors some sort of return.

Market crashes are nothing new. They have always been there. Many companies have survived them while still paying dividends to their investors. The dividends may not be high, but the fact that it is still there is very important.

The value of most portfolios takes a dip during market crashes; it is very painful to watch your investment portfolio value crater. If you are able to receive regular income during such a time, it makes a world of difference. Dividend stocks, therefore, come into the picture to save the day. This is one type of stock that you would find worthwhile to own during a market crash.

There are two very important principles that make dividends and market crashes a great combination.

- **Principle 1:** Dividends depend on the profitability of the business itself. They have nothing to do with the share price. This contributes greatly to the stability of dividends. Of course, there is no guarantee for dividends, but quality companies hardly ever cancel dividends because it affects the overall picture.

- **Principle 2:** The price of the shares in the stock market are simply a reflection of what people are willing to pay for the company's shares. It is a representation of human psychology and the forces of supply and demand—when people are irrationally selling, it can throw up anomalies. Share prices are volatile and variable. When you invest in dividends, you hope to have your shares for the rest of your life. It is the hope of every investor that the stocks they invest in will grow over time and will continue to pay them dividends. When a stock is doing well, there will be an increase in the share price. So, while you are making money through dividends, you can also decide to sell the share, which you will do at a profit.

The Investment Psychology of a Market

Crash

Many investors find market crashes to be utterly scary because they can bring about swings to the paper wealth of an investor. The swings can be very dramatic, and it can lead to changes in how investors see the prospects of most companies. When a crash is ongoing, this is the perfect time to learn how top investors have survived them and master the art. An investor must learn to manage their psychology in order to learn how to survive a market crash.

Here are some of the psychological aspects of a market crash that will help an investor to do well in a market crash.

Focus on the Long Term

A successful investor, Warren Buffet views the market as if it is an individual. He calls it Mr. Market. On a daily basis, Mr. Market has prices at which he is willing to buy and sell shares and, if the investor is happy with such prices, they can do business. If they are not happy, they can ignore it.

A proverb by Warren Buffett, is one to keep in mind. “Buy when others are fearful; and sell when others are greedy”. This is the right psychology to keep in mind. Just realize that your portfolio will go down; but if you invested in the right stocks, you would win in the long term. You will also receive a strong dividend income at this time.

If an investor is able to invest in high quality stocks, they are less affected by the changes that the market brings on a daily basis. Even if the market were to mark some of the stocks up or down, they would be affected very little by this; high quality stocks maintain their value. Some investors have come to view the market as a voting machine in the short run and as a weighing machine in the long run. The prices shift occasionally in the market, especially in the short term. These shifts sometimes present an incredible buying opportunity for investors. Top investors often ignore the noise of a market crash because their focus is usually on the long term.

Preparing For a Market Crash

Market crashes are nothing new to top investors. They've survived them before, and they have the assurance that they will survive them many more times. The timing however sometimes catches them off guard. Markets behave in a cyclical manner and, therefore, they are bound to move up and down with time. When a market is moving in such a rapid manner, this is a great opportunity to buy. Such opportunities can, however, be very short-lived and are only enjoyed by those investors who watch the market.

Top investors have created what they call shopping lists. These lists contain companies that they regard as great investments—when the price is right. With a strategy structured in this way, when there is a market crash, the investor can keep calm and act.

The most important thing is to keep cash in your brokerage account ready to be deployed in a market crash. This should be between 20% - 40% of your portfolio, depending on the market risk.

If the market has had a long period of upward movement, it's time to increase your cash holdings to close to 40%.

If the market has just had a mega crash, then start deploying your cash to buy stocks, and reduce it closer to a 20% holding.

Learning From a Market Crash

No one can really be totally prepared for a market crash. Even with all the preparation one may have done, crashes can still be difficult. A crash has the potential to destroy a lot of value, even if the investor chooses a portfolio of strong companies. While you may remain afloat, it may not be the same as if you are investing without a crash. In 1989, the Japanese Nikkei hit an all-time high. After a market crash hit, it has never again reached such highs.

A market crash can be a great learning opportunity. While it may be costly, the lessons can help you in the future. After going through a market crash, you should take stock of the things that you have learned and apply them to your investments. This makes you a stronger investor and you know better how to prepare for the next crash.

Utility stocks, healthcare stocks and consumer staples are known as defensive stocks. They are great during a market crash. A lot of them pay a decent dividend. A lot of them hold their value during a market crash. If they go down in value, they do a lot better than the rest of the market.

Utility Stocks

Utilities are a very important part of every society because life without access to these utilities seems unfathomable. Utility companies have taken advantage of the fact that they are overwhelmingly important. Utility companies are rated among some of the largest in the world. These large companies can generate stable and consistent revenues. This is why many investors are interested in investing in utility companies during a market crash.

What Are Utility Stocks?

These are the stocks of companies that provide basic utility services like water, electricity, waste management, gas, internet and telecommunication services. These are well established companies that consumers need for everyday survival. Some provide these services in a mixed bag. Investors prefer to have their money in these companies because utilities provide a consistent return.

Advantages of Utility Stocks

Whenever you are investing, you should make sure that you assess the advantages and disadvantages of stocks. Every type of investment carries some sort of risk and there is no investment that is risk-proof. When it comes to utility stocks, here are some of the most important advantages and disadvantages to consider.

Strong Dividend Payments

The cash flows of utility companies are usually predictable. For this reason, they pay generous dividend payments. It is quite common for investors to find utility stocks that have dividends above 5% with dividend payout ratios below 50%. Because of their strong dividends, utility stocks are great income plays. Whenever the company earns money, the investors, in turn, receive a paycheck. Always remember that every stock behaves differently, and you should try by all means to ensure that you research the utility company's history before you make an investment.

They Are Monopolies that Grow with the Population

Of course, experts do not agree with the idea that some people have those stocks can only go one way: up. A stock may be very strong, but the possibility of a decline cannot be completely ruled out. The utility sector, however, is more defined and investors are better able to see ahead. The future is quite clear. Utility companies fulfill the most basic needs of consumers. They have a strong customer base. This has helped utility companies to build a strong infrastructure—and they have the capacity to continue increasing it. Because the human population grows every day, these companies also continue to grow.

Utility companies in the United States have their target audience increasing by more than half a percent per year, which is also the population growth rate per year. This continuous expansion directly translates to a continuous increase in revenue. The companies continue to grow, which gives rise to operational efficiencies, which in turn reduce costs and go toward increasing profits.

Utility Stocks Act as Economic Shields

There are some places where economic recessions happen every 5-6 years and last for about a year on average. Whenever consumers develop concerns about an economic recession, they tend to cut down on their spending and save more money. The result on the corporate side is a reduction in revenue, and the stock values take a dive across the market. Utilities may have some slight dips here and there, but they are quite resilient during recessions.

When there are concerns about economic conditions, many consumers are usually grounded and stay at home. This leads to an increase in the use of utilities. Utility stocks take only slight dips because of continued usage; they recover quickly from these dips.

Disadvantages of Utility Stocks

Utility stocks are worth being considered by investors because of their impressive upsides. However, this does not imply that they do not have a downside. There are certain disadvantages that come with investing in the utility sector.

Relatively Slow Growth

Large utility companies are known for stable growth that favors long-term gains for investors, but the actual growth rate is very slow. The best utility stocks usually come from the largest and most well-established companies in the market. These companies depend on the growth in population for their growth in revenue. Therefore, their growth rates are very slow. They cannot be compared to something like the development of a new technology where revenues may increase dramatically. Therefore, if you are that investor who finds slow growth undesirable, you should look elsewhere other than the utility sector.

Potential for Losses

Utility stocks are commonly touted as stable investments. They are known to provide long-term growth and very stable dividends. However, investments can never be completely safe. It is possible to have losses from investing in the utility sector. The only way to be sure your money is completely safe is to keep it in cash. If you put it elsewhere, always leave room for the possibility of something befalling it.

There are some companies that fraudulently pose as if they are making profits when, in actual fact, they are not. Investors, on the other hand, can jump into investments with the belief that the possibility of returns is definite. You cannot be completely safe from losses, even when investing in the utility sector. This is why I always emphasize the need to do thorough research before shelling out your money; and always keeping a reserve in hand.

How Much to Invest in Utility Stocks?

Allocation of money to different stocks that form your portfolio is an intimate process that depends on different aspects of your personal financial life. Your appetite for risk, your goals, and your investing style have a large bearing on the allocation of money. When your portfolio is well-diversified, it usually consists of both stocks, bonds and gold.

The 5% rule is very helpful to investors who want to create the best mix in their portfolios: do not put more than 5% of your investment into a single stock. If you are interested in utility stocks, not more than 5% of the total value of the portfolio should be in a single stock. You also do not have to max out the 5% on all of the utility stocks in your portfolio.

Diversify your income across multiple sectors. This is described more in detail in the chapter on "Setting up a Diversified Portfolio".

Your goals as an investor also have a great bearing. Your investment goals will differ from those of the next investor. For example, you might be interested in long-term retirement income, while the next investor is more into capitalizing on short-term momentum. Your investment goals will have a large bearing on the investment decisions that you make regarding the allocation of money among different assets in your portfolio.

Healthcare Defensive Stocks

Think about the last time you went to a doctor. Maybe that was yesterday. Maybe that was years ago. You paid the doctor, you paid for the medicines and maybe more. Would you not go if there was a recession?

If you really needed to go and you had the money, you would find a way to pay.

That's what makes healthcare stocks a great defensive play during a market crash.

Make sure you avoid healthcare innovation stocks that behave more like technology stocks and invest more in established healthcare companies. Pharmacy retail, biotech stocks and drug distribution stocks are examples of such stocks.

Consumer Staples

Consumer staples are stocks of companies that produce, distribute, and sell household goods, foods, beverages, grocery items etc. These are items that people are unable to eliminate from their budgets.

Example stocks would be Coca-Cola, Kroger, Woolworths etc.

Since they have a regular income, they are able to provide a strong dividend that isn't generally cut during recessions.

How to Spot Safe Stocks with Low Debt?

It goes without saying that it is vital for an investor to filter out bad stocks from the defensive sector. Just because a company is in utilities, healthcare or consumer staples, doesn't mean that it is a good investment. Some companies have mismanaged their finances during the good times and are burdened with too much debt to be able to deal with a recession.

Safety stocks are those stocks that cushion you against unnecessary losses. They have lasting value. There are some stocks that are trendy—their value is based on hype. You should align yourself to stocks that have real, significant, and durable value. Some stocks are safe, even if their price is well below their actual value. For different reasons, stocks of great companies may go down. This is the best time to buy—bargains are also good in the stock market. For solid companies, the low value is usually a temporary slip.

How Do You Spot a Safe Stock?

Spotting a safe stock is dependent on several factors. Included in this section are some of the metrics to look at when identifying a safe stock.

Cash

A company should have cash at hand. The stocks of such a company are good because it is evident that the company has some money to spare. When sales dip, the cash held by the company keeps it going and it acts as a sort of insurance. Besides paying for the day to day running of the business, cash helps to pay for the growth of the company and also to maintain its dividends.

A good way to measure a company's cash on hand is the cash ratio. The cash ratio is the cash divided by the liabilities of the company. A good cash ratio is above 0.5. Ideally, you want a cash ratio to be above 1.

Little or No Debt

When a company has debt to pay off, it takes away the money that could otherwise have been used for profitable activities. Debt payments during bad times have the potential to drag a company under. A company should be able to channel all the resources that it makes to its growth. Repayment of debt reduces a company's potential for growth.

The Debt-to-Asset Ratio

The debt-to-asset ratio of a company is useful in the evaluation of a company's financial leverage. It is calculated by dividing the total liabilities of a company by the total assets. This ratio gives us a measure of how much a company is financed by debt and by funds that it wholly owns. If the debt is bigger, it means the company is not stable.

Debt/Equity = Total Liabilities/Total Assets

For example, if a company has $100,000 worth of liabilities, and $20000 assets, is highly leveraged and a very risky investment. If, on the other hand, a company has total liabilities of $50,000 and total assets of $100,000, it is a low-risk company and a very good investment.

Free Cash Flows

When a company has taken care of all its operating costs, the money that is left is the free cash flow. Free cash flow can be used to add to a company's cash and reduce its debt. The stocks of a company that does not spend more than it makes are safe. Companies that overspend may be successful in the short run, but in the long run, they will flame out.

Free cash flow is a subset of cash flow. It refers to the amount of cash that is left over when the company has paid all its expenses as well as capital expenditure. Free cash flow is easily calculated from the cash flow statement and is calculated as follows:

Free Cash Flow (FCF) = Operating Cash Flow (OCF) – Capital Expenditures

Example of Good Free Cash Flow

The following information is for XYZ Company for the fiscal year ending 2019.

Cash flow for Operating Activities = $1.608 billion

Capital Expenditures = $1.157 billion

The free cash flow of the company would therefore be calculated as follows:

FCF = $1.608 billion – $1.157 billion

= $450 million

As is evident, XYZ has a high free cash flow. This is good because it can be used to expand operations, deleverage the balance sheet, and pay dividends. If the free cash flow is able to cover these things, it is a good free cash flow. If, however, it is low enough to not cover some or all of these things, it means the free cash flow is not good enough.

Debt to Free Cash Flow

The best way to measure the strength of a company's cash flow is the debt to free cash flow ratio. The debt to free cash flow is a good way to check if the company has too much debt. If the debt to free cash flow is over 5, it is too highly leveraged.

In the above example, company XYZ has a debt of $900 million.

The debt to free cash flow is 2, which means that company XYZ has a good cash flow position. A debt to free cash flow ratio of 5 or below is considered a sign of financial strength.

Chapter Quiz/Summary

1. The market always goes up (True/False).
2. You should buy stocks only when everyone else is greedy and buying stocks (True/False).
3. A good way to prepare for a market crash is to hold 20-40% of your portfolio in cash (True/False).
4. Utility, healthcare defensive and consumer staples are good safety stocks during a market crash. (True/False).
5. Utility stocks always go up during a market crash. (True/False).
6. All utility and defensive stocks are safe during a recession. (True/False).
7. Two utility stocks have a debt to asset ratio of 0.2 and 0.7. Which one has a better debt position?
8. Two healthcare stocks have a debt to cash flow ratio of 3 and 9. Which one has a better cash flow position?

Answers:

1. False
2. False
3. True
4. True
5. False.
6. The one with a debt to asset ratio of 0.2
7. The one with a debt to cash flow ratio of 3

Dividend Capture Approach

Dividend capture is an investment strategy that focuses on the buying and selling of stocks that pay dividends within a particular time period. It is a short term strategy.

The investor buys the stock just before its ex-dividend date in order to capture the dividend. The investor then sells the stock on or after the record date, at a higher price than the purchase price. The approach focuses on the receiving of the dividend and not just the selling of the stock at a profit.

For the dividend capture strategy to be worthwhile, the stock must be the one that pays a sizable dividend. The stocks should also have a very high trading volume to take advantage of the regular cash infusions that result from the payment of dividends. The strategy is often tackled with a one-size-fits-all approach. As explained, investors prefer to buy the stock just before the ex-dividend date and sell it on or after the date. This means that they do not hold the stock for a long time. Other investors sometimes decide to hold on to their stocks for a couple of days before they sell them off.

For the strategy to work, the stock must be sold at a price that is higher than the purchase price, not less. The strategy also works if the price of the stock drops below the amount of the dividend. That capital is no longer a part of the value of the company because it is allocated to shareholders. The strategy, however, does not always play out because it is not always the case that prices will drop below the price of the dividend. The share price of a company is dependent on several factors, and the dividend is just one of those things. Sometimes the share price can be affected by demand. The strategy is built on the premise that you do not need to hold the stock long-term for you to collect the dividend payment.

The traditional investment approach focused much on the buying of stocks and holding on to them until such a time when they appreciate. The dividend capture strategy is very popular with short term traders who have no intention to hold a stock for a long time but still want to capitalize on the price movements and payment of dividends. Sometimes the investor will hold the underlying stock for just a single day before they let it go, as long as the holding period is long enough to capture the dividend. This strategy is a very active strategy, which means the investor has to be actively engaged in the market to take note of the trends.

Most companies pay their dividends on a quarterly basis, but an investor who knows how to use the dividend capture strategy can get a dividend at least six times within the year. When the investor using the dividend capture strategy buys a dividend-paying stock, they have to sell it off thereafter and use the proceeds to buy another stock that is about to pay out a dividend. This sounds like it is easy, but it is not; there are several factors that contribute to making the strategy workable.

Many factors affect the effectiveness of the dividend capture strategy. For example, there are tax laws that stipulate that a stock must be held for 1 year before it gets a special tax rate. If it is not held for that period, it is taxed at the regular income tax rate for stockholders. In some cases, there can be very high trading costs which, at the end of the day, affect your profit margin. This can defeat the major goals of the dividend capture strategy. It is also the case that the stock price of the company that is preparing to make dividend payments usually goes up. The prices will decline soon after dividends are paid.

Despite the factors stated above, strategists almost always come up with ways to ensure that they make a profit out of the work that they do. The key to making it work is the timing because, if you get it right, you will make meaningful gains. The dividend capture strategy is mostly dependent on the history and the patterns of stocks. This will help you to determine what will possibly happen before and after the ex-dividend date. When you analyze these events in history, you may come up with the correct day to buy and sell the stock. While this strategy is used by a lot of experts to make money, if you are to venture into it for the first time, you need to be properly prepared, so you do not wind up with staggering losses.

Special considerations to make include the fact that when the stocks are heavily trading, the price is less likely to reduce before the ex-dividend date. Also, if a stock is on a strong uptrend, it is likely to appreciate. This will result in the investor getting a dividend as well as the profit of the sale. On the other hand, stock prices can fall far below what you expect after the ex-dividend date. This may prompt the investor to sell the stock at a time that is more profitable, not on the ex-dividend date. They may decide to wait until the stock has gained value. This may be a few days after the ex-dividend date, but in some cases, the price may continue to fall.

Hypothetical Examples of the Dividend Capture Approach

Here are some examples of how the dividend capture approach.

Apple

Let's say that if Apple, in June of 2027, went ex-dividend after they declared a dividend of $0.51. On the day before the ex-dividend date, the stock closed at $147.23. It was possible to purchase shares at this price or less. If the investor were to hold the shares at the ex-dividend date, they would be entitled to the dividend of $0.51. On the day following the ex-dividend date, the stock opened at $148.06. This means that if the trader sold the shares, they would lock in a profit of $0.83 on top of the $0.51 dividend they would have received per share. At the time this scenario happened, Apple was in a strong uptrend. So, the trader made a profit of $1.31 per share from the trade.

United Airlines

Let's say United Airlines declared a $0.5025 dividend on the same day that it went ex-dividend. On the same day, the stock closed at $69.72. On the following day, the stock price was at $69.49. This means that the trader would sell the stock at a loss of $0.23, but still receive a dividend of $0.5025. At the time, the stock was in a trendless period. So, the trader made a net profit of $0.2525 per share from the trade.

Advantages and Disadvantages of the Dividend Capture Strategy

On the surface, a dividend capture strategy may seem to be straightforward and simple, but the case is not always so. There are several advantages and disadvantages to the strategy that you might want to learn about if you are interested in the strategy.

Advantages

Here are some of the advantages of the dividend capture strategy:

- The strategy allows the investor to make quick entry and exit. This means that your trades are handled in a matter of days, and you are done. This eliminates the risks of having your stocks decline in value while you still hold them. Usually, when that happens, it will become very difficult to sell the stock because the value will have gone down.

- The dividend capture strategy be used successfully in any market condition, as long as the investor times the trades correctly.

- There are several ways to implement this strategy and an investor can choose which one works better for them. The investor is free to decide when to sell the stock, that is, on or after the ex-dividend date, depending on what the trade-offs look like. This means that most of the decisions concerning a particular trade lie in the hands of the investor.

- One other advantage of the dividend capture strategy is that it is definite that you will find dividend-paying stocks in the market on any given day. If you are a fan of this strategy, you can be sure of continuity because there are stocks being sold every other day. This is the reason why most day traders make use of this strategy. The dividend-paying stocks are available to them every single day.

Disadvantages

The disadvantages of the dividend capture strategy include the following:

- When you employ the dividend capture strategy, you have a higher chance of making a profit. But the money that you make can be beyond certain thresholds and can be taxable at a higher rate. The taxes can really be a burden and weigh down on your earnings.

- All dividend stocks have the tendency of plummeting on the ex-dividend date. Unless the investor sets up a strategy that helps them to counter the decline in prices, they will be forced to wait for the recovery of the stock prices before they sell the stocks.

- While the strategy may be well-timed and profit the trader, the transaction costs can be very high as to negatively impact the profitability of the strategy. If the costs are high, the investor may unknowingly incur losses because the costs will eat into the profits the investor has made.

- The prices of stocks can be very inconsistent because of volatility in the market. This hampers the effectiveness of the strategy because the investor may predict the capital gains to be at a certain level during the dividend capture strategy. However, if the market is very volatile, the capital gains may deviate from what is expected and this will affect the capital gains of the investor. Sometimes it may lead to losses.

Other Criticisms of the Dividend Capture Strategy

The dividend capture strategy has been criticized in some cases for not producing tax advantages. The dividend returns are taxed at the ordinary capital gains tax rate of the investor. The reason is that dividend capture trades are not held long enough to benefit from the tax advantages and favorable treatment that the long-term investor receives from their dividends. This can however be tackled if the investor is wise enough to employ the strategy using a tax-advantaged account such as an individual retirement account.

It is also very difficult to account for the transaction costs of this strategy. While it is very dangerous to trade without accounting for these costs, it is also very difficult to account for them. Companies are paying dividends on a daily basis and this strategy is a very active one; the trader could have to account for trading costs on a daily basis. You will also find that the more active the strategy, the more commissions are paid.

The dividend capture strategy can be time-consuming, but it is very worthwhile. Depending on how much time you have to spare in your day, you can make time for day trading on a daily basis.

All you need to do is to learn about the basics of this strategy such as how to time the buying and selling of stocks. When you master the art, you can start off with lower capital and increase as you sharpen your skills.

I hope that having gone through this chapter; you are now well-versed with the dividend capture strategy. It may be difficult for you to engage in it as a college student because it is capital intensive and very active. You must make a high initial outlay to be able to trade and you have to make time to actively engage in the market on a daily basis. This, however, should not scare you away. Because, not in all cases, you don't have to do it yourself. You can make use of the services of experts and professionals who will help you to carry out your trades and time the market. All you must do is to ensure that the costs do not overshadow the profits that you make. Make sure you understand the risks involved in this method.

Chapter Quiz/Summary

1. A dividend capture approach involves buying a stock after the dividend is paid. (True/False)
2. A dividend capture approach involves buying a stock before the ex-dividend date. (True/False)
3. A dividend capture approach involves selling a stock after the payment date. (True/False)
4. A dividend capture approach involves selling a stock after the record date. (True/False)
5. A stock C is at \$0.61 on December 3rd. The ex-dividend date is December 5th. The record date is December 6th; and the payment date is December 20th. The stock is at \$0.7 on December 6th and \$0.65 on the payment date. The dividend paid is \$0.06 per share.
    a. On what date do you buy for the Dividend capture approach?
    b. On what date do you sell?
    c. What's the profit from the dividend capture trade?
6. What is the risk to the dividend capture strategy?

Answers

1. False
2. True
3. False
4. False; it can be on the record date
5. A. December 3rd or 4th

   B. December 6th or after.

   C. ($0.7-$0.61) +$0.06=$0.15 profit per share (if selling on record date)
6. The stock can decrease in value after the ex-dividend date.

Dividend Investment Traps

There are many times when investors just select stocks and press the buy button without giving it a second thought. This is especially easy for them if they have made a number of successful trades in the past. However, it will not be long before Wall Street gives you a reality check, because stocks can and do crash in the short term.

Other investors have come to think that they are unlucky, and investing is not for them. They have seen their picks going lower and lower losing a lot of money. Sometimes they buy high and sell low, and when they do that, they incur losses. As if that is not enough, when they exit the market, the prices suddenly shoot up. This is because of investment mistakes that investors make without knowing. This chapter will go over these.

Dividend investing is quite sophisticated and such mistakes are quite expected. This is one strategy that pays well but is complex in its nature. When you fail to use the dividend investing strategy properly, it can brew disaster for the investor. If an investor learns some of the pitfalls that affect investors, they can avoid them. It goes a long way in safeguarding the investor's money.

Here are some of the common dividend investing mistakes that are made.

Mistake 1: The High Dividend Trap

While coming across dividend stocks, you might come across stocks that have an extremely high dividend yields. Sometimes, you might see a dividend yield of 15% or 20%. These yields sound impressive; and you might think you've just struck gold.

However, the issue is that the company might be using all their profits to pay dividends. Or even worse, it might be financing its dividends through debt.

How do you tell the difference? Is it a really strong company that has more money than it needs? Or is it a failing business that's trying to trap investors by luring them with abnormally high dividends?

Let's have a look.

Dividend Yields Can Be Misleading If a Stock Just Crashed

As we learned earlier, the dividend yield is annual dividend percentage yield paid by the company.

The dividend yield can be a perilous trap if you are not careful. When calculating the dividend yield, the denominator is the price per share. If the price per share goes down, while the dividends remain unchanged, this means that the dividend yield should rise. For example, let's say Chevron paid of dividend of $3 when it's share price was $100. That's a dividend yield of 3%. However, the month after the dividend was paid, the share price crashes to $50. The dividend yield now becomes ($3/50)*100 = 6%. The dividend yield now shows as 6%.

Date	Dividend Paid	Chevron price	Trailing Dividend Yield
March 6 (Payment Date)	$3	$100	3/100*100 = **3%**
April 6 (Current Date)		$50	3/50*100 = **6%**
June 6 (Next Payment Date)	??	??	??

This may or may not be a buying opportunity. If the share price crashed because Chevron was losing business, maybe next time they can't afford to pay $3 dividend. You won't get a 6% dividend. So, the 6% dividend is a mirage.

If the share price crash was due to some other external factors and Chevron's earnings are still great, then they might still be able to pay the dividend of $3. It's important to understand why the share price crashed. Using this information together with fundamental analysis helps you to better figure out how the stock may be behaving.

When you perform a proper analysis, you will be able to develop a holistic view of the performance of the company. You will also be clear about its liquidity and solvency. Liquidity is a measure of how quickly a company can convert its assets into cash. Solvency measures the ability of a company to meet its obligations. The payment of dividends is done out of cash and the cash is made from earnings. The company should, therefore, have a history of consistency when it comes to earnings and earnings growth. You should never fall into the trap of only observing high dividends while turning a blind eye to duration.

There are a lot of things to observe about a company besides the high dividends. A company can get into debt and, for the reason of wanting to save face, still pay dividends. You must find out if the company is in any form of large debt before you invest. This might be an indicator that the high dividend payouts may not last for long. It would be bad for you to invest in a company that purports high earnings, only to find the earnings falling significantly a few months into the investment.

The payout ratio is a financial metric that is used to present the proportion of the earnings that the company pays out to its shareholders in the form of dividends. The payout ratio is expressed as a percentage of the total earnings of the company. In some cases, the payout ratio represents the dividends that the company pays out, expressed as a percentage of the cash flow of the company. The payout ratio can sometimes be referred to as the dividend payout ratio.

When a company has a low payout ratio, the implication is that the company is reinvesting most of its earnings into expanding its operations. If the payout ratio is above 100%, it shows that the company is paying out more in dividends than its earnings can sustain. This is often viewed by many as unsustainable and may be an indication that the company is using other means, such as using debt, to source the funds to pay dividends. The payout ratio is calculated as follows:

Payout ratio = Dividend Income / Net Income

The payout ratio is a good metric for determining whether the earnings of a company are growing or not. A lower payout ratio also implies that the company is earning enough to sustain the dividends it is paying out.

We ideally want a dividend payout ratio less than 50%; and avoid companies with payout ratio greater than 70%.

Example 1: Good Payout Ratio That is Growing

Consider the following information for company ABC:

Details	**2016**	**2015**
Dividend Payment	50,000	40,000
Net Income	325,0000	300,000
Dividend Payout Ratio	**15.38%**	**13.33%**

There are two important things to note here.

One is the payout ratio is only 13-15%. This is really low. That means that the company has plenty of extra money to invest in growing its business.

The payout ratio has also increased in the year 2016 as compared to the year 2015. If the company is still in the growth stages, this is a good sign. The payout ratio indicates that the payment of dividend is sustainable and can be consistent.

Example 2: Bad Payout Ratio

Consider the following information for XYZ Company:

Details	**2016**	**2015**
Dividend Payment	240,000	210,000
Net Income	325,0000	300,000
Dividend Payout Ratio	**73,85%**	**70%**

An analysis of the payout ratios above shows that the company is distributing more than half of the total earnings to the payment of dividends. This means the company has low retained earnings. The increase in the payout ratio in the year 2016 shows that the company has less retained earnings in comparison to the previous year. We want to avoid investing in this company as it may be a dividend trap.

Mistake 2: Buying Low-Quality Stocks

The desire to buy cheap stocks can culminate in big losses. For an inexperienced investor, it can be very tempting to go for stocks that are cheap because you might have low capital to start investing with. Stocks with a lower share price can include penny stocks, which may cost less than $5 per share. While these stocks may appear like they are the real deal, you are exposing yourself to a great deal of risk. Of course, the idea is that, when you invest in such companies, you are getting enough exposure to the equities world without having to invest a fortune. However, the truth of the matter is that, even if you do not have much capital, you do not have to specifically focus on low-cost investments.

There are some problems that you can encounter from trading in stocks of low price and quality. Penny stocks take up most of the space in the low-quality and low-price stock world. Penny stocks are usually unregulated and there is not much information provided about them to the investor. The trading volumes for stocks that are cheap are usually very low. It is very difficult to buy and sell such stocks and you may find yourself stuck with certain stocks and failing to get them off your hands for a profit. They are also very vulnerable to scams.

If you are to be a good investor, you must always remember that a low price does not always translate to good value. Some stocks may surely have a low share price but, at the end of the day, you will realize that the stock may not even be worth that low price. Stocks can be priced low to ensnare unsuspecting investors, but you will later find out that the company may have serious problems that it is struggling to get out of. In some cases, the company will show very little potential for growth. Remember, in the equities market, karma has it that you usually get what you pay for. If you buy cheap stocks, you can be sure to get low quality.

Mistake 3: Holding onto Stocks Past Their Due Date

It is true that some stocks can be held forever. Think about Coca-Cola or Walmart. These companies have growing businesses that are very competitive and do well in all types of markets. However, this is very rare. And, even for those companies, we need to monitor their earnings to ensure that they have earnings growth and net income growth.

The timing of how long a time is healthy for you to hold onto a stock is usually out of your control. There are many companies that have offered stock options to their employees but, by the time the companies folded, they had decreased in value. There are many factors that may cause the stocks that an investor holds to decrease in value. The investor may be careful with everything else but may find the company they have invested in losing value. It could be a new competitor that enters the market or, maybe, a new innovation and development that makes your company's' products obsolete. Sometimes you may try hard to keep your investment afloat, but the value of the company will continue to fall, and you end up losing.

Many investors have a terrible time letting go of certain stocks. The reason why people tend to hold on to a stock is that they are afraid of missing out. The stock market can be a gamble at times. The investor may be thinking that if they hold on a little longer, they might get more income. You should know that holding on to a stock for too long does not maximize its value but rather exposes you to more risk in the market.

Other Dividend Investing Mistakes to Avoid

Besides the mistakes explained above, there are other dividend investing mistakes that are often made by investors. The effects of these mistakes may just be as far-reaching as other mistakes and may cause the investor to lose out on their investment. Here are some such mistakes:

Misusing an Investment Strategy

There are a number of dividend investing strategies out there, and each investor is attracted to a strategy of their own. Strategies are chosen by investors who believe that they are the best for them. But this may, however, not be the case in your situation. This is one misstep that is very dangerous, and you should avoid it. You must make a comprehensive assessment of your situation and other important financial metrics. This will help you to come up with the best strategy for you. Appreciate the fact that not every strategy works for everyone. Learn as much as you can about dividend investing so that you are better able to figure out what works for you and what doesn't.

For example, a long-term dividend investor might want to avoid using the dividend capture strategy; while a trader might want to only use the options strategy and dividend capture strategy.

Misjudging Your Financial Needs

This is a common mistake among new investors. They are often fooled into thinking that dividend investing is rewarding enough to replace their paycheck. You need to run your numbers well and be conservative in your figures. You should never invest in dividends with the expectation that the dividends will cover all your living expenses. You have to include a factor of safety in your calculations. For example, if you living expenses are $4000 a month; you want to get a dividend income of $6000 a month (a factor of safety of 50%) before feeling comfortable in retirement.

Investors often underestimate their expenses and, at the same time, overestimate their dividend income. This is another pitfall. You should always be careful with the estimation of your expenses and your future needs. You should allow enough of a margin to allow for a comfortable lifestyle.

Failing to Reinvest Dividends

Dividend investments often grow if the investor masters the ability to reinvest dividends, even when they have demanding needs like funding their lifestyle. Reinvesting dividends can be vital. It causes you to create a dividend snowball. For any dividend investing strategy to work, you need to reinvest as much as possible and not take out of it before it has grown. Rather, wait until you can really afford to spend the money before you do so.

If you must live off your dividends, try to make sure that your needs are not in excess of the dividends you are receiving. If you manage to cover your needs and have some excess funds, you can reinvest them. As your dividends grow, you will discover that there will be more to reinvest. One good thing to do is to minimize your monthly budget. Make sure your needs are as lean as possible and let go of anything that is not necessary. Align yourself to developing your finances for the future.

Investing in Companies That Are Not Growing

Before making an investment, most investors often look at the stock price. The stock price by itself is an irrelevant metric in determining the perfect trade for you. It will not help you in any way in determining the perfect investment strategy. The best thing to focus on is the dividend yield. Instead of looking at the chart of prices, it is better to look at the historical dividend payments of the company. You should not focus on identifying companies with stock prices that are rising, but on those whose dividend payments are regular and consistent. If you are dealing with growth strategies, looking at stock prices would be ideal, but with dividend investing, much of the focus should be on consistent dividend payments. With dividend investing, regular dividend payments are a better sign of growth than stock prices.

I hope that this chapter has helped to enlighten you on some dividend investing mistakes that are made by most investors. It is not good for you to venture into investing without knowledge. This will cause you to encounter significant pitfalls. As a young investor, you are making investments with vital capital, so you need to avoid any mistakes that will reduce your chances of losing money.

Chapter Quiz/Summary

Dividend Yield = (Dividend Paid / Current Stock Price) * 100

1. What happens to the dividend yield when a company doubles its dividends?
2. What happens to the dividend yield when a company stock crashes 50% in one day?
3. A stock X paid $1 per share dividend in September when the stock price was $100. It rose to $200 per share in October. What is the new dividend yield?
4. What is the one key to accumulating a dividend snowball?
5. How do I keep track of a company's performance?
6. What is the factor of safety that I need to keep in mind while coming up with a dividend income threshold?
7. If my living expenses are $3000 a month, how much dividend income do I need to retire?

Answers:

1. Dividend yield doubles
2. Dividend yield doubles
3. 0.5%
4. Reinvesting dividends in quality companies with growing dividends
5. Monitor earnings every quarter
6. 50% factor of safety
7. $4500 per month (50% factor of safety)

Setting up a Diversified Dividend Portfolio

When it comes to setting up a long-term portfolio, diversification is crucial. You should never make forget about diversification. It is vital to ensure that you are not overexposed in the market because you will not get all your investment decisions right. Some of them will go wrong; diversification will cushion you. This chapter will take you deeper into the concept of diversification and will help you with the process.

What is Portfolio Diversification?

Portfolio diversification is an age-old principle of investment that states that an investor should never put all their eggs in one basket. The concept is that the investor should broaden their horizon by not investing in a small number of stocks in the same sector. Instead, one can invest in a variety of dividend stocks in different industries, in utility, mining, technology etc. We will specifically discuss asset allocation, but it is very important to understand that the major aim here is to spread risk across asset classes, markets, and economies to safeguard your investment.

The Importance of Diversification

Diversification, as already mentioned, goes a long way in avoiding exposure to a small number of assets. When you invest in a small or single type of asset your exposure to risk is great; if anything happens that brings down the value of the portfolio, your whole investment will be affected. When you invest across different asset classes, tap into different markets, and even go across countries, you spread your risks greatly. If one part of your portfolio does not do well, the others will, and you will be cushioned from risk.

The risk of short-term market volatility can affect your portfolio greatly. When you diversify your portfolio, you greatly reduce risks that have to do with short-term volatility. Some asset classes may be affected, but because you have a wide array of them in your portfolio, the others will cushion you against total loss. In some cases, you can make capital investment plans that sometimes do not go according to plan. Diversification protects you from the negative effects.

It is apparent that markets will always alternate between bull and bear markets. Bull markets are good for investors because there is not much negativity in the movement of prices; as long as the investment is set up well, the investor is almost guaranteed to get good returns. In bear markets, however, you will find that your portfolio will be declining gradually in value. If the bear market is prolonged, you may end up with losses. Diversification will help you to reduce the effects of a prolonged bear market because the assets that you hold will not be affected the same.

Sometimes the selection of stocks for investment is more like a gamble. You may select a stock that will not do well. In a diversified portfolio, you will find a good stock selection and some that are not so good. The good ones will cover your investment from the effects of bad stock selections. With diversification, you also get to enjoy the benefits of income generation and capital gains. The investor is also able to build their portfolio and align it in relation to long-term financial goals and their level of risk tolerance.

Diversify Across Different Industries

There are sectors that seem to be the real deal, but investors that are risk-averse will choose to diversify across different industries and sectors. Some prefer to niche down within a particular industry. For example, in the energy industry one can specifically choose to invest in gas, oil, and other forms of energy. If one form of energy does not do well and prices are tumbling, there obviously will be another form that is doing well.

Diversifying across different sectors is very important especially if you are dealing with the stock market. Certain sectors will perform better or worse than others. During the heated days of the coronavirus pandemic in 2020, many industries and sectors were affected, but they did not all take the blow the same. While the airline industry and restaurant sector were hit badly during this time, other sectors, such as health care and technology, did extremely well during that time. The large manufacturing companies that engaged in the manufacture of health kits and protective material did very well. If one investor had stocks in such a company and another company in the transport sector that was not doing well, the total performance of the portfolio would still not be that bad.

Diversifying Across Different Asset Classes

A well-diversified portfolio incorporates various asset classes. Such a variety comes in handy in enhancing your exposure to assets that belong to different classes. However, the wider asset variety makes it difficult for investors to determine the asset allocation splits that might work best for them. While expanding across different asset classes is of paramount importance, be sure to take some time to acquaint yourself with the specific asset classes that are accessible to you. If you are a dividend investor, prior knowledge with regard to how other stocks that are part of your portfolio assist you to protect your dividend stocks. Find out the level of risk that is involved for all the asset classes in a bid to maintain a balanced portfolio.

Blue-chip stocks are perceived to have a low-risk level because these companies are established and are very stable. They are usually leaders and pacesetters in their sectors. Growth stocks have a higher level of risk because they are usually thought of as stocks that are behind unproven products. The companies may not have been around for long and may not have established a reasonable track record. In the fixed income sector, you can also consider bonds which are at the forefront of the sector. This asset class also comes with its own risks and rewards; you might want to look at them before you add them to your portfolio. There are also assets like US Treasuries. These areas are as risk-free as anyone would expect.

When you diversify across these different asset types, you will have better peace of mind because you hedge against risk. You do not have to worry about what will happen if the market goes in the opposite direction than what you expect. Some people also include commodities like gold and other precious metals. These help you to hedge against what is going on in the traditional stock market. Diversification will work very well if it is carefully structured. All you need to do is to understand the nuts and bolts of each financial instrument that you intend to include in your portfolio.

Our Ideal Asset Allocation for a Dividend Portfolio

The best way through which you can balance risk and reward is through asset allocation. With this strategy you will come up with the perfect mix of assets and financial instruments in your portfolio. The aim in all this is to build a portfolio that helps you to achieve the ultimate goal of growing your wealth over time. You should be able to strike an equilibrium between risk and profit potential. Of course, each investor has a different risk profile and financial objectives. To be more specific, the asset allocation may differ due to age and time horizon. This section will focus specifically on the ideal asset allocation for a college student.

People can go to college at any time, which is the reason why you will find people of different ages in college. However, most college students are young and have several decades before they must live off their retirement savings. These people usually employ asset allocation strategies that are more aligned to financial instruments that have a greater risk. This means that your focus may be a lot more on stocks, especially dividend-paying stocks, than low-risk financial instruments.

On the other hand, if you have worked for the better part of your life and are nearing retirement, you will want to allocate more of the portfolio to fixed-income assets that have a lower risk profile.

We have two portfolios that we recommend to generate dividend income, based on your age and risk profile.

Dividend Portfolio 1

If you have a portfolio that is based on an income model, it means that all, or most, of the assets have minimum risk. They generate regular income which comes in the form of dividend stocks and stock appreciation. Here is the portfolio I like to use for diversifying my dividend portfolio:

- 30% Commodity Dividend Stocks
- 30% Utilities Dividend Stocks
- 40% Technology Dividend Stocks

This strategy gives you a diversified income of dividends across a variety of industries. For your Commodity portion, you want to be a little more active and invest during times when commodities are at the bottom of their commodity cycle. For example, you should buy commodity dividend stocks when oil is $20 per barrel and sell when it goes over $100. This requires being more of an active investor. We also need to invest in companies with solid balance sheets, like companies with strong dividends and low debt to asset ratio.

Utility stocks generally provide high dividends and have a Buy and Hold strategy. They may sink during recessions, but they hold up better than the general market, among the last stocks to crash and the first to recover.

The Technology section of the portfolio has the best growth potential. In this sector, we recommend looking at dividend growth stocks; that have growing dividend yields during recessions. These stocks must have strong cash flows, earnings and low debt. Avoid stocks that prefer doing cash buybacks instead of paying dividends.

Invest in stocks that have growing revenue, net profit and growing dividends.

Dividend Portfolio 2

This portfolio has less risk as compared to the previous one. It has a lower allocation to technology and higher allocation to utility stocks. There is also a 20% allocation to inflation indexed bonds or i-bonds.

- 10% Commodities Dividend Stocks
- 20% i- bonds or tips
- 20% Technology Dividend Stocks
- 50% Utility Dividend Stocks

The 20% in i-Bonds bonds adds a little stability to the portfolio. It is indexed to inflation. So, if inflation is at 8%, it'll pay you 8%. If inflation is at 4%, it'll pay 4%. The only disadvantage is you can only invest a maximum of $10000 per person per year. You can increase your investments over time. i-bonds are only issued by the US Government and require a social security number. Also, note that there are penalties for withdrawals before 5 years. Alternative to i-bonds are tips.

Disadvantages of Portfolio Diversification

Diversifying portfolios is ideal for most investors, but it does have its drawbacks. One of the drawbacks is time. Having to diversify across different asset classes can be very time-consuming. You must take time to study the markets and assets to find out which ones fit your desires and can be part of your portfolio. Besides being time-consuming, it can be very costly if the broker charges flat commissions. As an investor with a day job, you wouldn't want to engage in diversification if it costs you a lot of money.

Maintaining Your Portfolio

The Importance of Rebalancing

When you are investing through an actively managed fund, you will have no trouble with having to constantly check the balancing of your portfolio. The balance that you strike at the beginning, however, is not the same as that which will prevail until the end. There are a lot of changes that happen in the market, and you may have to occasionally rebalance your portfolio so that you continue to get positive returns. Maintaining a big allocation of assets that are underperforming may weigh down your portfolio.

Now, let's look at an example. Let's say you choose to invest in Dividend Portfolio 1. Three months after you set the allocation, there is a huge increase in your commodity stocks, and a crash in the technology stocks. Your commodity portion becomes 50% of your portfolio, while your technology section becomes 20%. In this case, you should sell some of the stocks in your commodity portfolio; and reinvest those in technology dividend stocks or utility dividend stocks. This is especially the case if your commodities are at the top of their commodity cycle.

Now, let's look at a second example. Let's say you bought Apple stock. You followed our rule and made sure it wasn't more than 5% of your portfolio. 1 year later, Apple stock has tripled due to the release of its new iPhone. So, now it's 15% of your portfolio. It may be difficult, but it's time to sell some Apple stock to ensure it's still at 5% of your portfolio.

So how often do you rebalance? Do it every year. Sometimes, in times of high market volatility, you can do it every 6 months.

So, the two takeaways of rebalancing your portfolio are:

1. Ensure that no single is more than 5% of your portfolio.
2. Rebalance your portfolio every 6 months to a year to ensure that you maintain a balanced portfolio.

Earnings and Net Income

Once you've invested in individual stocks, it is important to review earnings of the companies you've invested in every quarter. That's why we recommend no more than 10 stocks in your entire portfolio.

Now, how do we do this? It's easy to do this in Google. Just type in the name of the company you want to check out earnings for.

Etsy Etsy Inc >

NASDAQ: ETSY

Quarterly financials

DEC 2021 | SEPT 2021 | JUNE 2021 | MA >

(USD)	Dec 2021	Y/Y
Revenue	717.14M	16.16% ↑
Net income	161.56M	8.76% ↑
Diluted EPS	1.11	2.78% ↑
Net profit margin	22.53%	6.36% ↓
Operating income	143.98M	10.81% ↓
Net change in cash	160.79M	62.21% ↑
Cash on hand	-	-
Cost of revenue	208.97M	38.59% ↑

Check out the parts highlighted in green above.

First, ensure that the earnings are **Year/Year (Y/Y)** and not Quarter/Quarter. **Y/Y** ensures that you remove any seasonal variation.

a. Revenue should be higher. This is the case for Etsy; which is a good sign.

b. Net income should be higher. Net income is higher, which is good. But notice that it is growing slower than the revenue, which is a warning sign.

c. Cost of revenue increase should be negative or lower than revenue increase. In this case, we see that cost of revenue is increasing at 39%; which is more than double the revenue increase. This is a warning sign for investors and should be monitored. The company could struggle in an inflationary environment.

Monitor earnings to see how your stocks are performing over time. It is normal for companies to have lower income during a recession. But it's an alarming sign if revenues are going down while cost of revenues are going up.

We generally do not want to sell quality stocks that are paying us good dividends. But there are occasions when good companies go bad. Think of General Motors, General Electric, Lehmann Brothers etc. Most of the time we can avoid bad companies by checking out their debt profiles. But sometimes, they get bad over time or just get unlucky. So, earnings are a great way to spot that.

In conclusion, portfolio diversification is one of the concepts that are very important for an individual who wants to make the most out of their investing journey and reduce risk. This concept has been discussed extensively in this chapter to help start out. Diversification, however, does not guarantee that things will always go the way you plan. Things may not turn out so well for some asset classes, but diversification does improve your chances of achieving your financial objectives within your intended time horizon.

Insider Trading

One great to tell if a company is struggling is to review the insider trades of a company every 6 months or so.

If a company has a lot of insider selling, it means that they expect the company price to go down.

If a company has a lot of insider buying, it means that they expect the company price to go up.

This data is available at Yahoo Finance Insider Transactions tab.

Make a note of the number of purchases versus number of sellers and the dates/prices that the holders were buying/selling at.

Chapter Quiz/Summary

1. You should invest your entire dividend portfolio in commodities because they pay high dividends. (True/False)
2. You should invest your entire portfolio in Apple stock, because it has been going up for the last 10 years. (True/False)
3. You should invest all your dividend portfolio in technology stocks because that is the future. (True/False)
4. You should maintain a diversified, rebalanced portfolio in Technology, Commodities and Utilities that pays you a strong dividend income. (True/False)

5. If one of the stocks in your portfolio goes up 100x, you should just hold it forever as it may keep going up. (True/False)
6. How often should you rebalance your portfolio?

Answers:

1. False
2. False
3. False
4. True
5. False, you should sell some to maintain a diversified portfolio
6. Every 6-12 months

Tax Strategies

Disclaimer: For proper tax advice, contact a tax consultant in your local jurisdiction. This is not official tax advice, as the tax laws are different in every state and country.

Sometimes the return on investment is greatly reduced by investment expenses and brokerage fees. Taxes, however, are a bigger drag on investment returns. Investors who overlook tax issues tend to leave a lot of money on the table. Many investors will only look at taxes when they are nearing year's end. You should not let that happen to you. You must learn as much as you can about taxes and keep the information in mind throughout the whole year. Markets change frequently and it is wise to make tax-wise changes in your investment.

When you hold stocks and other assets that will remain in your hands for over a year, you should hold them in taxable accounts so that you enjoy the advantage of long-term capital gains. Dividend-paying stocks should also be held in taxable accounts. When you hold assets that earn short term capital gains and taxable interest, you should hold them in tax deferred accounts.

Many companies pay dividends when the dividend payments do not deter them from meeting their obligations when they become due. The dividends are also paid out if the company's assets are not less than its liabilities. When there are serious threats to the solvency of the company, that company will not pay dividends. Companies will always want to be proactive in the payment of dividends so that they can reduce the exposure of their assets.

Find Tax Free Dividends

The taxability of dividends depends on several factors. It depends on your residence and your level of income. In some countries, certain types of dividend investments are tax free to the investor. Given that there are 196 countries in the world and their laws keep changing, we cannot go through this in detail. It's best to consult a local accountant and ask them about tax free dividend sources in your area.

Changing your tax residency

As you may already know, different countries have different rules on taxing income. The same goes for taxing dividend income. As of 2022, there are several countries that do not tax dividend income. Hong Kong, Estonia and Latvia are a few countries that do not tax dividend income.

Also keep in mind that there are countries that do not have a capital gains tax rate; like Singapore, New Zealand, Switzerland etc.

Of course, there are many other reasons why one may want to move countries that have nothing to do with tax rate; but that's beyond the scope of this book.

It's just a good idea to ensure what your options are; and keep up to date on these options just in case you're looking to get more for your money.

Investing in a tax advantaged account (Roth IRA in the US)

Undisputedly, retirement accounts are the best way to save on taxes. These accounts are accessible to most people and experts also recommend them whenever the reduction of taxes is in question. When you invest in a retirement account, you reduce your taxable income and, at the same time, your investments will grow tax free until the time you retire.

List of Tax Advantaged Programs Across the Globe

USA – IRA, Roth IRA

Canada – Registered Retirement Savings Plan

Australia – Self Invested Super Fund

UK – Self-Invested Pension Plan

India – Personal Provident Fund (PPF)

Do Not Sell Assets

Not selling assets is a commonsense approach that helps you to avoid adding to your income when it is inconvenient for you to do so. One good formula for avoiding taxes on investments is not selling the assets that you hold until you are in a position that allows you to increase your income. The selling of your assets should be strategic. The most significant investments should be sold in years when you have the lowest income. This will have the effect of stabilizing your long-term income. You will be able to stay in the same tax bracket despite having earned a lot of money.

A Flexible Spending Account

If your employer offers one, you can try out a flexible spending account. This account allows you to funnel your paycheck directly into a tax-advantaged account. You can use the money in a flexible spending account to cover most out-of-pocket medical expenses. A variety of medical items are available to you through this account.

Deferring Bonus Checks

At the end of the year, a year-end bonus increases your income and puts you in a tax bracket that is much higher. In order to avoid this, you can defer your bonus check and ask your employer to pay you in the first month of the following year. The money will still get to you but, at the same time, you will have evaded an inflated income. It works better if your employer agrees to it and is not bothered. This really works best if you plan to quit your job the next year and your taxable income will be lower in the next year.

Other Tax Strategies

1. **Don't sell within 1 year – Get Long Term Capital Gains**

Investors are rewarded in most countries for holding stocks long term. In the United States, capital gains for stocks that are held for 1 year or longer are taxed at 15% instead of 25% (as of 2022). This is to disincentivize short term trading. So, try your best to keep your winning stocks for at least 1 year before selling.

2. **Selling losing stocks during a profitable year**

You can reduce your capital gains tax for a year with some capital losses. So, let's say you've made $3000 when you sold Microsoft stock earlier in the year. Come tax time, you notice that your Tesla stock is down $2000. If you sell your Tesla stock now, your capital gains reduce from $3000 to $1000 ($3000-$2000).

This is a great strategy to reduce your taxes during great bull markets.

3. Selling winners during a market crash year

If you've made some capital losses during a year, some countries (like the USA) allow you to write off that against your income (for up to $3000). So, if you made $50000 last year, and you lost $10000 in Google Stock, your income now is ($50000-$3000) $47000.

You can also now sell $7000 worth of winning stocks during the year without any additional capital gains.

Chapter Quiz/Summary

1. One way to reduce your tax is to never sell stocks (True/False)
2. One way to reduce your tax is to use a retirement account (True/False)
3. One way to reduce your tax is to not tell the Government (True/False)
4. Is it better to sell stocks within 1 year or after 1 year?
5. One way to reduce tax is to defer your annual bonus to the next year (True/False)
6. What is a good tax advantaged retirement account in the US?

Answers:

1. True
2. True
3. False
4. After 1 year, as there is reduced capital gains tax
5. True
6. Roth IRA / IRA

Conclusion

Dividend investing in times of inflation can be very difficult but it's also a great opportunity. Sometimes all you need to do is to take time to understand the metrics of dividend investing and learn from other investors as well. It has been a great delight putting this piece together because, even for me, it has been a great learning curve. Dividend investing is undoubtedly one of the best forms of investment. Once you have learned all the dynamics, you cannot help but fall in love with it.

We've gone through a lot of different topics in this book. However, there is a lot more to learn in detail about dividend investing and investing in general. Here's a couple of books I've written about inflation investing, that you would find really useful that go into detail on inflation investing.

Inflation Hacking by Kendrick Fernandez

Investing for the Long Run by Kendrick Fernandez

The end… almost!

Reviews are not easy to come by.

As an independent author with a tiny marketing budget, I rely on readers, like you, to leave a short review on Amazon.

Even if it's just a sentence or two!

I am very appreciative for your review as it truly makes a difference.

Thank you from the bottom of my heart for purchasing this book and reading it to the end.

BONUS

Using Options to Hedge Your Portfolio and Get More Passive Income

Think about 'options trading' as just that, an option. It's a complicated for beginner traders, that's why it's an extra in the book.

But if you learn how to use it, it's an additional tool that you can use to generate more passive income and hedge the risk in your portfolio.

In this chapter, we're going to do a brief intro to options and then some strategies you can use to complement your Dividend Investing strategy. If you'd like to learn about Options trading in detail, then we have a book that goes through the entire process from scratch. The book has worksheets and is written with the sole intention of getting you proficient in options trading.

The book is called "The Only Options Trading You'll Ever Need" and you can get it here.

What are Options?

In finance, an option is a contract that allows the holder of the contract the right to buy or sell an asset on or before an agreed future date. The selling/buying price of the stock is determined by the option.

The buyer has to pay a premium on the option to the seller.

A single options contract is for 100 shares of a company. That is the minimum number of shares that can be traded using an options contract.

Options can be very confusing for investors, so this chapter is structured to explain everything that you need to know.

Call Options

This is the most common type of option. This option is ideal for buying, not selling. The buyer of an option hopes that at a future date when they 'call' the option the stock will have risen beyond the strike price. This means that they will pay the earlier agreed-upon price—a price that is lower than the actual value. The investor bets that the stock will increase in value and this is often referred to as 'going long'.

Put Option

The buyer of a put option has the right to sell, not buy, an asset at a given time. This is the counterpart to the call option. The buyer of a put option expects that the price of the asset will have gone down since the contract date. If this happens, the investor sells the asset at a price that is higher than the actual price in the market.

How Are Options Traded?

The Securities Exchange Commission (SEC) regulates the options market in the US. These options are traded on major exchanges. Regulated options are much better to trade in than over-the-counter ones. Over-the-counter (OTC) options are unregulated and are riskier. To trade regulated options, you must engage a brokerage firm which will assist in handling your contracts. There is an options table online that you can then check out to see how well you are doing.

As a new options trader, you must be very careful with your investments. There are a lot of financial risks involved in the options market and regulators prefer that ordinary people do not get in too deep.

The risks involved can be far-reaching, therefore the investor should apply to their brokerage for an options account if they want to enter the market as a retail investor.

Selling Covered Calls

When investors sell covered calls, they have the option to sell their stocks at a given price to the buyer of the option. The buyer pays the seller a premium. So, the seller receives income through call options. Selling covered calls is great for people who own stock that has gone up in value significantly. Instead of selling the stock, they can receive an income for waiting to lock in profits.

Looking at it this way, selling covered calls can be described as a strategy for options trading. This strategy involves selling call options against the shares of your preowned stock. The reason why the strategy is described as 'covered' is that you own the stock and there's no need to buy it to exercise the option.

There are plenty of ways to make a lot of money in the stock market, but many investors limit themselves to only a few. Selling covered calls is one of the methods that many investors miss out on. Options do much better than traditional stocks and, to trade covered calls, the starting point is a stock that you already own. When opening the trade, you sell the call option. The buyer of the option is given the right to sell that option at an agreed-upon date. You earn some income when you sell the option. What it means is that the underlying stock is 'out of the money' until the expiration date of the option.

When an option is out of the money it means that its strike price is above the actual market price. If this happens, you get the chance to keep your full income from the trade. However, if the option is 'in the money' and is exercised, you have to sell the option to the holder. Since you already own the stock, you do not need to buy more shares on the open market to have the transaction completed.

Suppose you own 100 shares of a stock that is trading around $60. Let's also assume that you are willing to sell in the event that a 15% increase takes place, to $69 within a space of one month. You then decide to contact your broker so that you can sell at $69, who then enlightens you to the fact that the $69 call option is trading for $1 today. Considering that you own 100 shares, you get a premium of $100 for selling the option, from which you will subtract commissions and other expenses. On top of the $100 that you would have gotten from selling the option, you then agree to sell your shares for $69 each before a specific date within the same month. If your stock is above $69 on the date of expiration, you receive an additional $6900 (100 shares X $69) to the $150 that you got at first. This brings you to a total of $7050. However, if your stock is below $60 on the expiration date, then you get nothing out of the call. This is good because you sold the call to somebody else, and you get to keep the $150 premium. Moreover, your stock remains with you with no further obligation. You can even decide to sell another call option against the same stock in the next month, and you can generate a recurring income stream from the stock this way.

The Advantages and Disadvantages of Selling Covered Calls

Covered calls are a good way to earn income from the options premium and the appreciation of the stock price. This is a good way to accumulate wealth. If you are looking for ways to increase your passive income, this could be one of the good ways to do so. The strategy also helps to reduce downside risks that may affect your finances. The advantage is that you already own the shares under the options contract, as explained earlier. There is no need for you to go out into the market to buy so that the transaction can be completed.

On the other hand, there are some disadvantages associated with the trading of covered calls. One of them is that the selling of covered calls limits the amount of upside potential; when stocks go up above the strike price, you are forced to sell them for a price that is less than the actual worth currently prevailing in the market. In the above example, if the stock goes to $100; you still sell your stock at $69 only. This caps your gains.

One other disadvantage is that if you decide to sell the underlying stock before the expiration date, you might have to buy the options contract back. The transaction costs may increase while, at the same time, limiting your gains and increasing the total losses that you incur.

Selling covered calls is still a great way to earn passive income and to limit the risks that come with holding a stock in your portfolio. This is an ideal trading strategy for the holder of a stock long term. You, therefore, would want to trade in a way that minimizes the risks of losing your money in that stock. Of course, selling covered calls comes with disadvantages, but this should not stop you from trying it out. Honestly, there is no trading strategy that is completely risk-proof. All you must do is to trade carefully and to dedicate yourself to doing what it takes to minimize the risks involved.

Selling Cash-Secured Put Options

This is a great way to earn extra income. A cash-secured put has to do with the selling the option to buy 100 shares of a stock at a lower price. The goal is that the put expires worthless so that the premium is kept, or to be able to acquire a stock at a price that is below the current price.

For example, you want to buy a DBY stock trading at $20, but you think that it is too high at this price. Instead of buying you decide to sell one put at $18 that expires in the next 2 months for the premium of one dollar.

Because this is a cash-secured put, you will have to keep the cash in a money market account. There are two things that could happen:

1. You would receive a premium of $100 for 1 contract ($1 premium X 100 shares). Remember than any options contract has a minimum of 100 shares.
2. DBY can fall below $18 before the expiration date, and you might get assigned DBY shares. So, you would be buying 100 shares of DBX for one contract and spending $1800. Before starting the trade, your brokerage would check to ensure you have access to $1800.
3. If DBY is above $18, you keep the premium, and cannot buy the stock.

The potential profit of a cash-secured put is limited to the premium received. You achieve maximum profit if the underlying stock trades at above $18 until the expiration date. You then have to subtract the trading fees from the premium received. The potential loss is also limited to the difference between the strike price and the premium plus trading fees.

The selling of cash-secured puts is a bullish way of trading, although it is not as bullish as outright stock ownership. If an investor is bullish in a strong way, they would go for strategies like long calls, bull call spreads, and poor man's covered calls. Investors only sell puts on stocks that they expect to stay flat, or to only rise slightly, and not drop too much as well.

When Should You Sell Cash-Secured Puts?

It is best to sell cash-secured put options when there is either a slightly bullish or neutral outlook on a stock. It is great when you have a stock you really want to buy but the stock is very expensive. For example, if Microsoft is at $300 per share, and you want to buy it at $200 per share; you can sell a put option with a strike price of $200.

There are several things that you must consider when determining the perfect time to sell options.

The Risks Involved

The risk involved in the selling of cash-secured puts is only a little less than that involved in outright stock ownership. You should never fool yourself to think that there is no risk involved. There are people who have sold puts on respectable entities and have come away with staggering losses. In the stock market anything goes—ruling out risks is one thing you should never do. Companies, no matter how big they are, can go bankrupt, so the selling of cash-secured puts can go really well if things are going well. But when things go bad, cash-secured puts can do very bad. The best thing to do is to select companies with a strong technical outlook, competitive advantages, and earnings per share that are rising.

The biggest mistake most investors make is to assume that when a stock has dropped, it can't possibly drop much further. This is a very wrong way of seeing things and you should avoid it. A stock can be oversold today, and it can be oversold even more tomorrow.

If a stock goes to zero, you lose the entire amount of the cash secured put. So, in the above example, you would lose $1800 if the stock goes to zero.

Volatility and Implied Volatility

The volatility of the stock market is a very important concept that investors should understand. It is vital for an investor to know the stocks that have the highest potential for a price movement and take advantage when they can. Stock market volatility, by definition, is the range of movements in prices over time. A trade that is more volatile has the potential for significant gains, as well as significant losses.

There are several measures that are used in ascertaining the volatility. These include the standard deviation and the stock's Beta. You will realize that there is no particular set of stocks that is more volatile than the other. We can talk of stocks that are 'currently' volatile because they may not be volatile in the next review, while another set of stocks is. Stocks may be stable today, but still possess great potential to be volatile.

Implied Volatility

Implied volatility refers to a projection on the market with regard to the direction of movement in the price of a security. Investors use implied volatility to forecast the possible changes in prices. They can even use this metric to determine supply and patterns for specific stocks. The way implied volatility works is much of a muchness to historical volatility. The main difference between implied volatility and historical volatility is that the latter evaluates past changes.

The pricing of options contracts is often made easier through the use of implied volatility. It often results in options that have higher premiums. Forecasting the likely movement in the price of a security can turn out to be correct, or may not be. The forces of supply and demand, as well as the time value, are major factors in the calculation of implied volatility. Implied volatility is higher in bear markets and lowers in bullish markets. It does help in trying to quantify market sentiment and uncertainty but is calculated based only on prices rather than other fundamentals.

How Does It Work?

Investors often use implied volatility as a tool for forecasting changes in stock prices in the future. such predictions are done after considering some important predictive factors. Usually, the implied volatility is presented in the form of percentages and standard deviations over a defined timeframe.

When the market is bearish, the projection by investors is oriented toward the notion that the prices will fall as time progresses. For this reason, the implied volatility is higher. This is contrary to what happens when the market is bullish. In this case, the investors look forward to an increase in prices so the implied volatility is lower. Usually, investors reflect negative feelings toward bearish markets due to the increased amount of risk that they are associated with. Another important point to note is that implied volatility is not a clear indicator of the direction in which prices might move. For instance, high implied volatility may imply that the price could move toward any of the two extremes, either high or low. Another possibility is that the prices may also alternate between the high- and low-end extremes. Low implied volatility might mean relatively constant prices as it is unlikely that there may be broad changes.

For an option contract, the implied volatility is the value of the volatility of the underlying instrument which will return a theoretical value when input into an option pricing model.

To simplify the concept, the implied volatility is just the expected volatility in a stock.

The IV Rank

To make implied volatility work for options, we look at **IV Rank** for the stock. The IV Rank compares looks at the historical volatility of the stock over the last 52 weeks. It compares the historical volatility with the current volatility level.

So, if the Implied volatility is 100%, this means that the implied volatility is at the highest in a year. If the Implied volatility is at 0%, this means that the implied volatility is at the lowest in a year.

The Use of IV Rank With Options

The IV Rank helps an options trader to determine if the option prices are relatively high or low. This is important in devising an options trading strategy. In options trading, the IV Rank is the at-the-money implied volatility in relation to the highest and lowest values over the past year. If the IV rank is at 100%, it means the implied volatility is at its highest over the past year. The ideal options trading strategy in this case would be one that looks to sell options as the price of the options is high; and you receive a higher premium.

If the IV rank is low, it's a good time to buy options as the options premiums are lower.

Glossary

- **Blue-chip stocks:** The stock of a large company with a recognizable brand, whose market cap is over a few billion dollars and is considered by investors to be very safe.
- **Commodity stocks:** The stocks of companies that produce and distribute commodities like agricultural products, precious metals, industrial metals, and energy.
- **Dividends:** A sum of money that is paid by a company to its shareholders on a regular basis, that is quarterly, monthly, or annually. It is paid out of the profits.
- **Dividend yield:** It is the dividend per share, divided by the share price. It could be a company's total dividend divided by its market capitalization, expressed as a percentage.
- **Growth stocks:** These are stocks that offer a higher growth rate as compared to the rate prevailing in the market. These stocks grow at a faster rate than other stocks.
- **Inflation:** It is the general and progressive increase in the prices of goods and services in the economy. The units of

that economy's currency will buy less than they would if the prices were stable.

- **Intrinsic value:** The value of a stock calculated based on financial models.
- **Options:** A contract that gives the holder the right to buy or sell an underlying asset at a specified price on a specified date.
- **Spread:** A spread is the difference between two prices or yields. It is also the difference between the bid and the ask prices of a security.
- **Utility stocks:** Utility stocks, as the name suggests, are stocks in utility companies that provide basics like natural gas, electric utilities, and water.
- **Value stocks:** This is a stock that trades at a price that is lower than the intrinsic value, making it more appealing to investors.

References

Alvarez, S. (2022, February 20). *What Is The Intrinsic Value Of A Stock?* Investopedia. https://www.investopedia.com/articles/basics/12/intrinsic-value.asp

Faulkenberry, K. (2018, November 24). *Dividend Investing: 6 Important Advantages*. Arbor Asset Allocation Model Portfolio (AAAMP) Value Blog. https://www.arborinvestmentplanner.com/dividend-investing-advantages/

Healy, J. (2019, March 13). *Constant Dividend Growth Rate Model Explanation With Example.* www.myassignmentservices.com. https://www.myassignmentservices.com/blog/constant-dividend-growth-rate-model-explanation-with-example

Smith, T. (2021, June 28). *What Is The Maximum Loss Or Profit With A Covered Call?* Investopedia. https://www.investopedia.com/ask/answers/032615/what-maximum-i-can-lose-if-i-make-covered-call.asp

Inflation Hacking

Introduction to Inflation

Inflation is the rate at which a currency experiences a decrease in its purchasing power. It happens over a long period in most economies. However, there are examples of very high inflation rates over short periods, known as hyperinflation. Economists argue that inflation is almost always a result of an excessive increase in the money supply in an economy.

The general population feels inflation by the increase in the prices of goods they purchase. Things like groceries, fuel, and utilities get expensive over the length of time when an economy is experiencing inflation. Each unit of that economy's currency loses its value in terms of what people can exchange it for. When economies continue to suffer relatively high inflation rates over long periods, people can afford fewer things. If they have money saved in interest-free bank accounts, the value of their savings also decreases.

What causes Inflation?

When there is more money available, and the quantity of goods remains the same, the demand for money will be lower and basic economics will apply. Now, people would be willing to pay more money for the same item, which will cause an increase in the price of that item. An increase in the overall money supply would mean that buyers can pay more for the same things across the board. As a result, there is an increase in the price of items, and the economy will experience inflation. They refer to an imbalance between the money required by an economy for its trade-related needs and the amount of money supplied. It is worth mentioning that an overall sustained increase in prices has to occur for inflation. A singular rise in prices due to demand does not point towards inflation.

Even though most economists agree that an increased money supply is the main reason behind inflation, there are three key drivers of inflation when the supply of money increases.

Demand-Pull Effect

This phenomenon occurs when the population suddenly has a lot more money to spend. Naturally, the demand for items increases. When this demand is unmet by the manufacturers and producers of goods, the demand for goods increases, causing the demand to drive up prices.

Cost-Push Effect

This effect occurs when the demand-pull effect applies to intermediary goods such as oil, utilities, and other raw materials. As the retailers factor in these costs when they price their products, an increase in their price causes an increase in the finished goods' price.

Built-In Inflation

This effect is a result of an economy that has been experiencing inflation for a long time. Employers increase their wages to accommodate the trends. When their wages increase, the cost of labor increases for the producers and manufacturers. This causes an increase in the price of finished goods.

How do economists determine the rate of inflation?

Economists can model inflation trends and can make projections for future economic periods. They do this by various methods. One is by looking at historical data and using macroeconomic changes to produce a forecast for the future. These forecasts help Governments and Central Banks monitor their monetary and fiscal policies, respectively.

The metric used to measure inflation is the Consumer Price Index (CPI). To calculate the CPI, determine the weighted average of a basket of everyday consumer goods and services such as food, healthcare, transportation, etc. It calculates how the average price of these products and services change over time. This gives a general idea of the rate of inflation an economy is experiencing.

As we have explained earlier, inflation is an increase in the prices of a basket of everyday items that change over time. That makes it a lot easier for almost everyone to determine the rate of inflation in their region. However, it's important to remember that the inflation rate you calculate may not be the same as the one determined by your regional or national government. The main reason for this is that those institutions will most definitely be using a basket of goods that will be quite different from yours. For example, they might be taking the average price of unbranded wheat or rice, whereas you would be comparing a specific rice brand that you use regularly. Let us look at different large economies that measure their respective CPIs.

United States

In the US, the Bureau of Labor Statistics determines the CPI. The Bureau collects samples of tens of thousands of products that get purchased by thousands of families across the United States to track their prices. They look at all types of products and services for this exercise. They do this by selecting a popular item through a process called initiation. For example, they can choose a specific brand for a particular type of cheese purchased by a large number of families in the US. The sample product changes every four years. The statistics are in the link below:

https://www.bls.gov/cpi/

Australia

The Australian Bureau of Statistics is responsible for the calculation of the Australian CPI. It determines the CPI by calculating the change in thousands of everyday items' prices and grouping them into 87 categories and 11 broad groups. The bureau then tracks the difference in these items' prices every quarter and then publishes the CPI. The 11 groups are housing, food/non-alcoholic beverages, Transport, Recreation and culture, Alcohol and tobacco, Furnishings, household equipment and services, Health, Education, Insurance and financial services, Communication, Clothing, and footwear. The statistics are in the link below:

https://www.abs.gov.au/statistics/economy/price-indexes-and-inflation/consumer-price-index-australia

Here are the links to inflation data for other major world economies.

China
https://data.worldbank.org/indicator/FP.CPI.TOTL.ZG?locations=CN

Japan
https://www.stat.go.jp/english/data/cpi/

Germany

https://www.destatis.de/EN/Themes/Economy/Prices/Consumer-Price-Index/_node.html

UnitedKingdom

https://www.ons.gov.uk/economy/inflationandpriceindices

India

http://mospi.nic.in/cpi

France

https://data.worldbank.org/indicator/FP.CPI.TOTL.ZG?locations=FR

Brazil

https://data.worldbank.org/indicator/FP.CPI.TOTL.ZG?locations=BR

Canada

https://www.statcan.gc.ca/eng/subjects-start/prices_and_price_indexes/consumer_price_indexes

How You Can Measure Inflation Yourself

Measurement of inflation is very complex, and there are many ways to measure it. Different metrics can give you different results. Since every person spends money on different items, inflation is different for every person or family.

Let us discuss how you can determine the rate of inflation to an accurate degree on your own to become more aware of how much you are spending and if you need to take any steps towards protecting your financing against the harmful effects of inflation.

The best way to calculate inflation at home is to track the prices of the goods and services you use regularly. As a result, you will determine how inflation directly impacts you instead of how general inflation affects other people. You can calculate inflation by following the steps given below.

- Create a selection of everyday goods and services you use. For example:
    - 1kg of your favorite brand's rice or flour.
    - Price of a fixed unit of your favorite snack, e-g, a chocolate bar.
    - Your monthly mobile phone cost.
    - Your monthly price of utilities.
    - Price of a movie ticket at your local cinema.
    - Price of 1 liter (or gallon) of fuel in your area.
    - Price of a private medical check-up in your area.

These prices should be easy to collect every month. You can track the changes in these prices on a quarterly, semi-annually, or yearly basis to see how much they have increased. You can then see the rate at which prices rise with inflation in your area. An example calculation could be as follows.

Price of 1kg rice on January 1st, 2021: $4

Price of 1kg rise on March 1st, 2021: $4

Price of 1kg rise on June 1st, 2021: $4.2

Price of 1kg rice on September 1st, 2021: $4.2

Price of 1kg rice on January 1st, 2022: $4.5

Inflation calculated on a semiannual basis:

January-June 2021: (4.2-4)/4% = 5%

The inflation rate was 5% on a semi-annual basis between January and June of 2021, taking rice as an example.

Do the same for all items in your list and calculate the average rate of inflation.

Why do some economists think inflation is good?

Businesses rely on a steady stream of cash flow to function. They count on constant sales to become and stay profitable. Ongoing sales are only possible if people keep spending money. People make purchases mostly because of specific needs, but they also make purchases to benefit from lower prices. Just look at how incredibly successful sales are for business.

What exactly does a sale imply? It implies that if you don't purchase an item during a given time frame, its price will increase. Inflation essentially acts as a massive sale for most, if not all, items in an economy. People believe that spending now is better than spending in the future because prices will increase. Also, prices increase while wages do not. This results in people spending more instead of saving, which keeps the businesses going.

An economy with many thriving businesses continues to grow, creating more employment opportunities, increasing wages, and raising living standards for people. Those economists who believe that a low rate of inflation is beneficial to an economy support this view.

How Inflation Can Hurt You

We have explained earlier that inflation causes a rise in the price of items. These items are all sorts of things you use daily, such as food, utilities, clothes, and fuel. However, inflation also causes increases in prices of essential and emergency services such as healthcare, transportation, education, and insurance. The important thing is that all modern economies experience inflation. However, your financial circumstances might not survive high rates of inflation.

You could lose your job, or your business might suffer a loss, consequently reducing your income. However, even if you have a stable job, your purchasing power will decrease if your wages do not increase over time. You will be unable to afford the same quantity of items that you could only a few years back, your rent will increase, which eats into your expendable income, and any savings you have in the bank will lose their value over time.

How to safeguard your finances against inflation?

We have discussed in detail what inflation is. It is essentially the value of your money going down over time. Another way to look at it is that the value of items goes up over time. The logical way to protect your finances against inflation is to invest in items instead of cash. But that is easier said than done. With hundreds of asset classes to choose from, it might become so confusing that you might end up with your standard savings account. But investing in assets, bonds or commodities should not be this hard. We certainly do not think so. The next sections of this book will discuss different types of assets that protect against inflation. We will discuss how you can invest in these and the characteristics of those assets that enable them to act as a suitable hedge against inflation.

Precious Metals

Precious metals are those metals that have a remarkably high value compared to other metals. This higher price can result from various factors such as scarcity, use in industrial applications, and market sentiment. Investors have long used precious metals to hedge against not only inflation but also adverse market risks. The price of precious metals usually rises in times of economic certainty because investors choose to buy them as 'safe-havens.' This means that they are considered safer than other asset classes, such as equities. However, the prices of precious metals increase over the long term anyway.

Precious metals are almost always easy to purchase. They are easy to store because of how little space they take when physically stored. They also have reasonably high liquidity, which means that they can be sold for cash whenever required. These factors make precious metals an excellent choice for an asset class to hedge against inflation. We will discuss a few precious metals in detail below.

Gold

Gold is by far the most famous metal to ever exist. Humans have been in love with Gold for as long as we can trace record history. It was always thought to be valuable and has maintained its status as an undisputed safe-haven asset for many millennia and continues to maintain its position even today. Investors use Gold to diversify risk in their portfolios, hedge against inflation, and safeguard against worst-case scenarios such as war. It has long been considered a store of value, and continued to rise in value throughout history.

Why does Gold have value?

Gold has held steady value throughout time, which is why it is often relied on as a hedge during tough times. It has importance as part of a diversified investment portfolio. Gold's value can increase in response to events that cause a decline in the value of paper investments (stocks and bonds) to decline. Although short-term volatility in Gold's price is almost inevitable, it has always maintained its value over the long term, thus offering an excellent investment opportunity.

How effective is Gold against inflation?

As we quote Gold against the U. S. dollar, the dollar value loss due to inflation makes Gold more expensive. This expensive Gold provides a hedge against inflation. Moderate inflation levels do not affect gold prices, which tend to remain stable, but high inflation rates lead to higher gold prices. This makes it an effective hedge during inflationary periods, especially in the long run.

Below you can see the performance of Gold over the last 100 years. You see the outstanding performance of Gold during the 1970s. The 1970s were not only a highly inflationary period, but it was also the period where the US Government removed the US dollar link to Gold.

Over the last 100 years, the growth rate has been 4.5% per year, which is higher than the average annual rate of inflation in the United States (3%).

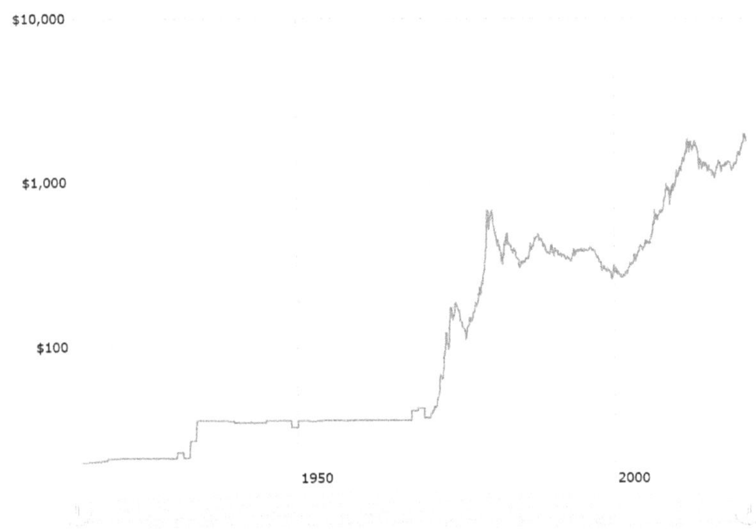

Source: Macrotrends

2021 = $1850

1921 = $20.61

Rate of growth = 4.5% per year

How can you invest in Gold?

You can purchase Gold in several ways. You can buy physical gold bullion from traders and online stores. You can also invest in Exchange Traded Funds that have a significant quantity of Gold in their portfolios. You can also purchase Gold on the commodities market online.

Silver

Silver is a rare metal with a lot of versatility. It was one of the first native metals to be mined. Crafting jewelry and making currency, silverware, dental fillings, and mirrors are just a few ways we use Silver. Silver iodide seeds clouds that can produce rainfall. In addition to its antibacterial properties, it also offers several health benefits. Silver is the best conductor, so it has significant industrial use. Other applications include the manufacture of contacts, switches, and fuses. The value of silver is of little wonder.

Why does Silver have value?

Silver has long been a form of money and a store of value. Today, it has become the most widely used coin-making material ever. The continuing cognizance of silver and its store of value have maintained the worth of silver over the centuries. As it has moved out of currency, silver supply and demand are primarily rooted in jewelry, industrial applications, and investment options.

How effective is Silver against inflation?

Silver remains an affordable asset for investors as a hedge against inflation. With a lower price point than Gold, it can be more appealing to the smaller retail investor. With its correlation to stocks and bonds, it can be an excellent asset to diversify a portfolio. Due to its industrial applications, the price of silver moves more with inflation, requiring a much smaller investment to hedge against inflation.

Below is the 100-year chart for Silver. It shows a growth of **3.7% per year**, which slightly outpaces the inflation rate. Silver is undervalued when compared to Gold.

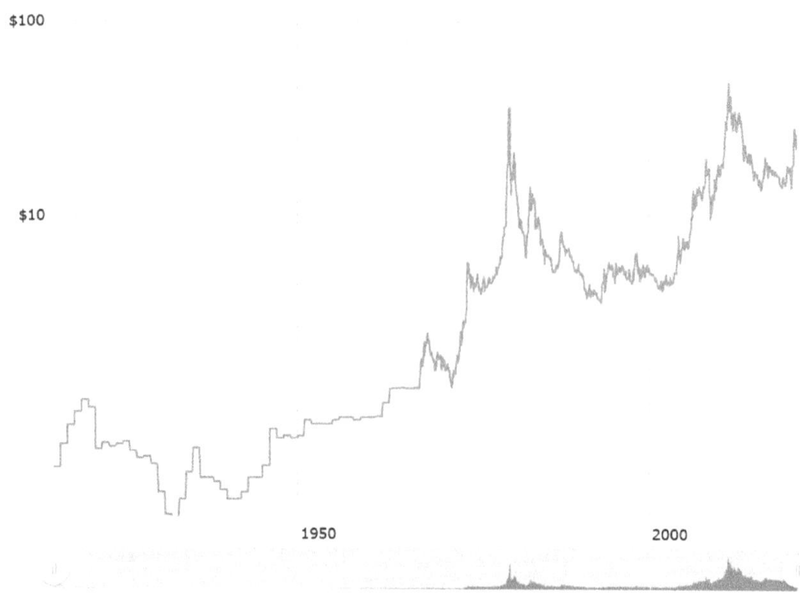

Source: Macrotrends

2021 Price = $25

1921 Price = $0.61

Rate of growth = 3.7% per year

How can you invest in Silver?

There are multiple ways to invest in Silver. The traditional method involves buying actual bullion bars bought and sold over the counter at major banks. Additionally, investments can be made in silver coins and rounds, silver exchange-traded products, a silver certificate of ownership in place of actual bullions, silver accounts allowing direct buying and selling of silver, and in the form of investment in silver mining companies.

Platinum

Platinum is a scarce precious metal known for its strong conductivity, resistance to corrosion, and durability. It has tremendous economic importance, and its applications include jewelry, catalytic converters, oil refining, electronics, and dentistry. A diverse range of applications has ensured high demand for Platinum, with a resulting significant economic role.

Why does Platinum have value?

Although Platinum has a short financial history, having been discovered only about 300 years ago, its scarcity often confers its value. The rarity of platinum deposits and the difficulty in mining them has made it the highest symbol of value and quality. It has become a significant attraction for investors looking to diversify their portfolios. Platinum is mostly in one country, South Africa, which limits its availability. Moreover, the imbalance in the limited supply and excess demand of Platinum lends it even greater value.

How effective is Platinum against inflation?

It has been identified as a moderately good investment for portfolio diversification and hedging against inflation. It is traded around the clock on global markets and often tends to fetch a much higher price than Gold in financially and politically stable periods. Due to its intrinsic value and correlation to stocks and bonds, even a small percentage of Platinum can offer inflationary protection.

Below is the 50-year-old chart for Platinum. As you can see, it does increase over time. The rate of increase tends to match the rate of inflation. However, an important thing to note in the chart is the peaks. The peaks happen at different times as compared to Gold and Silver. So, a small position in Platinum can hedge against inflation and serve as a great diversifier in your precious metals portfolio.

Source: Macrotrends

2020 Price = $1029

1970 Price = $226

Rate = **3.1% per year**

How can you invest in Platinum?

Platinum is traded as an exchange-traded fund (ETF) on the London and New York stock exchanges, offering a good investment vehicle. Platinum is also available in the form of coins and bars available at different foundries, as well as in the form of Platinum accounts where it can be instantly bought or sold. Another way is to create a futures contract where Platinum is bought or sold at a predetermined time and place.

Palladium

Palladium might not be the most popular precious metal, but it is a highly effective asset for investment to protect against inflation. It is the fourth precious metal we will discuss in this. As a by-product of Platinum mining, Palladium holds immense investment value.

Why does Palladium have value?

The industrial, jewelry and investment usages of Palladium have contributed to its sporadic growth and value. It has quickly become the most valuable of the four precious metals, primarily due to its application in the automotive industry as a raw material in hybrid vehicles' catalytic converters. Acute shortages have also driven Palladium prices up. With climate change and anti-pollution policies in effect worldwide, demand for Palladium has only increased, and it has been trading above Gold for the past year. Its value is also derived mainly from its application as an inflation hedge.

How effective is Palladium against inflation?

Like other precious metals, Palladium is also priced in U. S. dollars, giving it an inverse relation to the dollar. Therefore, appreciation in the dollar rarely influences Palladium, and depreciation in the dollar reduces purchasing power, making metals like Palladium an ideal hedge against inflation. Palladium has been steadily increasing in value since the start of the 21st century, which has greatly benefited investors.

In the Palladium chart below, you can see that it is the best performing of the precious metals with a growth rate of 8.7%; due to the increasing demand for palladium. Palladium has applications in catalytic converters of automobiles, and consumers are shifting away from diesel to petrol vehicles recently, which is great for palladium in the short term. But remember that if electric vehicles increase their market share, it might hurt palladium in the long term. So, it's best not to have a considerable investment in Palladium.

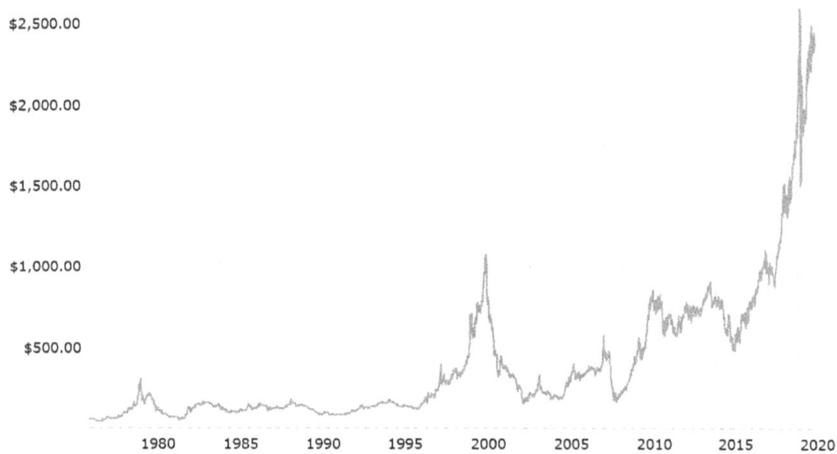

Source: Macrotrends

2020 price = $2365

1970 price = $58.5

Rate = **8.8% per year**

How can you invest in Palladium?

Investors may gain exposure to palladium by investing in palladium-focused businesses. Direct investment in Palladium producers includes Norilsk Nickel, North American Palladium, Stillwater Mining. Alternatively, investors can buy bullion bars and coins made of Palladium for portfolio growth. Exchange-traded funds are also a good investment vehicle. Palladium-backed ETFs track the precious metal like an index fund but trading on a stock exchange.

Gold Mining Companies

Since gold prices are the same everywhere, companies with lower costs per ounce of gold mined to make the most profit. The gold mining stock price is mostly contingent on Gold's price, especially with companies whose primary business is gold mining. That said, gold mining companies can produce lucrative output for investors.

Why do Gold Mining Companies have value?

The value of gold mining companies is derived mainly from the value of the Gold. Their primary worth comes in their ability to offer the potential of leveraged upside to Gold's price. When gold prices rise, mining companies can increase their total production to grow their total sales. There is also a strong relationship between the price of Gold and gold mining stock. A 10% increase in gold bullion price can translate into a 20-30% increase in stock prices. Limited supply also poses barriers to entry, which further lends to the value of mining companies

How effective are Gold Mining Companies against inflation?

Gold mining stocks provide a hedge against inflation. Gold rises with inflation but typically also produces earnings in non-inflationary times. Therefore, gold mining stocks offer a better inflationary hedge than base metal mining stocks, as higher prices translate into higher profits. However, over-taxation of companies in inflationary times can sometimes reduce earnings. Gold mining stocks also provide a broader portfolio and gold investments, reducing overall volatility and increasing risk tolerance.

How can you invest in Gold Mining Companies?

Gold mining companies are available as shares on the stock market. The decision to invest in a particular gold mining company should be an informed one supported by understanding the mining industry's cyclical nature. Additionally, investors should identify companies who can weather inevitable downturns with low production costs and strong balance sheets.

Gold Streaming Companies

Gold streaming companies act as middlemen in the gold mining sector. They pay an upfront fee to mining companies in exchange for a percentage of their revenue or a right to purchase their future production at a fixed cost. Their investment aids cash-strapped mining companies in exploration and production projects, which grants gold streaming companies exposure to a range of companies in the gold sector.

Why do Gold Streaming Companies have value?

Despite a rise in metal prices, investors still prefer to buy stocks from streaming companies than gold mining companies. The extensive exposure range makes streaming companies a much safer, more reliant investment, and they hold their value in the lower-risk investment they offer. As bigger gold miners are fully valued, this practically makes streaming companies the more attractive investment choice.

How effective are Gold Streaming Companies against inflation?

The lower risk involved in gold streaming companies makes them a good hedge against inflation. The interest rate and production upside can typically provide a return on investment, even if Gold itself is shorted as a hedge. Streaming companies have been trading at all-time highs even when mining companies were trading at all-time lows. Gold streaming companies have even reported increased dividends. Despite the poor price performance of mining companies, streaming company performance has remained unharmed. As streaming companies hold highly diversified portfolios of mines and other assets, the concentration mitigates risk.

How can you invest in Gold Streaming Companies?

Stocks for various gold streaming companies are available on the stock exchange. Some of the largest streaming companies include *Wheaton Precious Metals, Franco-Nevada, Royal Gold, Osisko Mining,* and *Sandstorm Gold.* Investment decisions should be the product of thorough research into the company's performance and risk mitigation abilities, although diversification primarily assures low risk.

Gold Mining vs. Gold Streaming Performance

Below is a chart of the Gold Miners VanEck ETF vs. SPDR Gold Shares ETF since 2000. As you can see, Gold Miners do underperform the value of Gold ETFs because most Gold mining companies are poorly run and inefficient.

Investments in Gold Mining companies require a lot of expertise in individual gold mining companies and about the gold market in general. Finding the right investment at the right time is the key to success in gold mining companies, but investing in Gold or gold ETF seems like a safer bet.

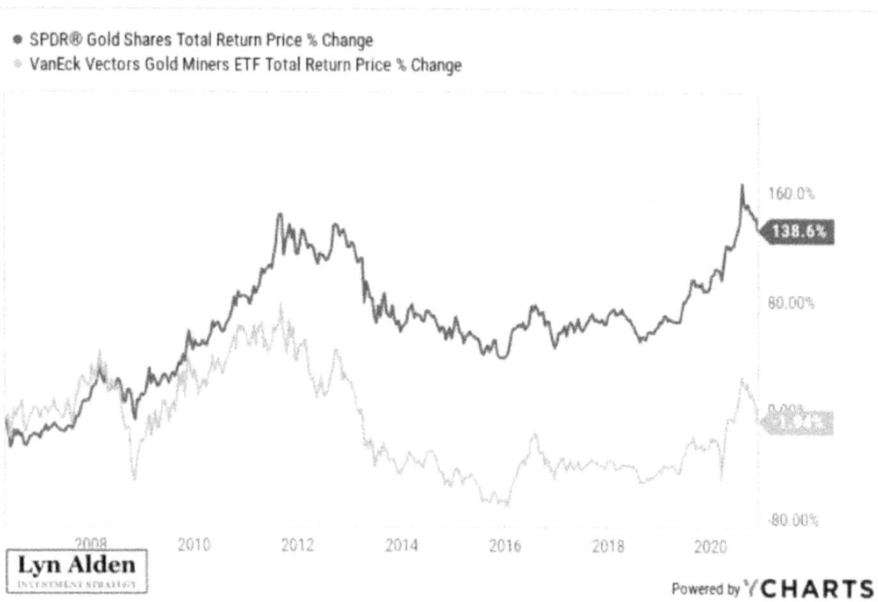

Source: Lyn Alden Investment Strategy, www.lynaden.com

In the chart below, we compare the performance of 3 popular Gold Streaming companies vs. Gold Etf (Gold ETF is in purple). As you can see, all the Gold Streaming companies outperform Gold.

Gold Streaming companies, in general, are a significant investment and the best way to invest in Gold.

Source: Lyn Alden Investment Strategy, www.lynaden.com

Commodities

Commodities are those goods that investors perceive to have value without giving any significance to their origin or brand. For example, wheat can be grown in any part of the United States, and it would get traded as wheat. Most of these goods are in constant demand throughout the world, such as cocoa, oil, rice, cotton, and copper.

Commodities are an asset class that is traded almost exactly like securities. They are available on unique exchanges called mercantile exchanges. Investors typically group commodities into two main categories, soft commodities and hard commodities. They refer to soft commodities as cultivated goods, such as wheat, corn, and soybeans, or ranched goods, such as cattle. And they refer to hard commodities as goods that require drilling or mining to extract from the earth, such as oil.

Why do commodities perform well against inflation?

As we explained earlier, inflation reduces the purchasing power of a currency. Another way to look at it is that things become more expensive. Items that are in demand all the time become more expensive consistently, which is where commodities come in. When you invest in commodities, you are essentially trading in your currency that will devalue over time because of inflation and getting something that will increase in value. If you keep your investments in commodities over a long period, they will almost always provide an effective hedge against inflation.

Oil

Oil is arguably the most important source of energy we have today. Even after various power plants shifting towards renewable sources, oil dominates the transportation sector. It continues to be the primary source of plastic.

Why does oil have value?

Oil is the top energy source for the world today. Countries such as the United States and China consumed a combined 33 million barrels per day in 2019. These countries also like to keep large reserves of oil for future uses, and because for all other countries that are not exporters also need oil, oil has a consistent demand. This is true even when oil loses value because other factors (mostly speculative) determine oil's value.

How effective is oil against inflation?

Besides the abnormal price actions such as the one in 2014 and 2020, oil can still offer protection against inflation in the short term. Investing in oil directly might not be the best way to protect yourself against inflation as the oil markets can be very volatile. However, let's look at oil-focused ETF and especially the energy companies such as Exxon and BP. We can see a very healthy appreciation in value when checking their share price performance. Both Exxon and BP experienced incredible gains between 2010 and the start of 2020 by almost doubling the price. Exxon's share price was 56.57 on 2nd July 2010 and jumped to 102.65 just four years later.

The historical chart below shows that oil tends to track within $20 - $140 per barrel. So, it's best to invest in oil companies when it is close to the lower end and sell closer to the top end of the range.

Source: Macrotrends

How can you invest in oil?

The safest way to invest in oil is by investing in oil-focused ETFs and large energy companies. These companies understand the risks associated with oil as an investment, and how to manage the risks. Keep in mind that oil might serve to be a short-term hedge against inflation because of the changing trend towards energy sources for the future.

Copper

Copper has remained an integral part of the industry for thousands of years. Once can mold copper into various shapes, due to its' highly malleable nature; making copper an excellent choice of metal for wires and motors. It is an excellent heat and electricity conductor, making it a viable option for various other industrial uses.

Why does copper have value?

Copper has applications in almost all types of industries throughout the world. Investors who trade copper speculate on the global demand due to an ever-increasing industrial activity. More recently, in growing economies like India and China, copper demand outpaced copper production. The growth of the housing market also contributes towards increasing demand for copper due to its electrical uses. Investors continue to value copper as a reliable hedge against inflation. It is also used heavily to manufacture motors, investors, batteries, and wiring for electric vehicles. The average use of copper by weight per vehicle is 83KG, and with electric vehicle demand expected to increase in the coming years, copper will remain a precious commodity.

How effective is copper against inflation?

According to Bloomberg intelligence, copper consistently outperformed every other primary asset class except energy when measured against every 1% annual increase in the United States Consumer Price Index. Its base trading per pound increased by almost 50% between December 2016 and December 2018.

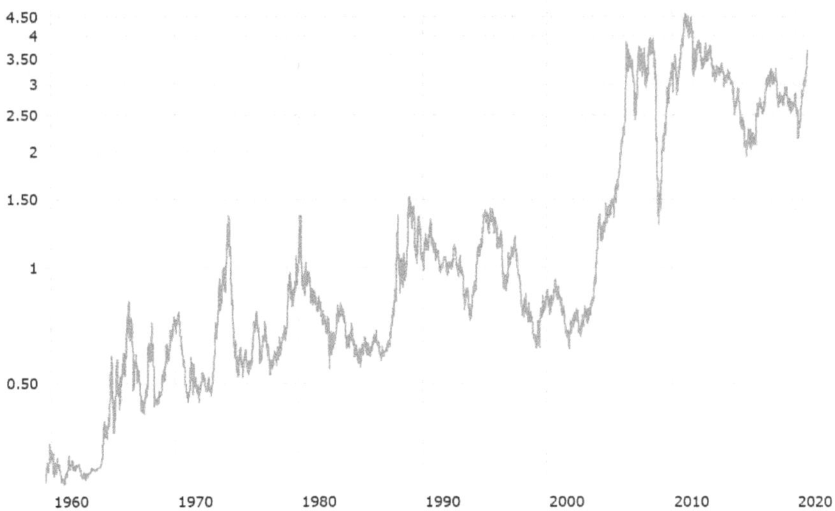

Source: Macrotrends

The historical chart of copper above shows an average increase of approximately 4% per year, which outpaces inflation. Copper offers a lot more future promise due to its use in electric vehicles and construction projects.

How can you invest in copper?

Copper is an excellent long-term hedge against inflation when traded individually. Its lot size may be an issue as it comes in a 25,000 pounds lot. So, if the trading price for one pound were 3 USD, you would need to invest 75,000 USD. However, the best way to invest in copper is by investing in copper mining companies. These companies make their livelihoods from copper and have better measures in place, which provide more stable returns than the metal itself.

Corn

Corn is among the most popular global food sources. A crop native to Central America, corn has been grown in almost all parts of the world for centuries. It is used as a food source, making ethanol, producing high fructose corn syrup, and producing a variety of alcoholic drinks. The United States is the largest corn producer, with an annual production of over 350 Million Metric Tons.

Why does corn have value?

Global demand for food continues to grow by the day, which is met with various food sources. One of these is corn. Corn continues to remain in high demand in the United States, China, and the European Union for various purposes. Ethanol demand is an important price driving factor for corn as various Governments have to meet biofuel targets. Its price is related to the price of oil, and if oil prices rise, ethanol will become an even more attractive fuel source which would drive up the price of corn. With increasing temperatures due to global warming, corn output gets easily affected. A lower corn supply results, and corn gets more expensive.

How effective is corn against inflation?

Corn is an excellent hedge against inflation because of its various price drivers and its overall global requirement as a food source. Because of the food source point, inflation will inevitably cause its price to rise. Owning corn instead of currency will provide the required protection against inflation. Corn has consistently proved to be less volatile than other grains such as wheat and soy, making it a more stable long-term investment.

Below is the long-term chart for corn prices. The long-term chart shows that though corn prices have increased, they haven't kept pace with inflation. The reason for this is that improvements in technology are a strong deflationary force for food prices.

It is best to be careful with investing in corn producers, being very selective in choosing companies with high cash flow, and investing during times when they are corn shortages due to an external stimulus. Investing in corn can be a good diversifier during certain times.

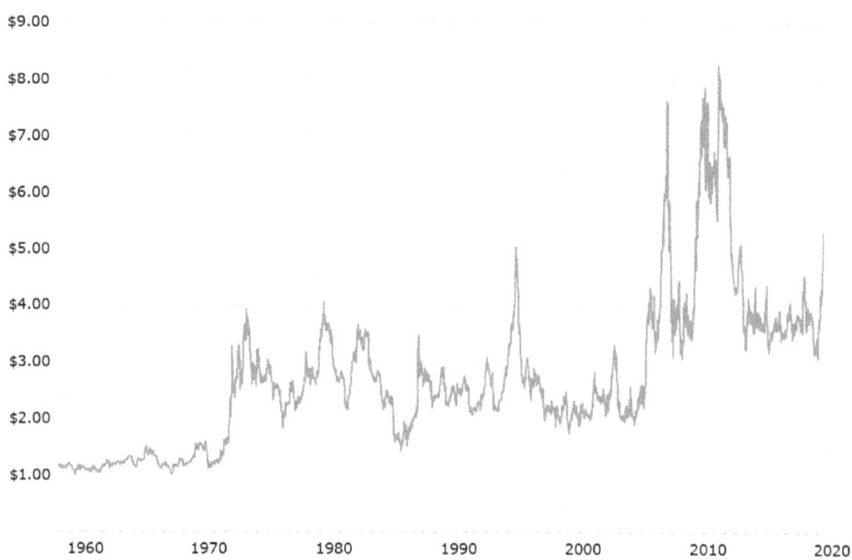

Source: Macrotrends

How can you invest in corn?

You can invest in corn in a variety of ways. The first and foremost option is futures contracts and options. Although these are speculative instruments, they can provide the necessary hedge against inflation if the price moves in your intended direction. A less-speculative mode of investment is to invest in corn-focused ETFs and companies. There are no companies that purely deal with corn. However, the companies you should be looking for are those that are in business with corn producers. Producers of fertilizers, pesticides, and animal feeds can be viable investment options.

Wheat

Wheat is cultivated worldwide for its cereal grain seed, a staple for almost every country. Wheat stems from a grass type referred to as Triticum grown in numerous places worldwide. Wheat happens to be the most widely cultivated food crop on land, used mainly for bread, different kinds of pasta, and other bakery goods. China,

Pakistan, USA are some of the top wheat-producing and exporting countries in the world.

Why does wheat have value?

Wheat is the powerhouse of starch and energy, with components, like protein and vitamins essential for health. It is an important carbohydrate source for most countries. It is easily digested and can be highly nutritious when combined with other proteins. Wheat, alongside maize and rice, plays a significant contribution in supplying food to the nearly 9 billion in the world today. People cultivate wheat worldwide, and its worldwide demand is the primary reason behind its universal appeal.

How effective is wheat against inflation?

Regardless of a country's economic conditions, wheat continues to appeal to all and is an excellent investment. It gets ample attention because of constant global demand. Similar to other commodities, wheat poses an attractive investment opportunity while being an inflationary hedge. With rising prices, raw materials and food commodities such as wheat also rise. Wheat, being a necessity of a large number of the world's diet, allows it to remain attractive to investors in inflationary period.

While inflation can be dangerous for various other investments, the opposite is true with commodities. The increase in wheat value allows investors to balance their losses that they may have experienced elsewhere. Wheat is used widely for food production, making it a potent inflationary hedge.

From the historical chart, we see that food prices have increased with time; but have not kept pace with inflation.

Diversifying with small investments in strong wheat-producing companies can serve a purpose at certain times of high inflation. We can see considerable increases in wheat prices during the early 1970s and late 2000s due to increased money supply in the economy.

Source: Macrotrends

How can you invest in wheat?

To hedge against inflation, you can consider investing in wheat. The most straightforward way to invest in wheat is through wheat options like other commodities. Options allow you to speculate on wheat prices and enable you to pick a position according to your level of risk.

You can also invest in stocks of companies that deal directly with wheat, such as cereal producers, fertilizer manufacturers, and agricultural machinery manufacturers like John Deere.

Lumber

Lumber refers to wood that is available such as planks and beams, after being processed. It trades on mercantile exchanges like other commodities. Its main uses are in residential and commercial construction, for various flooring purposes, and manufacturing furniture. Major lumber producers are the United States, Russia, China, and Canada. All of these producers have large swathes of the forest for lumber production.

Why does lumber have value?

Lumber is by far the most used construction material in the United States, which, along with China, are the two largest lumber-consuming countries. Global demand for lumber also remains high and is expected to grow. This is primarily driven by the ever-increasing demand for residential and commercial properties, wood furnishings, and various kinds of wood-dependent furniture.

How effective is lumber against inflation?

Lumber prices soared in 2020. Between early March and October 2020, lumber's price increased from around 280 USD to over 900 USD, which is an excellent indication of how lumber performs when the market is experiencing extreme levels of uncertainty. The ever-growing pressure from environmentalists against the reduction of forest cover is a strong driver of lumber's price. Trees do not grow as fast as crops, so the race to make logging sustainable gets faster every year, which consistently drives lumber's price upwards. These reasons make lumber a relatively much better hedge against inflation than other commodities.

Below is the historical chart for lumber. It usually has a steady price, but at certain times, we see substantial price hikes. For example, in 2020, there was a considerable increase in demand for lumber due to people doing more home renovation, which saw lumber hit all-time highs in 2020.

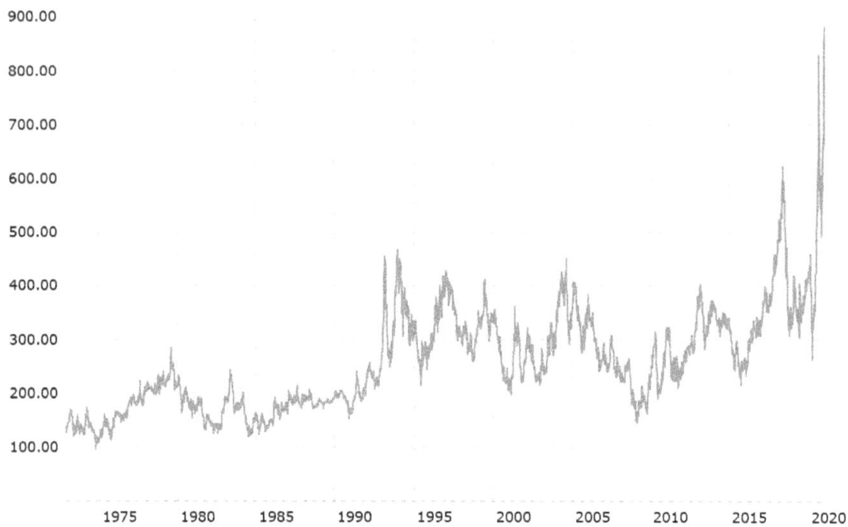

Source: Macrotrends

How can you invest in lumber?

Lumber trades in planks per 1000 board feet. Online investment portals allow you to trade lumber futures and options. As always, these are speculative instruments that can incur a loss if the price does not move in your favor. However, hedging against inflation is a long-term investment, and small price changes will not affect the overall long-term performance. Lumber stocks are an excellent investment if you do not want to invest in lumber directly. Various listed companies engaged in logging have provided consistent value appreciation over the years and can be viable options for hedging against inflation.

Cotton

Its universal application as a textile raw material has ensured a thriving global trade for cotton. According to the World Wildlife Fund (WWF), cotton is the most widespread, non-food profitable crop globally. Its role in the global textile and fashion industries, cosmetics industry, pharmaceuticals, in addition to its industrial applications, make it a worthy investment commodity to consider.

Why does cotton have value?

Demand and supply dynamics for cotton largely influence its trading price. Based on these factors, economists have projected a moderate, steady growth of the cotton sector. Given its demand, cotton has a large and relatively stable presence on the stock market, making it a preferred investment choice. Cotton investment also allows for exposure to other agricultural commodities and offers a great way to broaden a portfolio.

How effective is cotton against inflation?

As global economies grow, commodities like cotton grow with them. With a finite supply of cotton, limited by seasonal changes, cotton is more likely to retain its value and act as a hedge against inflation. Cotton has a statistically high hedging potential against inflation, with a positive correlation between inflation rates and asset returns. It performs exceptionally well in long-term investments.

The historical chart shows that cotton price hasn't increased because of better technologies to manufacture cotton. Cotton can be a good diversifier during periods of high inflation, but investments need to made in strong producers with high cash flow at specific periods.

How can you invest in cotton?

A standard option for cotton investment is stocks. Stocks run a lower risk middle-ground between more direct options. They can be bought directly in cotton manufacturing companies or textile-based companies that use cotton as a raw material. On the other hand, Cotton ETFs offer the benefit of a bundle of assets; due to diversification, market movements have less influence on ETF performance. Additionally, you can invest in cotton futures through regular brokerage accounts, which can be very profitable.

Strategy

As you can see, most commodities increase over time; but don't always keep up with inflation. This is because of the increase in technology and the decay of commodities over time. Precious metals don't decay, but commodities do. Thus, it's best to avoid a buy and hold strategy for commodities.

My favorite strategy is a buy low, sell high strategy. Buy when the commodity is cheap (relative to the M2 money supply) and sell when high. Many producers also tend to have decent dividends, so factor in the dividend when analyzing the stock benefits.

Strong Currency

A strong currency can effectively protect you against inflation. The simple logic behind this is that inflation will cause your cash holdings to lose value. To retain the same value of your holdings or to experience an increase, you will need more of the currency you use to spend. To get more of your local currency without investing in any other asset classes, you can purchase a currency of another country that has historically performed better than your local currency. When your country experiences inflation, its exchange rate will also get affected as the local currency will lose its value. This means that other countries' currencies will gain value against your local currency. This implies that even if the other country's currency has not improved in value on its own, it will still be a better option as you can get of your local currency after it has devalued.

How to evaluate the strength of a currency?

The simplest way to assess the value of a currency is to compare it with another currency. Currencies are always traded in pairs, and their values are represented in this way as well. The USD, for example, has no value on its own unless it is used to purchase another currency or to purchase goods. To value the US Dollar, we would need to determine how much of another currency we can buy with 1 USD. If the currency we want to purchase is the British pound, then we would need to see how many US dollars we will get for one British pound. Whatever value we get for this will be the exchange rate of the British pound with the US dollar and will be traded as a pair called GBP/USD. If you were buying British pounds for US dollars on the 12th of December 2020, you would need 1.32 USD for every GBP.

To determine the strength of a currency, we would need to look at the history of the price of a currency pair over a period of time. This trend will tell us how a currency has fared against another over a specific period of time. A strong currency will experience an increase in its value against another currency over a period of time. Taking the example of the GBP/USD pair, if the 1.32 value decreased to 1.16 over a 6-month period, you would need fewer dollars to buy the same number of pounds. In this case, you will 1 dollar and 16 cents instead of 1 dollar and 32 cents to purchase one British pound. This means that the British pound would have gotten weaker against the US dollar.

The main driving forces behind currency value appreciation are the demand of the currency as well as the ability of a country to register a trade surplus year on year. A trade surplus means that it earns more foreign exchange than it uses. This results in the country having an excess of a foreign currency, in most cases the USD, which results in the value of its own currency getting higher. A prime example is the Norwegian Krone which has experienced an increase in value over the past five years against the USD.

Example of strong currencies in past periods

With over 175 currencies traded in the forex markets every day, there are plenty of options to choose from. However, when we are talking about protecting against inflation, we must consider how certain currencies have performed over the years against our local currency. Having said that, some currencies are considered safe havens regardless of where you live. This is because these currencies experience appreciation in their value due to a number of other factors that are global while also being consistent.

United States Dollar

The United States Dollar has historically been a great safe-haven currency for non-US investors and remains immensely popular amongst them. It is mostly ideal for investors whose home currencies have performed poorly against the USD historically.

It is an excellent diversifier for those in non-US countries with weaker currencies. However, the USD has not performed as other stronger currencies in terms of its intrinsic value, such as the Kuwaiti Dinar or the Omani Riyal. The Federal Reserve Bank of New York is an institution of the United States Government and the only body that can issue the USD.

Although the US is very slowly losing its status as the global financial superpower, all major commodities are traded in USD, countries keep their foreign reserves in USD, and most international debt obligations are met in USD. This provides the dollar with an unparalleled demand globally for the moment, especially for non-US investors. These reasons make the USD a great currency diversifier.

USD Performance

The most effective way to measure the USD's performance is by using the US Dollar Index (DXY). It is a measurement of how the USD has performed against a basket of different currencies instead of a single currency. Below is the lifetime chart of the DXY.

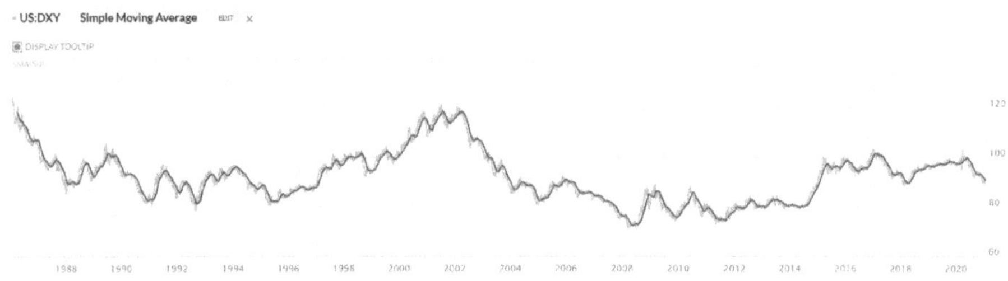

Source: Marketwatch

The USDX was at 79.335 on the 1st of January 2010, and it was at 97.296 on the 1st of January 2020. The USDX shows a remarkable increase of 17.961 or 22.6% in the USD's strength against the major currencies of the world. Keeping in mind that this is the performance of the US dollar against other strong currencies such as the Euro, Japanese yen, and British pound. If the currency you have used to purchase the USD is not a primary world currency, the chances are that not only will you be soundly protected against the risks of inflation; you will experience an overall appreciation even after adjusting for inflation. The USD is an excellent hedge against inflation, especially for non-US investors.

Let's suppose you're an investor located in the US. In that case, however, it's better to diversify your non-US currency exposure as there is some long-term risk to the US Dollar due to political instability, humongous trade deficit, and debt.

How to invest in the United States Dollar?

You can invest in the USD by buying it directly from money exchanges. You can also buy it on various online investing platforms as a pair with another currency. Another way to invest in USD is by investing in a USD-focused ETF such as an ETF that tracks the USD's performance against six major currencies. The US dollar is one of the most focused currencies in speculative circles. You can invest in it by way of futures and options where you will profit if the price changes in your favor.

Japanese Yen

The Japanese yen has also held its position firmly as a safe haven currency for the last two decades. There are several reasons for this. One reason is that Japan has remained the top creditor nation in the world for a long time, which means that Japan always holds a considerable portfolio of debt issued by other countries. When economic uncertainty seeps into the markets, Japan starts selling these debt instruments. The buyers have to purchase the debt in yen, and as a result, the yen experiences a surge in demand and gets stronger while other currencies get weaker. Another reason that keeps the Yen stable is that Japan is an attractive market for raising finance due to its near-zero interest rates. Since the debt obligations are met in the yen, the demand for the yen always remains high.

Japanese Yen Performance

An interesting dataset that can instantly paint a clear picture of the Japanese Yen's performance is its trend against major currencies since the start of the pandemic in 2020. While other currencies got weaker because they were issuing more debt to support their economies, the Yen registered incredible strength against both the US dollar and the British pound. The JPY/USD rate in early March was 110, and the rate in December of the same year was 105. An incredible increase of about 5% during a global pandemic. It indeed remains a credible and secure safe haven to hedge against inflation.

Historically, we see that the Japanese yen has strengthened a lot in the last 30-40 years. A high volume of Japanese exports and their population's considerable savings rate is the main reason for its strength.

Japanese Yen currency is an ideal diversifier for people in the United States.

Source: Macrotrends

How to invest in the Japanese Yen?

The Japanese Yen follows the same path for investment options as other safe-haven currencies. Buying the currency from Forex markets in cash is one of the easiest ways to acquire the currency and build your portfolio. The Japanese yen is also a focus of various Exchange Traded Funds specializing in its nature as a safe haven currency. Investing in these ETFs might be a more suitable option if you do not prefer owning the currency itself. If you want to invest by way of speculation, the Yen allows for an abundance of investment in the options and futures markets. However, these come attached with more risks than ETFs and cash holdings.

Swiss Franc

The Swiss Franc is a strong safe haven currency, mostly because of Switzerland's stability over many centuries. The country remains politically neutral, which adds to the strength of its currency. The Swiss National Bank adopts a policy of zero inflation which results in the franc not losing any value. Because of these reasons, the Swiss Franc appreciates in times of economic uncertainty and thus continues to be valued as a safe haven currency globally.

Because the Swiss Franc enjoys immense popularity amongst investors, it is consistently in high demand. This demand keeps pushing the Swiss Franc value higher and trades on all major Forex markets. Its code is CHF. It mostly trades as a pair with the United States dollar, the Euro, and the British pounds in codes USD/CHF, EUR/CHF, and GBP/CHF.

Swiss Franc Performance

The Swiss Franc continues to enjoy its status as a safe haven alongside the Japanese yen. Historical data shows that the Franc has consistently appreciated against the US dollar for a better part of the last two decades. You could buy 1 USD for roughly 1 Swiss Franc in the middle of 2010, whereas currently, you need 0.9 Swiss francs to purchase 1 USD. Even though this may seem like a small appreciation in value for ten years, it is essential to keep in mind that we base this appreciation against the all-powerful United States dollar, which itself is a stable currency. So, if the Swiss franc appreciates against the USD, it will certainly protect your financial position against any risks that inflation poses.

Historically, we see that the Swiss Franc is powerful against the US dollar and that the Swiss Franc has strengthened significantly over the last 20 years.

Switzerland is a stable non-EU country with neutral politics and is very business-friendly.

Source: Macrotrends

How to invest in the Swiss Franc?

The easiest way would be to buy Swiss francs from currency exchanges. The next best option would be to buy Swiss francs as pairs in the online forex markets. Various online platforms allow you to do this. As with all other currencies discussed above, Swiss Franc focused ETFs are an excellent investment if you don’t want to buy the currency on its own. You also have the option of investing in Swiss franc futures and options. Be advised, though, that futures and options are speculative instruments and are riskier than owning the currency independently.

Thai Baht

Thailand has experienced an explosion in tourism in recent times. The government has invested heavily in making the country an ideal tourist destination for people worldwide. It is popular amongst European travelers looking to get away from their cold and rainy weather to the warm beaches of Thailand. What this translates to is a high demand for the Thai Baht. When demand for a currency is more elevated, its value usually goes up. Thailand has also consistently posted a trade surplus for a better part of the last decade, which has enabled the Thai Baht to appreciate significantly in value throughout the same time frame.

Thai Baht Performance

The currency has appreciated against the USD, the Euro, the GBP, and many other major world currencies in the last decade. Very few currencies have shown such a performance against a large basket of world currencies, which makes the Thai Baht an excellent investment for US-based investors.

We can see this in the 20-year historical chart for the Thai Baht against the USD below.

The primary reason for this is due to the increased tourism from Western countries to Thailand.

The Thai Baht is an excellent diversifier as it doesn't follow the charts of other Western countries. However, as with all diversifiers, do not invest too much in it.

How to invest in the Thai Baht?

The Thai Baht trades in similar ways to the other currencies we have talked about above. The easiest way is to purchase the currencies from online or in-store exchanges. Like other similar currencies, many ETFs focus on the Thai Baht as a core investment and take precautions to offset any abrupt volatility. These are safer than buying the currency in cash.

A Short message from the Author:

Hey, are you enjoying the book? I'd love to hear your thoughts!

Many readers do not know how hard reviews are to come by, and how much they help an author.

Thank you for taking the time to share your thoughts!

Your review will genuinely make a difference for me and help gain exposure for my work.

Real Estate

Real Estate is a lucrative alternative to stocks that offers lower risk and higher returns on investment. It can be a desirable investment as a tangible asset that can be controlled. Most commonly, real estate investments materialize returns through rent from properties, which provide a constant source of income. Profits can also be made through appreciation, as property can be sold after its value goes up beyond the cost of investment. For long-term investments, real estate can be leveraged to expand your holdings.

The passive, stable income earned from real estate is one of the significant benefits of this investment. Such an income can cover monthly expenses and make a profit while allowing investment in several properties, which mitigates risk. This also provides investors with long-term financial stability, as properties appreciate over time. Real estate is also a sought-after investment in periods of high inflation, as the property value increases with inflation, acting as a hedge against it. All in all, it is a good source of sustained cash flow and profits.

Below is a chart of median housing prices in the US over the last 100 years. The dip around 2008 is due to the housing credit crisis. In general, we see that housing prices tend to track inflation.

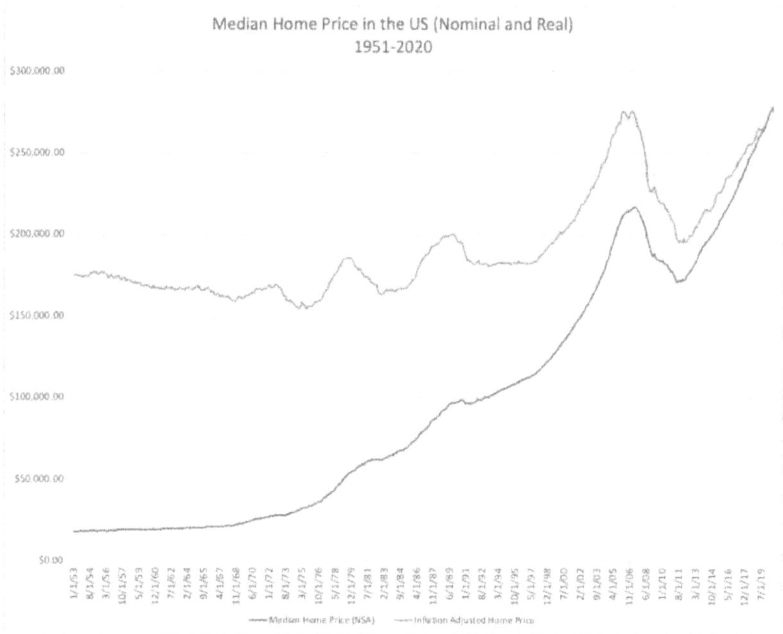

Source: DQYDJ, www.dqydj.com

How to identify real estate markets with good cash flow

Real estate with good cash flow and low debt can translate not only into profits but also allow further investment in other properties. For this reason, it is vital to identify markets that expound on this benefit to get the most out of real estate investment. The process of identifying profitable real estate markets requires a lot of research. This should involve analyzing market performance through research reports and newspaper articles, particularly relating to properties you might be interested in. You should also keep an eye on microeconomic factors that shape each market, including job growth, housing prices, rental rates, construction starts, and supply and demand forces. All of these factors determine the growth and value of a market and indicate the sort of returns that can be expected in the future.

Additionally, capitalization rate or cap rate calculations come in handy when deciding on real estate investments. Cap rates are determined by dividing a property's net operating income by the current market value and reflect an estimation of potential returns on a real estate investment. This formula can provide a look into the initial yield of an investment property and can aid the decision-making process to maximize profits.

Additional calculations that can help appraise potential investments include price-to-rent ratios, which compare median home prices with median rent, and can determine likely demand for rental properties, which in turn predicts rising value.

An excellent way to value real estate is by using the RV ratio. The RV ratio is the Rent-to-Value ratio which determines the percentage of a month's rent of a property to the total purchase price of the property. For example, a house that costs $200,000 to purchase and has a monthly rent of $1,000 has an RV ratio of 0.5%. An ideal RV ratio is above 0.7%. So, for the same house, if the purchase price remains the same at $200,000, and if the rental yield rises to $2000, this would produce an RV ratio of 1%, which is ideal.

Net Operating Income (NOI) analyses the profitability of income-generating investments, giving an estimation of a property's value. Some other key factors that can indicate good cash flow properties include a diversified economy with a rapidly growing job market and population growth, as well as increasing demand for rental properties and commercial spaces. You should also identify affordable property prices, as high investment costs can reduce net cash flow.

Residential Real Estate

Residential real estate includes all properties intended for living. This includes everything from single-family houses to multi-family residences. Housing being a necessity, residential real estate is less sensitive to economic conditions. This has made it a common investment choice, especially for the long-term.

Why does Residential Real Estate have value?

Globally, median house prices increased by 6.9% in 2019 and continue to grow at a rate of 1.9% in 2020. Historically, home prices have risen with inflation rates as the cost of materials increases. House prices are also subject to market forces, which leads to a higher value with increased demand. This often comes from urbanization, the advent of nuclear families and independent living, as well as the rise of the middle-class. Residential real estate is therefore viewed as a safe investment with guaranteed returns.

How effective is Residential Real Estate against inflation?

In recent housing bubbles, house prices have increased faster than inflation rates. With such trends, residential real estate is seen as an effective hedge against inflation, especially in the long run. In addition, as home mortgages come with lower interest rates, residential real estate increases in value while monthly payments remain stable, effectively countering the effects of inflation.

How can you invest in Residential Real Estate?

Owning rental properties can provide a regular income if they are rented while the property appreciates. Mortgaged ownership of rental properties is an investment that hedges against inflation. You can also invest in Real Estate Investment Groups (REIGs). REIGs operate by allowing investors to buy into a company that buys or builds residential apartments.

You can also flip houses by buying a home and increasing its value with specific repairs and updates before selling at a profit. Alternatively, homes can be purchased in a rapidly rising market and sold for a profit. To diversify your real estate portfolio, you can also invest in Real Estate Limited Partnerships (RELPs). RELPs buy and hold a variety of properties and make profits once the property is sold.

Real Estate Materials Retailers

Real estate materials companies are involved in the production and sale of building materials, home improvement products, and services, as well as rental tools and equipment. They also offer long-term commercial contracts. Materials companies' value and performance are inherently linked to that of real estate. With relatively stable demand, materials companies usually operate with high returns and profits for investors.

Why are Real Estate Materials Retailers suitable investments?

Real estate materials companies derive their value from the inherent link to real estate and property development. As the value of developed property and real estate increases, so does that of materials companies that provide building, improvement, and maintenance materials. Not only that, but demand for materials companies is also directly tied to demand for real estate. While they can be more dependent on market forces, materials companies can be counted on to offer returns on investment.

How effective are Real Estate Materials Retailers against inflation?

Inflationary periods mark an increase in the value of real estate. This increase also translates significantly to real estate materials companies, providing a sufficient hedge against sudden inflation hikes. Even when real estate values, like house values, drop due to lower purchasing power that lowers demand, demand for home improvement and maintenance remains relatively stable. Long-term commercial contracts do not respond quickly to inflation when signed before inflationary hikes, so they stay relatively stable in the face of rising inflation rates.

How can you invest in Real Estate Materials Retailers?

Real estate development companies that trade publicly can be invested in by buying shares on the stock market. Increasing dividends overtime provides higher cash flow to investors. Investment risk can also be diversified by investing in stocks from different companies. Some of the largest real estate materials companies include *Home Depot* and *Lowes*, the former holding 47% of the market share in the US and steadily growing. Suitable investments can be made in such companies by first identifying those with good cash flow, high returns, and risk mitigation strategies.

Real Estate Development Companies

Real estate development companies are involved in activities ranging from renovation and re-lease of existing properties to buying and selling of raw land, as well as the sale of developed lands. Developers are involved in the creation and renovation of real estate, and these processes can determine the value of the resulting property. Real estate investors often work closely with developers to increase their returns.

Why are Real Estate Development Companies suitable investments?

When a property is developed, its value increases. The appeal of property development, therefore, lies in the potentially higher operating profits and capital gains upon sale of a property. Real estate development responds to market forces, that is, it increases with demand and can guarantee returns and even increase the value of surrounding commercial and residential real estate. As demand for residential and commercial real estate is inherently linked, real estate development companies can ensure high returns on investment in property development.

How effective are Real Estate Development Companies against inflation?

Real estate development companies are expected to grow in inflationary periods. This growth can be attributed to the lower purchasing power of money during inflation, which leads to higher prices translating to higher earnings from development. As the cost of building materials is higher, the property value also increases. Especially in areas where there is a certainty of demand, development companies can offer a good hedge against inflation. Dividends from shares also grow in time and provide higher cash flows to investors, even with rising inflation rates.

How can you invest in Real Estate Development Companies?

You can invest in real estate development companies by buying stocks of publicly trading companies on the stock exchange, based on the company's performance and annual returns. You can also make long-term investments by raising capital for development projects, where you can earn a share of the profits from the sale of developed lands. Alternatively, investors can also offer loans to development companies to finance their projects and make profits on the interest paid on the loan.

Real Estate Investment Trusts (REITs)

Real Estate Investment Trusts (REITs) are formed when a corporation utilizes investor money to buy, operate and manage income properties. REITs are not subject to corporate tax, as they pay out about 90% of their income as dividends. REITs dabble in equity and mortgage-backed securities offering diversified exposure to real estate, as they allow indirect investment in commercial, residential, and industrial real estate. They are best for investors who wish to add real estate to their portfolios without traditional transactions.

Why are Real Estate Investment Trusts suitable investments?

REITs operate much like mutual funds but allow a lot more control over where your money goes. They enable investors entry into non-residential assets, which can be otherwise difficult for individual investors. As they are exchange-traded, REITs are also highly liquid, allowing faster cash transfers. They offer investors regular income, as well as opportunities for appreciation. REITs are also mostly affordable for individual investors. With pooled capital, they are able to invest in tremendous assets.

How useful are Real Estate Investment Trusts against inflation?

Over the past 25 years, REITs have experienced consistently growing dividends at almost twice the inflation rate. REITs provide natural protection against inflation. Their value is derived from real estate value, which increases with inflation. This allows for REIT dividend growth and provides a stable source of income throughout inflationary periods. REITs also mainly diversify risk, as they own a multi-property portfolio that remains relatively stable even if one asset reduces in value due to inflation.

How can you invest in Real Estate Investment Trusts?

Publicly traded REITs are listed on the stock exchange, and shares can be bought and sold through a broker. Alternatively, you can invest in REIT mutual funds, which themselves invest in REITs, and their share prices are not subject to fluctuation. ETFs are also available for REITs, which support the majority of their assets in equity REIT securities. They incur lower investment costs on higher returns and offer trading flexibility through diversification and risk management.

Cash Flow

Cash flow refers to the incoming and outgoing finances of a business. The cash coming into a business is primarily the earnings of the company. These earnings depend on what the business is focused on. Some businesses may earn through the service they provide, whereas others may rely on goods they sell. The outgoing cash is essentially the expenditure that the company has. Similar to the incoming cash, this too can be attributed to several different aspects. The salary paid to the employees, the liabilities, any bills or additional expenses, and the production costs (if a product is being produced) all contribute to cash exiting the business.

The cash that the business actually benefits from is the difference that gets left behind when the expenditures are subtracted from the incoming money. As a result of inflation, it is usually this different that is affected the most, and thus the entire cash flow is impacted.

Nominal Cash Flow vs. Real Cash Flow

The cash flow of a business that is calculated without considering the influence of inflation in the future is referred to as nominal cash flow. On the other hand, real cash flow is the cash flow estimated considering the effects of inflation. The latter then becomes a good way for comparing the current cash flow to that of the past. A high inflation rate causes the real cash flow to be a lot less than the nominal cash flow.

Why are high cash flow producing businesses a good investment?

A high positive cash flow implies that the business has more significant finances to support the business activities. It is when the profits earned by the business outweigh the expenditures. Investing in such a business yields higher chances of receiving more incredible and more profitable returns. A business that is already flourishing would get the opportunity of expanding even further with additional investment. Expansion of goods or services would directly correlate to catering to a greater audience and, subsequently, increased sales. Investment in a business that focuses on processing raw materials is an incredibly profitable idea. Extra funds would imply that the company has the facility of buying and storing more raw materials to process and utilize later. This would help save the business from suffering because of the price hikes of raw materials.

How can positive cash flows hedge against inflation?

As aforementioned, a positive cash flow means that the business is earning more than it is spending. This difference can be positively impacted by the additional investment made and negatively affected by external conditions such as the market inflation. During inflation, a business increases the prices of the product or service it offers its consumers. However, at the same time, the firm also has to sustain an increase in the production costs, and labor costs.

The greater the cash flow, the lower the business is impacted by the inflation rates. This is because the substantial earnings allow the company to recover any costs lost to the high inflation rate. Generally, if a business has a return rate of greater than 5%, it's stable enough to sustain the effects of regular inflation. A positive cash flow further allows a business to spend on other profitable investments that we have covered such as commodities and assets.

A business with a positive cash flow can raise its prices to maintain its real cash flow during high inflationary periods.

RV Rental Business (Renting out RV's)

The RV rental business revolves around customers renting RVs to travel and live in them. There are many different types of RVs that can be rented out in a RV rental business; including caravans, motorhomes, and campervans. Many people prefer to rent RVs whilst on a trip to cut down costs and to experience living outdoors.

Why is an RV Rental Business a good investment?

RVs are a highly sought-after option for investment. This is because they prove to be cheaper than hotels and allow savings to be made in the transportation costs. Keeping this in mind, investing in a RV business timely can help you obtain high returns.

How effective is a RV Rental Business against inflation?

RV rental businesses create cash flow by the rental fees paid by the customers. The maintenance costs along with any other expenses are deducted from this fee to determine whether the cash flow is positive or negative.

The business owner has the prerogative to increase this rental fee during inflation as the maintenance costs increase too. This makes the RV rental business to be highly effective against inflation. If a positive cash flow is created, this surplus can then be invested to buy or lease more RVs to rent out. The existing RVs can also be upgraded. In short, even during inflation, investments can be made that will contribute to creating more positive cash flow in the RV rental business. Some customers may even prefer to rent RVs for a longer period. Even though some discounts may be offered in such a circumstance, the business still benefits from the continuous rental fee of the RV.

How can you set up or invest in a RV Rental Business?

Setting up an RV business does not require any specialized skill. Rather, with a few simple steps, you can kick-start your business to start building cash flow. The main things you need to focus on is setting a suitable rental fee for the RVs and managing the costs. The primary costs your RV rental business will have would be the upkeep and maintenance costs of the RVs. These can include oil changes, tyre changing, and ensuring overall cleanliness. Another expenditure could also be the advertisement costs that you would have to pay. An initial cost that you will also have to bear would involve buying or leasing different RVs.

Online Apparel Store

Online shopping has always been profitable not only for the customers but even more so for the investors. They provide customers the facility of shopping a wide range of clothing whilst sitting within the comforts of their home. Buyers can browse and choose whichever piece of clothing they desire, check sizes, and then get the order delivered all through a few clicks.

Why is an Online Apparel Store a good investment?

One of the biggest reasons why a lot of customers are turning towards online shopping is the convenience it provides. It saves the buyers the hassle of traveling time to the store and allows them to save time by providing perks such as express delivery. Online apparel stores have become even more popular during the current pandemic situation. Customers can easily choose what they wish to buy, place an order, and get the clothes delivered at home, without any human interaction.

How effective is an Online Apparel Store against inflation?

An online apparel store is one of the easier business to create positive cash flow. This is because the investor reduces the expenditure that plays a significant role in traditional apparel stores. These include the costs of renting or buying the store location, the electricity bills, and hiring employees to help assist the walk-in customers amongst many others. Since these costs are absent for an online apparel store, the cash flow becomes positive thus helping an online apparel store prove to be highly effective during inflation. The biggest challenge is to ensure that the profit is higher than the advertising costs + manufacturing costs. Analysing your competition beforehand will help with this.

You can also expect to make a much higher profit if you source your merchandise from overseas. Countries like China, Bangladesh, India, Vietnam, and Thailand produce garments of an excellent quality and sell it for economical prices. This margin is itself a hedge against inflation particularly because you will always be able to find a vendor at your price point as their markets contain hundreds of suppliers.

The fact that during inflation the prices of the clothing being sold also increases add-ons to the creation of a positive cash flow. The most notable expenditure of an online apparel store, apart from the purchasing costs, is hiring a customer service team and building a website.

Since these expenditures are not directly impacted by inflation, the earnings made during the period outweigh the costs. This contributes to generating a positive cash flow even during the inflation period.

How can you set up or invest in an Online Apparel Store?

The most important part of setting up an online store is buying the services of a third-party website-creating platforms such as WordPress or Woocommerce. Your online apparel store will start operations as soon as the website is up and running. Another very important consideration is to ensure that there is enough stock to cater to a large number of orders in the business' inventory. This is where a positive cash flow becomes beneficial. With a great cash flow, an online apparel store can make certain that there is enough stock in the inventory to fulfil diverse orders from customers without making them wait.

The branding and advertising of the online apparel store is very crucial to deciding whether the business makes enough sales to create a positive cash flow. Advertising on social media platforms or collaborating with other already well-established businesses may help with achieving a decent amount of exposure to get your store going.

Online Aviation Merchandise Store

The aviation industry has mesmerized generations and has created an army of loyal enthusiasts. These people love everything about aviation and are willing to part easily with their hard-earned cash just to get closer to the industry. They spend hundreds of dollars individually on aviation related merchandise, aircraft models, and plane tags. https://aviationtravelshop.com/ is a popular aviation merchandise store in Australia.

Why is an Aviation Merchandise Store a good investment?

Aviation enthusiasts love to spend money on aviation merchandise and retailers leave no opportunity dry when they are designing products. For example, airplane tags are particularly popular among aviation fans. This is because these tags are made from real aircraft skin. This makes these tags very unique as they were once part of a magnificent machine that flew tens of thousands of miles over its lifetime. Fans of the industry also love buying aircraft models. Especially popular models are those of planes that are no longer in service such as the Airbus A380, the Concorde, and the Qantas 747. The industry fanbase is only growing by the day and demand for its merchandise will remain strong for the foreseeable future which makes an online store selling merchandise an excellent investment.

How effective is an Aviation Merchandise Store against inflation?

An online store that is running a successful sales strategy can be an extremely lucrative investment. The best part about this niche is that it targets a want-based audience. Most aviation enthusiasts understand that aviation merchandise does not come cheap which prepares them to shell out hundreds of dollars on individual plane models. The profit margins on these models are exceptionally high which greatly helps with driving up profits. Your online store can produce a healthy cash flow and provide you with a decent profit every month which will effectively shield you from any inflation induced worries.

How can you set up or invest in an Aviation Merchandise Store?

As with any online store, the first thing you need is the store itself. Ecommerce stores are easy to set up these days using popular platforms such as Shopify. Once you have the store set up, the next thing you would have to do is look for suppliers. Again, the internet is your friend. There are hundreds of suppliers out there for generic content but very free that sell official aircraft models and even fewer that sell original plane tags. This makes it very important to be extra careful when choosing your vendors. After your vendors have been finalized, you have to start selling your stock. Best areas to market your store are aviation related groups and pages on social media as well as by using paid ads on search engines.

Online Used Computer Parts Store

Since the turn of the century, almost every industry has become heavily dependent on computers. Almost all business transactions now involve the use of computers. With growing developments in data science and artificial intelligence, computers are extremely important now more than ever.

Why is a Used Computer Parts Store a good investment?

These advancements have also made new computers extremely expensive, making them unaffordable to a large majority of users. Instead of buying new computers, people are increasingly investing in used computers or choosing to repair their old computers to save costs. Setting up a used computer parts store, thus, becomes an excellent business investment. Considering that computer parts are not a perishable commodity, the risk of losses because of products being destroyed is reduced too.

How effective is a Used Computer Parts Store against inflation?

The used computer parts in the store can primarily come from two different sources. They can either be bought from private sellers who sell their computers part by part, or they can be repaired parts. Both ways, obtaining the parts does not add significantly to the expenses of setting up a computer parts business. However, in order to ensure that a positive cash flow is created, you need to make sure that other costs are also kept low. These include costs such as the rent of the store and the helping hands hired for the customers' assistance.

Used computer parts sell at a significant price and are subject to becoming more expensive as a result of inflation. This is because of reduced supply of parts for older computer models with the passage of time. This hike along with other factors contributes to making a used computer parts store an effective investment during inflation.

How can you set up or invest in a Used Computer Parts Store?

Setting up an online computer parts store should not be difficult given that there are so many online platforms that make it easy to do so. You can go with the standard Shopify route or you can go with the traditional WordPress path. The WordPress option will require you to use an eCommerce plugin such as WooCommerce or BigCommerce as described previously. Once you have the store up and running, you can start marketing it on computer parts related pages. Don't forget to mention that you check all parts for quality and performance before you sell them to increase confidence in your store as you are selling used items.

Good Debt Options

Good debt includes borrowing that can help build long-term wealth. With good debt, you can leverage the power of your money to create passive income streams that, over time, can build wealth. It is considered a sensible investment in one's financial future as it offers benefits that do not have a negative impact, unlike bad debt which drains wealth and is difficult to repay.

Why are good debt options a good investment?

While it might be a compelling idea to remain debt-free, it is almost impossible to do so without also forgoing lucrative investment opportunities that can build wealth in the future. Good debt options offer the opportunity to invest in the future in responsible yet rewarding ways that can improve your own net worth, give returns and improve the quality of life. Without good debt, investments in education or real estate, residential or commercial might not be possible. These can limit your opportunities in the future. Responsible management of debt can also improve credit scores, which can open doors for other investments.

In the short-term, good debt, like all borrowing, incurs monthly costs and can restrict cash flow. Over time, this investment can start to offer returns that not only cover the debt, but also translate into profits that can be further invested for gains. Investments in good debt can also keep you away from impulse borrowing that results in bad debt that can deplete your finances and make recovery difficult. Good debt comes with the guarantee that not only can it be paid back but can also offer returns in the future.

Long Term Property Finance

Long-term property financing refers to investments in real estate through borrowing. Long-term financing like mortgages is considered good debt, as they can offer higher returns on the investment when property values rise beyond the borrowed amount. Long-term financing is used for investments in property that will generate returns in the future. Mortgages are a common source of finance for residential real estate investments as well as commercial real estate as commercial real estate loans.

Why is Long Term Property Financing a good investment?

Long-term property financing offers several benefits to investors that make it a valuable investment. Long-term borrowing can come with low interest rates, as the property itself acts as a collateral to the loan. It also increases cash flow, when smaller amounts are being paid out on interest, and other sources of income and finance are open to cover expenses and be invested elsewhere. Payments on long-term loans are also designed based on investors capabilities on a regular basis, and these helps build credit for future borrowing. Additionally, long-term property financing is a lucrative investment based on the value of the underlying property, promising high returns.

How effective is Long Term Property Financing against inflation?

Inflationary periods are known to lead to increases in property value. For this reason, long-term property financing is not only a profitable investment, it can also hedge against inflation. Property that is bought before high inflationary periods with long-term loans will increase in value during times of high inflation, beyond the amount of investment. You will still be paying the same monthly instalments on your loan, but their value will fall. At this time, the property, be it residential or commercial, can even be sold so that it covers the borrowed amount and leaves a profit for the investor. Inflationary periods benefit borrowers by enabling them to pay off a debt that is worth less than it was at the time of borrowing.

For this to happen, you have to make sure that the debt on the property is **a long-term fixed rate mortgage**. If the debt is variable rate, then you run the risk of increasing interest rates with inflation.

How can you invest in Long Term Property Financing?

A common source of long-term property financing is mortgages. Also known as home loans, they allow individuals to invest in residential real estate as a long-term investment. Mortgages hold the property being bought as collateral with monthly instalments. Mortgages can also be taken out for commercial real estate, although these differ slightly in amortization periods and interest rates. A purchase-money mortgage can also be taken out, where loans are financed by the property seller. Once a balloon payment has been made, you can keep this source of finance or refinance with a traditional lender.

Hot Money Investments

Hot money involves the flow of funds from one country to another for short-term profits on interest rates or anticipated exchange rate shifts. Such investments are referred to as hot money because they can move very quickly in and out of markets. Hot money investments can occur locally, by investing in short-term certificates of deposit with unusually high interest rates. Internationally, foreign investors can move their money to different countries to take advantage of higher interest rates that combat local inflation rates. Foreign investors buy securities from emerging markets.

To make this investment, make sure that you have good knowledge of the foreign marketing that you are investing into. Preferably you are working with reliable locals in that market; or actually living there.

Why is Hot Money a good investment?

Hot money indicates currencies that can quickly move between financial markets, and ensure investors are able to benefit from the highest short-term interest rates available. As a short-term investment, hot money regularly yields quick high returns on investment as it moves from low interest rate countries to those with higher interest rates. Such investments diversify risk by expanding portfolios. It also counters lower returns in local markets due to low interest rates so that the same investment can make higher earnings in international markets.

How effective is Hot Money Investment against inflation?

Investments are typically made in foreign countries experiencing higher inflation rates than local markets. In high inflationary periods, interest rates increase. This is the optimal time to make hot money investments as rates continue to rise in foreign markets. Hot money investments benefit from high inflation rates commonly found during inflationary periods. An example of a productive hot money investment can be found in the 10% earning made by Swiss investors when they invested out of Swiss markets with -0.75% interest rates in Indian bonds at an interest rate of 9.25%. With government promises to stabilise exchange rates within 2% fluctuation, investors still made a 10% return in USD. Because the Government maintained a stable exchange rate of the INR to the USD for a full financial year, investors materialised gains in USD.

How can you invest in Hot Money?

Investing in hot money requires extensive market research and knowledge, as well as financial acumen. Such investments can be made in foreign countries with higher inflation rates compared to local markets, to maximize returns. Making hot money investments with short-term portfolio investments, including bonds, equities, and financial derivatives. You can also invest in short-term foreign bank loans, and foreign bank loans with short-term investment horizons. You should keep in mind that hot money investments do not work over the long-term and are not suited to those who are not willing to move markets quickly, as returns can only be made during a limited period of time.

Refinancing of Existing Property

Refinancing involves the replacement of an existing debt obligation with another debt obligation under new terms. With refinancing, the previous debt is paid off, leaving only the new debt to be paid on agreed conditions. This is done for a variety of reasons, including availing better instalment conditions or lower interest rates. A common type of property refinancing is mortgage refinancing on houses, usually to get a loan that better fits the homeowner's financial situation. Refinancing existing property is a good debt that also offers cashouts.

Why is Refinancing Existing Property a good investment?

Refinancing holds value as an investment for several reasons. It offers lower interest rates compared to the previous loan, which not only saves money, but can speed up the rate at which equity is built. It could also potentially decrease monthly instalments, thereby improving cash flow. This can also significantly shorten the loan's term without increasing monthly payments. Refinancing can also reduce the risk associated with the debt, especially if switching from variable-rate to a fixed-rate loan. Finally, you can consolidate various other debts under one through refinancing, which can provide reduced monthly payments and short-term relief.

How effective is Refinancing Existing Property against inflation?

Refinance activities have seen an increase north of 65% in 2020 in the U.S. As inflation causes interest rates to rise, refinancing to a fixed-rate loan can offer a hedge against inflation. Fixed-rate loans charge a specified interest rate that does not fluctuate with inflation. Essentially, with such a loan, you can pay the same amount of money, but it now has less value. Not only is money saved on such a loan during inflationary periods, it can also make monthly payments easier to meet. Refinancing can also be used to cash-out on real estate properties that have increased in value during inflationary periods. This allows access to a higher loan amount while maintaining ownership.

How can you invest in Refinancing?

There are many ways to refinance your property to a beneficial outcome. The most common is rate-and-term refinancing, where a new loan agreement replaces the original loan with lower interest. This is often applied to mortgages. Cash-out refinancing can be used where cash is needed, against real estate that has increased in value. This way you are able to gain the value of the property without selling it. Cash-in refinancing can be used to pay down a portion of the loan for smaller loan payments, which can improve cash flow. Alternatively, consolidation refinancing is used to pay off several debts with one new loan, which decreases monthly payments and increases cash flow.

Refinancing is best done when long term interest rates have been lowered significantly since you started your mortgage payments. A good time would be when the interest rates have been lowered due to a recession and you have the option to refinance at lower rates.

Inflation-Indexed Bonds

Inflation-indexed bonds or securities are produced to offer investors a safe and risk-free option to protect their portfolios against inflation. These securities are primarily issued by sovereign governments. They are designed to offset the loss in purchasing power of a currency by giving returns that either match or outperform the expected inflation levels of an economy. These are also referred to as real securities. This is because their returns are meant to offer profits that are usually adjusted for inflation. They are meant to protect your liquidity by ensuring a return that either beats or matches the negative effects inflation would otherwise have.

Also keep in mind that Inflation indexed bonds are not particularly great investment vehicles if you are looking for higher returns. This is because other asset classes such as gold and some currencies not only protect you from inflation but also vastly outperform it. As with all government securities, their rates of return are fixed and therefore you know exactly how much you will stand to make after a certain period. But the main difference with inflation adjusted bonds is that their principal changes during their life. This is how the bonds can offer protection against inflation. There are different methods used by different issuing authorities which determine how the principal changes.

For example, one issuer might choose to change the principal value of a bond by adjusting with the CPI on a semi-annually basis. So, a 10-year $10,000 bond with a fixed 2% rate will accrue $100 during the first six months. If the prevalent CPI has a figure of 3%, the principal value of the bond will increase by $150 after six months which will take the value of the principal to $10,150. The bond will accrue interest for the second six-month period on the new principal value. So instead of 100$ before, the new interest value would be $101.5. This will ensure that the bond will adjust with the CPI to account for all effects of inflation. At the end of the maturity period, the holder of the bond will receive all the interest that has been accrued on the inflation adjusted principal. The bond holder will also receive the adjusted principal value.

Why are inflation indexed bonds a good investment?

These bonds come with a unique feature which is that their principal gets adjusted for inflation. This contrasts with other inflation adjusted bonds which have variable interest rates that change as a response to changes in inflation. The benefit with getting principal adjusted is that if the economy happens to undergo a period of high inflation period at the beginning of the bond's lifetime, its principal will get adjusted to a fairly high value. Going forward, if inflation reduces over time and the economy does not experience near 0 inflation or deflation, then even with moderate interest rates that were fixed when the security was issued, the bond will yield a much higher return due to the high principal value.

For example, a 20-year $10,000 bond that has a 2% rate is issued with semi-annual adjustment. The economy registers a CPI of 7% for 2 and a half years, 5% for the next 2 and a half years, and 3% for the remaining 15 years. The bond would accrue $100 for the first six months. The principal would increase by $350 and the interest value would increase by $3.5. The principal would continue to increase by 7% p.a for the next 2 years compounded semi-annually. It would then increase by 5% p.a for the next 2 and a half years compounded annually. After five years, the principal will have a value of $12,983. You would earn interest for the new principal every time the interest gets accrued, which is semi-annually in this case. So, the interest value at the start of the 6th year would be $129.83 instead of the $100 that was accrued at the very start. This value would only increase as the 2% CPI would still cause principal adjustment for the remaining 15 years of the bond even with a 2% interest rate.

Inflation-Indexed Bonds performance against inflation

Inflation-indexed bonds are excellent investment vehicles against inflation. As inflation is usually measured by the CPI, and since these bonds get their principal adjusted according to the changing CPI, they produce returns that more or less beat inflation over a long term. However, this is only true when an economy does not experience deflation as the principal can also be adjusted to a lower value if the value of CPI becomes negative. Historically, with the exception of the deflation period experienced by the US economy between the end of 2007 and the middle of 2009, inflation-indexed bonds have consistently performed on par with their expectations.

How to invest in Inflation-Indexed Bonds

A sound way to invest in inflation-indexed bonds is by investing in Exchange Traded Funds that focus on similar securities. This is because these ETFs hold inflation-indexed bonds of different values, tenures, and maturities. They could be holding a 30-year $10,000 bond that mature next year, or a 10-year $5,000 bond that was issued last year. This has the potential to provide considerable protection against certain risks that you might otherwise be exposed to if you outright bought the security.

This is not to say that buying securities on their own is considerably worse. You can always invest directly in these securities by buying them from your local broker or bank.

Prime examples of top performing Inflation-Indexed Bonds

For investors who are particularly interested in investing in USD based investment, the Treasury Inflation-Protected Securities (TIPS) are an ideal choice. These bonds are issued in USD, they are linked with the US CPI, and in periods of inflation in the US economy, their principal also adjusts resulting in higher long-term USD return. These can be especially popular for investors whose local currencies have historically performed poorly against the USD.

One of the top performing ETFs that is focused on inflation-indexed bonds is the PIMCO 15+ Year U.S. TIPS Index Exchange-Traded Fund (LTPZ) which has appreciated by an impressive 23.98% since the start of 2020. This return far outpaces major inflation levels throughout the world. Over the past 11 years, the fund has produced an average year-on-year return of 8%.

Stocks

Stocks are shares of companies that you can buy any number of to take ownership of a company. You can buy shares of any company, whether private or public, but for the purposes of this text, we will be talking about stocks of publicly traded companies.

A publicly traded company is a company that has some or all of its shares listed on a stock exchange and made available for sale and purchase by the public. Any member of the public can own a share in any publicly listed company. The number of shares you purchase determines how much of a company you own. Some shares of companies allow you to vote on major matters of the company such as the appointment of directors.

There are two ways through which you can monetarily benefit from owning stock of a company. The first is the appreciation in the value of the stock you hold, and the other are the dividends a company pays to shareholders. Both can be used to protect yourself against inflation. However, most companies that pay dividends usually start performing poorly in times of inflation. This is because their cost of production rises. Some companies can pass on that increase in cost to their consumers, while others cannot. This increase in prices of raw materials for example, can affect the ability of a company to keep paying dividends due to lower profits. This makes the value of the raw material stock the better option to consider when choosing a company to invest in to guard against inflation. Dividends are also sometimes not paid for other reasons that are not connected to inflation. The historical performance of a stock paints a clear enough picture for investors to help them make the correct choice regarding their investments.

How do stocks perform against inflation?

Since there are literally thousands of stocks to choose from to perform this analysis. It is hard to generalise how stocks perform against inflation. This is also difficult because stocks in one country might perform exceptionally well for an investor in another country. This could be due to fundamentals supporting the stock's performance or it could simply be the exchange rate that provides a better return for the investor.

However, a better way to judge how stocks perform against inflation is to not look at them individually. We will see later that the best way to invest in stocks is by investing in ETFs or index funds. This is because these assets contain a pool of diverse stocks from different companies. This allows them to protect their positions against volatilities in the stock price of any one company. Historically, both the S&P and the Dow Jones Industrial Average have returned positive inflation adjusted figures on average. We will discuss them in detail in a later section of this chapter.

It is worth noting that stocks have become very speculative these days. Although this does not apply to mature companies such as Coca Cola, it applies to almost major tech companies. And even though these companies tend to produce exceptionally high returns, they can also experience extremely high volatility in their stock price. We will explore tech stocks in detail but one thing to remember here is that tech stock performance is not a measurement of how stocks generally perform against inflation.

How to choose the right company to invest in

It really is the question of the hour. With thousands of companies listed on exchanges around the world, it becomes very difficult to pick and choose the correct stock to act as a hedge against inflation. However, this is made easier if we simply follow the fundamentals of inflation.

For example, since inflation causes a rise in prices of **consumer goods**, companies that are related to this sector will fare much better than others. This is also especially true for companies that can pass on the increase in prices of their raw materials directly onto consumers. Examples of such companies included food producers, oil and gas or energy companies, utility companies, and healthcare, etc.

ETFs, S&P 500, and the Dow Jones Industrial Average

But individual stocks do come with various risks. One major risk is that the corporation can experience a setback from a lot of different sources. This can be a new competitor, change in regulation that governs the company's target market, a corporate scandal, or loss in the company's leadership by the shareholders. All of these are extremely difficult to predict from the historical data that shows the performance of a company's stock. A much better way to invest in stocks is by investing in ETFs that have been designed to protect investors against inflation or those that mimic the most popular index funds such as the Standard & Poor 500 and the Dow Jones Industrial Average.

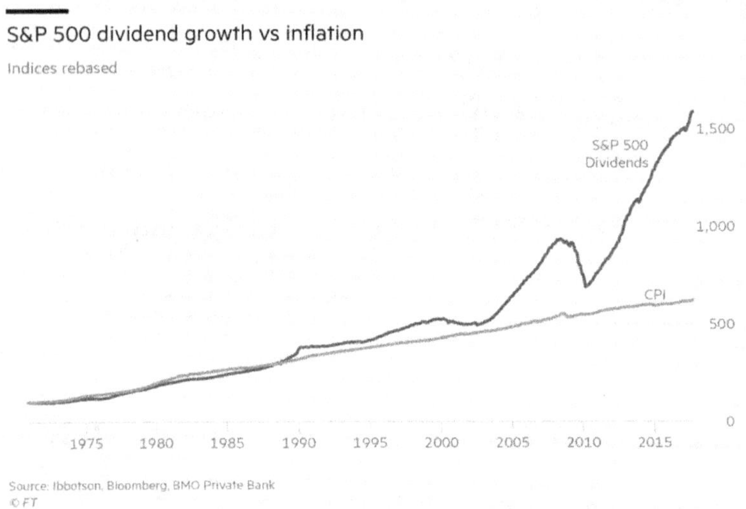

Source: https://www.pinterest.com/pin/497366352591275920/

https://i.pinimg.com/originals/6a/dc/1a/6adc1ab36d291cf60e93b0db7b5049b3.jpg

The graph above shows that the S&P 500 index has returned higher than the US CPI for a better part of three decades. This makes this index fund an extremely appropriate investment to protect yourself against inflation as not only does it provide a protection against the harmful effects of inflation, it generally also returns a profit on your investment.

Are tech stocks safe investments against inflation?

There is usually no problem with any specific industry in terms of a stock as an investment. Some tech stocks are excellent investments against inflation while others are not very fruitful. The distinction is between growth companies and value companies.

You will see examples of various tech stocks in the markets today that have lots of debt and no profits to show for their operations. These companies will have extremely high valuations and some analysts might even refer to them as overvalued. These companies leverage their tech association to lure in investors who are highly interested in the company's growth potential. And sometimes, these companies experience rapid appreciation in their stock prices.

However, a prime example of when this can go wrong is of WeWork. WeWork was valued in the tens of billions of dollars after receiving funding several times from SoftBank. However, in the end, the fundamentals of the company were so bad to investors that the much-hyped planned initial public offering of the company failed. There is always a possibility of this happening to highly speculative growth centered tech stocks.

It is important to do a fundamental cash flow analysis of the companies involved, so that you can pick out stocks that are profitable and would benefit from an inflationary period.

Cryptocurrencies

Cryptocurrencies have gained immense popularity in the past decade. They have been endorsed by central banks, global financial institutions, and even social media giants. Their popularity has been built on their distinct features and characteristics.

A cryptocurrency is a virtual currency that is essentially a software created by performing complex mathematical calculations as dictated by code. The process operates over a network that involves several computers located throughout the world and is protected by a technology known as blockchain. Because the currency is protected by digital cryptography, it is unique in the sense that it cannot be counterfeited or spent twice. A major reason for the rise in popularity of cryptocurrencies is that unlike all other currencies, cryptocurrencies are not issued by any central bank. This makes cryptocurrencies immune to any manipulation by sovereign governments or central banks. Cryptocurrencies are protected using blockchain technology in such a way that their transfers are possible directly between two pirates without the need of a third party. Transfers of cryptocurrencies take several minutes but they have extremely low costs.

Because of the way cryptocurrencies are designed, they are by nature scarce and each new mined coin takes more resources. These contribute to a steady increase in prices which investors have attributed to the possibility of using cryptocurrencies as a hedge against inflation.

Note: A cryptocurrency investment is extremely speculative, and it's not recommended to invest more than 0.5-1% of your portfolio in crypto.

Bitcoin as an Asset Class and an Investment

Bitcoins are a unique payment system and a form of a reward for a process known as mining, and is primarily used in the exchange of products, services, or currencies. Bitcoins are the pioneer of a decentralized peer-to-peer payment system with no third parties involved. Bitcoins were the first execution of a concept under the name of "cryptocurrency" that was speculated and surfaced over a cypherpunks mailing list in 1998. The proposed idea meant a new form of money using cryptography (rather than middlemen or a central authority) to administer its transactions and creations. The design was finally implemented in 2009 after the bitcoin software was applied as open-source code (OSS). Its popularity has grown in the past decade as developers continue to work on its development.

Bitcoins are owned by no central authority and are rather controlled by bitcoin users worldwide. Bitcoin development is limited to improving the technology without enabling a change in the bitcoin protocol. Users can use any version or software but to remain compatible with each other similar rules must be applied for a uniform crypto network.

The backend network of Bitcoins is much more complicated than how users view it as a mere computer program. It shares 'blockchain' technology, which is a public ledger. The ledger enables the user's computer to verify how viable each bitcoin is for every transaction that takes place. Digital signatures protect each Bitcoin transaction allowing users to use their Bitcoin addresses to exchange Bitcoins. Additionally, Bitcoin mining refers to the process that produces more bitcoins by solving a computational puzzle, rewarding the miner with bitcoins in return.

The electronic cash system is recognized as a standard representation of a cryptocurrency and happens to be the most popular digital currency. Bitcoins are used by individuals worldwide. In 2017 alone there were up to approximately 5.8 million cryptocurrency wallet users, of which a large fraction were bitcoin users, as per a research conducted by the University of Cambridge.

The value of Bitcoin consistently appreciates over the long term although it has experienced an exceptional level of volatility over the years. Bitcoins that could be purchased for $0.0008-$0.8$ per Bitcoin are now valued at $39,334.20 each (8th January 2021). Bitcoin gained its value due its rising demand and limited supply. The negative correlation between the supply and demand of bitcoins is what drives the price up. Over time Bitcoins have matured in the crypto industry, gaining the attention of investors as it is increasingly being looked upon as a credible derivative that can be used as a hedge against inflation.

Bitcoins possess the largest market capitalization of any cryptocurrency today. Most economists regard bitcoins as a top-performing asset class with the unique traits it holds. However, a consensus on the nature of bitcoins remains undecided.

With the growing popularity of bitcoins as well as the rise of their value due to limited supply, investors are more convinced than ever to own bitcoins. Investment decisions can strongly rely on bitcoins' nature, making it essential to establish a consensus on whether bitcoins represent a new asset class.

Bitcoins are now being regulated in various jurisdictions worldwide that comply with local and international laws and allow investors to purchase bitcoins through established exchanges or crypto platforms legally.

The return on bitcoins and the risk-reward associated with it requires conclusions drawn from statistical approaches. Bitcoins have shown an insignificant correlation with other asset class traits. It is not associated with regular stocks or commodities as it goes in the normal world.

Despite bitcoins being relatively new in the market, the returns consistently outsize the preceding year's figures since crypto had begun and are now seen increasingly as suitable hedge against inflation. Bitcoins are an ideal investment primarily due to their fixed supply that stores value and contains enough potential to appreciate in the long run. Investment banks and institutional investors are consistently piling into the use of cryptocurrencies.

Litecoin and Ethereum

Cryptocurrencies are not limited to the use of bitcoins. There are several other investment options that investors opt for depending on their trading style and bankroll. Some prominent alternatives to cryptocurrencies apart from bitcoins are Ethereum and Litecoin.

Ethereum

Ethereum is a software platform designed in 2015 to serve the purpose of supporting decentralized contracts and digital cash. With a market cap of $69,604,579,809 (1/10 the size of bitcoins), Ethereum is the closest alternative to bitcoins one can find.

It is speculated that Ethereum holds the potential to revolutionize data protection, the finance industry, and social media. It also claims to secure, codify, and trade anything. It has gained support from significant financial organizations such as Microsoft Azure and Amazon Web Services.

Litecoin

Another well-versed option in the crypto market is Litecoin, referred to as the silver to bitcoin's gold. Litecoin is an open-source and decentralized software that is a form of digital cash.

Litecoin transaction fees are relatively lower, considering it requires minimal resources. Litecoin also tops bitcoin with a processing speed that is four times faster, posing as an ideal option in terms of efficiency and costs.

The future of Litecoin depicts a potentially good investment for most investors and is regarded as a close call to bitcoins.

Historical Performance Against Inflation

In 2009 when the initial trading of bitcoins had begun, the digital cryptocurrency had undergone a lot of volatility. The fluctuations in price were seen in 2010 when the value of a single bitcoin rose from $0.0008 to $0.8. Since then, bitcoins have experienced significant crashes and rallies. Mt.Gox surfaced into a marketplace for bitcoins, having 150,000 bitcoins exchanged every day. However, due to its volatile nature and speculations for fraud the exchange was taken down in 2013. By 2020 Bitcoins were able to regain its losses which were previously incurred and possess a market cap of over $732 billion as of January 8th, 2020. It is now traded on numerous licensed and credible exchanges such as Kraken, Coinbase and Gemini.

Bitcoins are carefully designed with a deflationary approach, in addition to being a unit that stores value. It represents a similar gold standard creating opportunities for crypto users and investors to rise above the adverse effects of inflation.

Bitcoins are popular for their incredible potential to provide industries with protection against inflation and pose as an inflationary hedge, encouraging investors to own more bitcoins. Tycoon investors refer to bitcoins as the new gold for the 21 century and consider them as being naturally immune to the impacts of inflation.

The performance of bitcoins against the global pandemic tells us a lot about the potential of bitcoins against inflation. COVID-19 measures had led to the implementation of an inflationary monetary policy, which encouraged an aggressive supply. The lockdowns measures had given rise to key areas and food staples, largely affecting businesses worldwide (Similar to the 1970s when the USA encountered massive unemployment, which led to gold being the currency savior against inflation)

Bitcoin happens to be an ideal hedge against inflation in this scenario. Bitcoins possess a natural inflationary trait with a fixed 21 million bitcoin supply. This limit is what drives the value of bitcoins up and makes them immune to monetary inflation.

The supply shortage against the rising demand for bitcoins depicts an increase in the future per unit price which is gaining the attention of investors worldwide.

Prospects as a Hedge Against Inflation

The limited supply of bitcoins creates an inflation hedge, unique to other asset classes as it is immune to the changes of a political environment within a country. Investors that purchase bitcoins are not intending to contribute to a deflationary measure but are using it as a hedge against the consequences of inflation. However, despite the benefits cryptocurrencies are speculative and highly volatile. In the worst-case scenario, investors may even lose all their money rather than gaining anything.

Apart from inflation, bitcoins also pose as a hindrance against a disruptive law and order due to political instability. The prospects of bitcoins seek potential in preventing additional factors that can trigger more inflation.

Police states practicing seizure of private wealth and bank accounts closing due to unreliable governments can be minimized with bitcoins. Corrupted systems, export-protecting devaluations are namely few inflation triggers that bitcoins act as a hedge against.

Worst case scenario - Hyperinflation

We have already discussed inflation at length throughout this book. It is a reduction in the purchasing power of a currency. Hyperinflation is accelerated version of inflation. When the rate of inflation is exceedingly high, usually over 50%, an economy is considered to experience hyperinflation. It quickly erodes the purchasing power of a local currency, significantly raises prices for goods, and causes the value of savings to drop dramatically. It usually occurs in extenuating circumstances such as war or an abject failure of economic policy. Because the rate of inflation increases rapidly during times of hyperinflation, the rates are usually measured on a daily basis. These daily rates sometimes fall between 5% and 10%. When the monthly CPI goes over 50%, an economy experiences hyperinflation.

What causes hyperinflation?

Hyperinflation is usually caused by an excessive money supply or an extreme lack of confidence in a country's currency by its citizens and trading partners. The most common reason for hyperinflation is when a central bank starts printing excessive amounts of money for one reason or the other. This is usually a result of an economic depression. An economic depression is different to a recession in the sense that it lasts much longer, usually a couple of years. Because of this, the central bank decides to pump more money into the economy to stimulate economic activity to get out of depression. However, sometimes the rise in money supply is not met with a proportionate rise in economic output. Due to ensuing depression, businesses increase the prices of goods and services in order to remain profitable. These increases are met by purchases because people have the money to buy them. Because the central bank continues to print more money, consumers continue to purchase products with ever increasing prices. As a consequence, hyperinflation takes hold.

Another reason that causes hyperinflation is when a local population does have the same confidence in the value of a currency as before. When this happens, a constant low confidence environment spreads across the population. People start buying goods in more quantities than they do in anticipation of rising prices. This causes more people to start buying even more things for fear of missing out on essential goods and services. This causes prices to get out of control sometimes and hyperinflation occurs.

Options for Hyperinflation

If you ever find yourself in a country that is either experiencing hyperinflation, or it might soon, there are various steps you can take to protect yourself. As hyperinflation significantly erodes the value of the currency, commodities become expensive. The most in-demand items such as food, water, fuel, and utilities usually experience the highest increase in prices. Owning assets that produce these commodities, or owning these commodities outright is an excellent way to insulate yourself from the harmful effects of hyperinflation.

A lot of the strategies listed below are from the people who experienced hyperinflation in the Weimar Republic post World War I. This was the last case of hyperinflation in a developed country.

Owning Farmland or a Home Garden

There are several assets investors choose to turn to whenever investing in balancing out the effects of inflation. Gold is a popular and effective asset to consider. However, investing in a commodity such as owning farmland or home garden can pay off better than other asset classes.

In other words, the rising prices in food and other organics play a significant role in inflation. To benefit from this, investors invest in farmlands that pay off better during inflation. Higher prices would increase the value for crops, allowing the farmer to make up for higher rent expenses for the land.

Investors are more inclined than ever in owning home gardens or farmlands as the demand for food continues to rise while farmland supply decreases significantly. Investing in farmland is profitable as it offers constant returns as per historical evidence and effectively poses as a hedge against inflation measures.

Farmland is referred to as gold that can yield. Such an investment enables investors to be more exposed to opportunities for financial gain. The valuable commodities that are produced from the farmland give an edge over investing in other options available.

Converting Everything to Foreign Currency or Precious Metals

During hyperinflation, the average value of a country's currency decreases notably. Converting existing cash or owning foreign currency(ies) or precious metals is the smart option to opt for during hyperinflation. Owning top-performing assets can act as a hedge against hyperinflation and its severe consequences. In some cases, it might even be very profitable. Investors have been using the tactic of investing in precious metals to prevent themselves from adverse risks and financial repercussions.

The prices of precious metals rise higher during inflation and are relatively safe compared to other asset classes. Investors who sense incoming hyperinflation are quick to respond by investing in metals like gold and silver.

As the currency value decreases, the value of precious metals increases, depicting a negative correlation. These metals balance out the effects of inflation giving investors an upper hand even during times of a financial crisis.

Similarly, local currency can quickly lose its value, and investors often turn to store their money value by converting cash or liquid assets to foreign currencies. Converting everything into foreign currency can protect investors from the impacts of the devalued currency i.e., losing their current monetary value. The foreign exchange rates may vary based on the different inflation rates amongst the many currencies available.

Postponing Payment of Debt

With hyperinflation, you can expect to witness a decline in the average value of a country's currency that is undergoing a financial crisis. Money now is more valuable than what it will be in the future.

The value of debt decreases during hyperinflation; however, it can become quite challenging to pay off debts during hyperinflation. This is because inflation often has little to no effect on income. With a diminishing value of income, individuals will be spending more on sky-high goods and will have lesser disposable income to pay off debts. But delaying these payments will be a lot more beneficial since the debt will be worth less and less as the value of the local currency continues to decline.

A financial crisis would encourage businesses to delay payments by purchasing supplies on credit. These businesses prefer to delay their payment dates to incur a 'less valuable debt' during hyperinflation. Failure to obtain credit for a business during hyperinflation may be as severe as putting the firm out of business. You can also do the same and seek to delay payment of as much debt as is possible. This is because it will be a lot easier to pay off the debt in the future as the value of the currency in which the debt was taken would be significantly reduced. If you also invest in commodities or other assets to protect yourself against hyperinflation, you would be able to pay off the debt with much more ease in the future.

Getting into Long Term Financing

When an economy experiences hyperinflation, central banks usually raise interest rates to control inflation by reducing the money supply. This makes borrowing expensive in the short term. However, the important thing to note is that since all these loans will need to be paid back in the local currency, the loans will be worth much less in the future and consequently, much easier to pay off. This is because the currency would have significantly lost its value making it a lot easier to acquire from the sale of goods or property. For example, if you take out a mortgage from a bank in a period of an extremely high level of inflation, your monthly payments will be in the local currency. However, the value of your property will most likely appreciate monthly and will be worth many times more at the time of the mortgage's maturity. This is because you will be making the payments in the now heavily discounted local currency. A mortgage is one example. You can also take other forms of long-term financing. The basic idea is to buy commodities or assets that have the greatest potential of appreciating in value over time as the value of the currency in which the loan has been borrowed continues to decline.

The Risk of Government Intervention

During a traumatic experience like hyperinflation, there is tremendous pressure on the Government to mitigate the pain due to hyperinflation. This element is very unpredictable. For example, long term financing of apartments might make you think that it's a great think to be a landlord during hyperinflation. However, during the Weimar Republic hyperinflation, rents were capped by the Government, leading to many landlords going bust.

During hyperinflation in Venezuela, it's natural for wheat and soy prices to rise. However, the Government imposed price controls which led to food shortages.

In Argentina, the Government outlawed exchange of Argentinian pesos for foreign currency.

The anonymous and decentralized nature of Bitcoin has proven to be a boon for those who held Bitcoin in Venezuela. Venezuelans have widely adopted use of Bitcoin in their daily life through P2P

(Peer-to-Peer) networks. Other countries with high inflation problems (like Zimbabwe) have struggled to do so.

The unknown elements of hyperinflation make diversification especially important. You never know what is an asset during hyperinflation, and what is not.

Conclusion

Sectors that Outperform during Inflationary Periods

We have talked at length about the types of sectors that have traditionally performed very well during inflationary periods. These sectors can be traced back to the fundamentals upon which inflation is based. These fundamentals dictate that sectors that deal with goods that are in demand all year round are very likely to perform well during times of inflation. The reason being their ability to transfer the increase in the cost of their raw materials directly onto consumers because people always need what they are selling. These sectors commonly include food and beverage producers, agriculture companies, and healthcare providers.

Other sectors that perform really well during inflationary periods are those sectors that either produce or provide services to utility companies and energy providers. Examples include power generation companies and oil and gas companies, These sectors experience healthy appreciation in their stock prices during times of high inflation because they are directly related to the core energy requirements of the population.

The Importance of Diversification in a Portfolio

While we have discussed numerous ways through which you can confidently protect your finances against inflation, we would suggest not putting all of your eggs in one basket. The main reason for this is that even though all of the avenues we have discussed are quite effective at countering the effects of inflation if they are used together, their effects can become more certain.

There are countless combinations you can try to create a diverse portfolio to protect your investments. This is my favorite allocation.

10% Precious metals

15% Commodities

20% High Quality Tech Investments

20%	Foreign stocks (non-US developed and emerging)
10%	Real estate (REIT's, REIM's)
10%	Speculation (Crypto / Mining Stocks)
15%	Cash in Multiple Currencies/Inflation Indexed Bonds

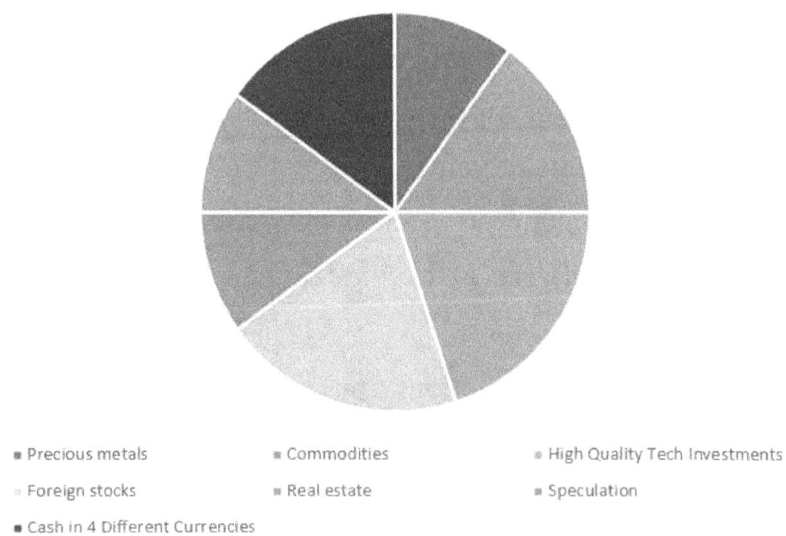

There are a few reasons why this specific combination is ideal.

- Firstly, because having stakes in commodities, tech investments, and foreign stocks ensure that more than 70% of your portfolio is highly liquid. This means that you can convert your holdings into and out of cash quickly and easily.

- Secondly, investing in precious metals, commodities, and real estate is almost guaranteed to perform well during inflationary periods even if the other assets in your portfolio do not or take a while to catch up with the others in terms of value appreciation.
- Thirdly, because investing 10% in speculative instruments provides a little risk exposure to your portfolio which can produce more than average results but even if it underperforms, it will still be only 10% or less which means that more than 90
% of your portfolio will be relatively safer and will go on to ensure that the entire portfolio makes a decent return.
- And lastly, a 10% investment in real estate provides much-needed strength to the portfolio as real estate almost always performs well in the long term. Because this is not as liquid as the others, you will be less likely to trade it more frequently which will ensure that your portfolio has a long-term appreciating asset as well.

Other Resources

As you come to the end of this book, I hope you realize that we only wish the best of success in your investing journey. Whether you utilize my strategies or not, we want you to do well.

Here are a few other resources that I recommend for investors:

Rule #1 Investing – This is hands down the best investing book I have ever read. Helps value investors which stocks are priced below their true value and buy a stock at a good Margin of Safety.

Investing QuickStart Guide – Great resource for beginner investors to get started with investing.

The Dando Investor – Another great investing resource

The Downfall of Money – A fantastic, detailed story of the finances during the Weimar Republic's hyperinflation in the 1920s

The end... almost!

Reviews are not easy to come by.

As an independent author with a tiny marketing budget, I rely on readers, like you, to leave a short review on Amazon.

Even if it's just a sentence or two!

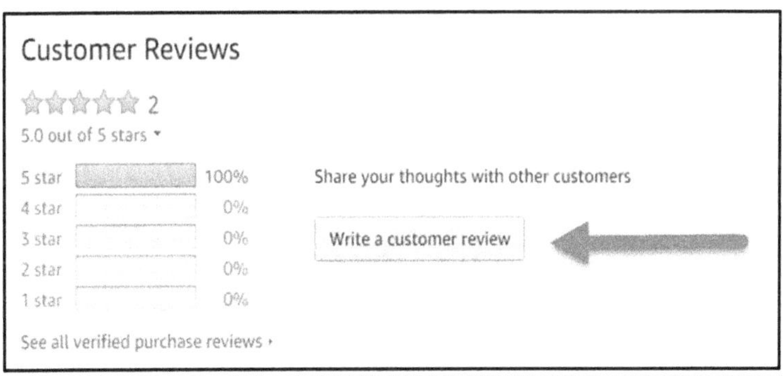

I am very appreciative for your review as it truly makes a difference.

Thank you from the bottom of my heart for purchasing this book and reading it to the end.

Finance and Investing for the Long Run

Investing for Teens and Young Adults to Make the Most of Their Money.

Introduction

This book is the key to your financial future; but it's not a one size fits all. Everyone is at different stages in their financial journey. There are some who are just getting started off in their career. Of those who are getting started, some have zero debt while others have a load of student debt.

There are others who make a lot of money but don't have much financial discipline or financial knowledge. They have a tendency to overspend and have not spent much time learning how to save or invest. They need help with budgeting and need to start building their knowledge base in investing.

There are others that are doing pretty well. They have zero debt, a great job and are well invested. But they have all their assets invested in one or two asset classes. One may be completely invested in the stock market, for example. They have exposed themselves to high-risk investments with little portfolio diversification. While this may not be an issue in the short term, it could lead to catastrophe in the long term. The best way to deal with this is portfolio diversification and allocate a portion of their assets in gold, safe stocks and cash.

Then there are some who are very financially responsible. They have a good job, great financial discipline. They have a large source of funds; but they have it all in cash or bonds. They have a great sense of apprehension when it comes to investing in other assets. While their strategy may be perfect for a stock market crash, they have exposed themselves to long term inflation. They either slowly lose purchasing power long term due to increasing prices; or risk becoming poor due to an inflationary collapse. An increase in allocation in stocks, gold and real estate may serve them well in the future.

No matter where you are in your financial journey, this book will help you out. I recommend using this book as a reference and the different chapters as placeholders depending on the stage of your journey. For example, if you are just getting started on your journey, you can learn about budgeting, compounding, planning and increasing income, while saving the other chapters for when you've saved more money. If you have 100% of your money saved in cash; you can focus on the precious metals and portfolio construction chapters.

Thank you for purchasing this book; and I hope you get the most out of it.

The Importance of Long-Term Financial Planning

"Most people don't plan to fail, they fail to plan."

— John L. Beckley

Planning plays a critical role in every sphere of life, and finances are no exception. Planning is the foundation for implementing a vision and allocating resources accordingly. It also helps to highlight unforeseen risks and the development of feasible countermeasures to these.

Financial planning entails developing elaborate frameworks for managing money to meet our life goals (Timmerman & Volkov, 2020). A well-planned approach is vital in controlling income, investment, and expenses, ensuring the planner can account for their finances. Financial planning also ensures that individuals allocate their income in line with their priorities, underpinning their ability to achieve personal goals. A financial plan lays down the framework to ensure that we do not fall into financial problems and lower our quality of life.

Long-term financial planning is especially critical to achieving long-term goals (Topa, Hernández-Solís, & Zappalà, 2018). It goes beyond the short-term circumstances, setting us on a pathway to implement our vision, augment financial growth, and increase our quality of life.

Long-term financial planning is also key to increasing savings. It gives teens and young adults insights into their income and expenses, helping them optimize their spending and investments. While saving is possible without a long-time financial plan, it is less effective. Topa, Hernández-Solís, & Zappalà (2018), claim that a long-term financial plan augments the individual's ability to both set saving targets and, crucially, achieve them. It also plays an integral role in creating a saving mindset since it helps individuals to follow a specific spending pattern. For example, long-term financial planning plays a significant role in long-term projects such as buying your first home (Garg & Singh, 2018). It enables individuals to save part of their income for an extended period, making their vision of buying a home possible. With a financial plan, young people can save beyond their goals, and use this excess money to accomplish other objectives.

A long-term financial plan not only guides young people through their life's journey but helps them to turn dreams into reality. A financial plan is important in creating wealth thus enhancing a person's living standards.

A long-term financial plan is critical in ensuring that we meet our daily needs optimally and gradually increasing our quality of life (Timmerman & Volkov, 2020).

A long-term financial plan helps teens and young adults to optimize their spending. This supports their lifestyle together with improving their quality of life and, hence, mental health. The plan, therefore, sustains their quality of life and gradually increases it (Lusardi, 2019). It helps a person attain the kind of peace of mind which is pivotal in augmenting their quality of life. With a long-term financial plan, individuals can use their funds to cover their expenses, splurge with their families, and invest for future goals without worry. Thus, the plan helps individuals manage their income optimally and with peace of mind.

The fundamental role of a long-term financial plan is preparation for the future. Frameworks and approaches adopted to cater for future occurrences tend to foster preparedness. Long-term financial plans help account for future expenses. There are numerous risks and unforeseen circumstances that might unexpectedly require funds. For example, sickness, death, accidents, or job losses may require emergency funding

(Lusardi, 2019). Without these 'rainy-day' funds set aside, individuals may end up borrowing or facing considerable financial strain. Long-term financial planning plays an integral role in setting aside emergency funds to cater to unforeseen circumstances. It ensures that individuals can pay for varied funds on time without worry.

Financial planning also pays a key role in reducing mental health and physical health issues. A good financial plan reduces financial uncertainty, which reduces stress and anxiety. According to money and Mental Health Institute, 46% of people in debt had mental health issues. Eventually, mental health issues lead to physical health issues.

Fundamentally, we are saying that financial planning is the key to a financially secure future.

How Compounding Works in the Long Run

"Compound interest is the eighth wonder of the world. He who understands it, earns it ... he who doesn't ... pays it."

-Albert Einstein

Compounding is a crucial tool that enables savings growth and helps pay down debts. It is a formula used to augment the time value of money, increasing the principal amount and interest earned over time. Compounding guarantees that assets grow exponentially over the years. It differs from linear growth since capital gains or interests are invested in increasing earnings (Baid, 2020).

Compounding makes our pot grow faster than when it earns simple interest. In cases of simple interest, the initial amount earns a particular interest over some time, and therefore only the principal sum attracts that additional revenue. This generation of additional earnings over time is created by the reinvestment of the initial capital plus its earnings over a particular period. In compounding, the interest applies to the principal amount as well as the interest that the principal amount had earned earlier.

So, we are not only earning interest on our original sum, but also on the interest that sum has already earned. Interest on our interest, in other words. This is why compounding is often referred to as *miracle* compounding. It plays an integral role in the growth of savings and investments (Alikar et al., 2017). It assures individuals of continually increasing earnings over time, ensuring them optimal returns. In the long run, compounding increases the amount of income generated through capital gains on investments.

Banks and other financial institutions credit compound interest using compounding periods. These periods can be daily, monthly, quarterly, semiannually, or annually depending on the prevailing conditions. In all of these cases compounding tends to increase the amount invested exponentially.

Inevitably, though, there is a catch. While it offers brilliant returns on our investments, it also applies to our debts!

Compounding increases any debt owed. In such cases, interest accumulates on the borrowed amounts and previous interest charges that have been applied to that borrowed amount. The sum required to pay off a debt, therefore, increases since one has to pay for the unpaid principal sum and the compounded interest which accrues on it. In the long run, compounding increases the cost of a debt. Good news for the lender' less so for the debtor.

So, just as compound interest makes our savings grow quickly, so it makes our debts increase faster than we might imagine.

As mentioned earlier, compounding ties in neatly with the principle that invested money (and savings) grow over time. Due to money's earning capacity, the funds we can invest now becomes worth more in the future. This theory enhances the core financial principles that if money can earn interest, it becomes worth more the sooner it gets disbanded (Alikar et al., 2017). Consequently, compounding aligns with the principle of *present discounted value*, with time playing an essential role in determining its future value. While the interest rate is also crucial, the period over which compounding takes place determines the pace of t growth of assets/ It increases the time value of money in the long run.

The earning capacity of funds increases with the frequency of its compounding periods and the time frame taken to arrive at the final sum.

For example, for one year, three compounding periods would increase the future value of an investment more than one (Baid, 2020). Similarly, funds that have gained a compound interest over three years earn more than those that earn for three months. Therefore, the longer the time frame, the more the earnings in the long run.

As we said earlier, compounding earns interest for the initial amount and accumulated earnings over the same period. Compounding is crucial in finance; it is the foundation behind many investment strategies. Its ability to increase earnings significantly, especially in the long run, is attractive to investors.

One of the most common ways of earning compound interest is through **dividend investment plans** offered by numerous corporations. This approach entails reinvesting dividends earned to buy more shares. Thus, the number of shares an investor holds in a firm grows with a consequent increase in value of their investment. Provided, of course, that the firm is doing well.

Another benefit of this approach is that it also assures an investor of a consistent increase in the cash dividends paid out by a firm. Again, with the proviso that the corporation sustains its profitability. This example provides an insight into the concept known as double compounding. This is where, on top of the growth in the number of shares owned, the investor also benefits from higher dividend payouts (Baid, 2020). Investors, therefore, continually increase the value of their investment, and the more they reinvest, the greater the increase in value they gain. In these cases, long-term investments mean that the investor earns even more. Compounding applies over the long term, which is generally a bigger earner for the investor than any short-term compounding can offer.

We can learn more about compounding over the long term by looking at how money accumulates over time when it earns annual compound interest. Compounding makes wealth grow faster; therefore, the more the frequency of the compounding period and the time frame of the investment, the higher the capital gains growth on the principal amount.

In other words, the longer the period of investment, and the greater the number of compounding periods, the more money we make.

Let's take an example to illustrate this. For argument's sake we will assume an annual investment interest return of 8% alongside a monthly investment of 250 dollars. If an individual starts saving at the age of 25, they accumulate 878,570 dollars by the time they reach 65. If another individual starts saving the same amount under similar conditions when they are 45, they accumulate 148,268 dollars by age 65. In this example we can see that difference of 20 compounding periods (that is, an additional twenty years of savings for the person who began at age 25) brings about a difference of 730,308 dollars (Alikar et al., 2017).

In other words, quite a lot of money.

More compounding periods means more cash earned. Or the earlier we start to save and invest the better the returns we will see. Investing for more extended periods will ensure that compounding will work to our advantage in the long run.

Compared to simple interest, compounding has higher returns on investment. Using the example of the 250 dollars monthly investments within the 40- and 20-year periods, the final investment is smaller using simple interest than when using compound interest. Investment during the two periods is 120,000 dollars and 60,000 dollars for the 40 years and 20 years of investment respectively. However, the return using from simple interest is 313,362 dollars for the person who starts saving at 25 and 108,441 dollars for the individual who starts saving twenty years later. In the first case, there is a difference of 565,208 dollars between compound and simple interest returns while in the second instance the difference is a much smaller figure of just under forty thousand dollars. This difference demonstrates that compounding is an effective way to grow savings. The chart below illustrates this point.

Figure 1: *This figure shows the difference in returns between different periods with compounding and simple interest at 8% per annum.*

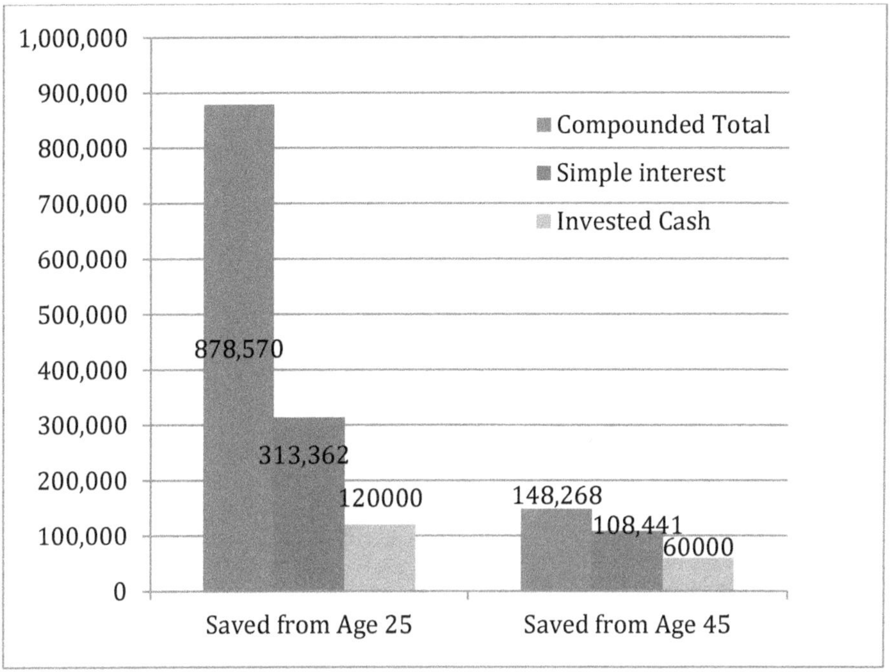
1,000,000
900,000
800,000
700,000
600,000
500,000
400,000
300,000
200,000
100,000
0
Compounded Total
Simple interest
Invested Cash
878,570
313,362
120000
148,268
108,441
60000
Saved from Age 25
Saved from Age 45

Inflation and Time Value of Money

Inflation is as violent as a mugger, as frightening as an armed robber and as deadly as a hit man.

- Ronald Reagan

The time value of money states that money held today is more valuable than that the same amount held on a future date. Getting paid today is better than getting paid tomorrow. However, the exception to this occurs when the money gains interest (that is lower than inflation).

So, while a pot of money will increase in value (by which we mean purchasing power) if it gains interest which is lower than inflation, if it is kept in our pocket or under our bed, it becomes less valuable over time. The rate of inflation reflects how prices increase over time (a more detailed explanation of inflation follows shortly). Therefore, the time value of money is subject to both risk and returns. One must take risk to gain returns in the future.

Net Present Value is a critical concept in explaining the time value of money (Muda & Hasibuan, 2018). It helps provide insight into how time affects the monetary value of items. It displays the differences between the present and future purchasing power of money.

Inflation plays a major role in financial planning since it affects the relative value of money over time. Additionally, it has ripple implications for future prices of goods and services, thus affecting an individual's purchasing power. Inflation is considered as the change in the prices of a range of products over a particular period. It is the actual change in prices of consumer goods and can be used to determine future prices of goods and services. Inflation refers to the increase in the price levels. For example, a 10% annual inflation rate indicates a 10% average increase in the price of goods and services every year (Alikar et al., 2017). Inflation has adverse effects on the value of money as a medium of exchange. With increased inflation, the value of our money keeps falling. In cases of extreme inflation, such as in Germany during the Second World War the price of goods grows much faster than the value of money, making it worthless. Stamp collectors might have in their collection German stamps from this period. They will see the cost of the stamp overprinted on the actual object. A typical stamp might cost 8 million marks. In other words, a person who was previously extremely rich, with 8 million marks in their bank account now has only enough money to buy a single postage stamp.

So, inflation is very important in determining the value of money. Calculated annually, it helps Government to develop policies to maintain the value of money.

An increase in inflation increases an economy's volatility and affects both how people trade and use money as an indicator of value. High inflation makes it more difficult to use the money to store value, affecting the time value of money.

But just as inflation can reduce the value of money, it also erodes the actual value of a debt, making it easier to repay (Muda & Hasibuan, 2018). This is the reason why banks are less willing to lend money during periods of high inflation. By the time the loan has been repaid, the value of the money paid back may be less than the value of the money initially lent. That is bad business. To counter this, in most cases, banks lend money at an interest rate higher than the inflation rate (Muda & Hasibuan, 2018). The volatility of a high inflation rate makes setting a lending rates a daunting task because there is limited stability in the markets.

Inflation is therefore among the most significant determiners of the time value of money. It also has ripple implications for the present and future value of money, affecting investment and lending abilities. It erodes the purchasing power of money. This is the number of goods it can buy in the future compared to the amount it could buy in the period set as the base year (Muda & Hasibuan, 2018). In most cases, this is the difference between what money can buy in the present compared to what it can buy in the days to come. For example, in 2014, we could purchase a movie ticket for 15 dollars; in the 1980s, we could have taken ourselves and nine of our mates to see Back to the Future for the same sum of money. (Kim, Anderson, & Seay, 2019). $15 in 2014 purchased 10% of the amount it did in the 1980s. Purchasing power, as a result, erodes with time, and inflation plays a critical role in this reduction.

The fact that prices will typically go up in the future, demonstrates that inflation eats away savings (Muda & Hasibuan, 2018). Keeping our money in a bank is better than keeping it under our bed. But, while the bank interests offsets some of the inflation, interest growth fails to increase in line with inflation rates in most instances. In other words, interest rates offered by banks are usually lower than the prevailing rate of inflation. Thus, our savings lose value with time.

Here is an example. The US Dollar has an average inflation rate of 2.93% (Muda & Hasibuan, 2018). Therefore, $100, 41 years ago, had the same purchasing power as $330 today. An item that cost $100 in

1980, will cost $330. If individual kept their $100 from 1980 in a box in their bedroom and brought it out today, they would need to add $230 to it to purchase the product they could have bought 41 years ago.

We need to understand the role of inflation in the time value of money if we are to make investments that negate these effects. The time value of money is essential in enhancing the quality of investments by tapping into money's earning capacity (Alikar et al., 2017). However, there is a downside to this with inflation playing a critical role in eroding the value of money over time.

Here's a few other examples of how prices have changed over the last 30 years.

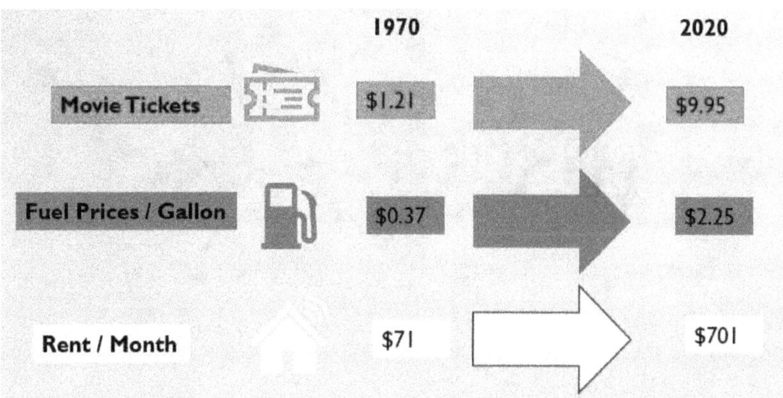

The time value of money and inflation are crucial determinants of investment returns.

They help to determine probable returns and thus play a central role in financial planning.

How to Create and Use a Budget

You can fool all the people all the time if the advertising is right and the budget is big enough.

- Joseph E. Levine

Budgets are fundamental to financial planning. They provide revenue and expense estimates, enabling individuals to project, understand, and manage their funds. Budgets play a key role since they ensure that individuals allocate their funds optimally to achieve their set objectives (Jones et al., 2017). They enhance control over finances since each person understands the percentage of funds required for each of their requirements.

By keeping track of what we earn and how we spend it, budgets are pivotal in ensuring that we have best management of our financial resources. Budgets are also instrumental in setting goals and developing strategies to help achieve the set goals. They are helpful when measuring outcomes. They are useful when we compare outcomes to hopes.

By accounting for income and expenses, budgets also play a fundamental role in planning for contingencies helping to mitigate risks.

Budgets are also called spending plans. They show how we balance income, expenses, and financial goals. They pump up the efficacy of financial plans for a specific period, estimating how much money we will make and spend within a set period. Budgets are crucial whether accounting for the incoming and outgoing funds an individual has, as well as in a household or corporation. This accountability is vital in optimizing the efficacy of financial plans and ensuring that individuals achieve their set objectives (Tyson, Eric, & Tony, 2018). A budget also helps people understand if they have enough income to cater for projected expenses. In cases where we do not have enough money, we can apply planning strategies to prioritize our outgoings and allocate money where it is most needed. Budgeting allows individuals to spend money appropriately since the spending plan allocates money for individual needs and aspects that are considered of high importance (Jones et al., 2017). Our budget helps balance income with spending. Consequently, we are kept from spending more than we make. And as Mr Pickwick said, that is one of the secrets to happiness. It is also a crucial tool in keeping individuals out of debt and ensuring they achieve their objectives.

By keeping track of where money is being spent, budgets ensure that we eliminate unnecessary expenses and enhance our ability to achieve our financial targets. They enable us to set realistic goals. With the insights on projected income within a given period, one can predict the goals we can achieve within this period (Tyson, Eric, & Tony, 2018).

The above shows that a budget is also a crucial tool in enhancing saving and debt elimination. Experts consider setting a budget to be one of the most critical financial habits individuals can adopt. It not only enhances accountability but also plays an integral role in financial decision-making.

The process of creating a budget is subject to individual financial goals, estimated income, and expenses. Some prefer to write the budget by hand, while others prefer budgeting applications or spreadsheets.

There are several elements which are important as we develop a workable budget. First, we need to input our net income. That is the money we receive from work, parents, interest on savings which we use to spend, kindly relatives or indeed any other guaranteed source. By net income, we mean the money we receive after statutory elements such as tax and pension contributions have been removed. Second, this revenue is the foundation for operating our budgets; one cannot spend amounts that are not within their reach (Fedosov et al., 2021). Listing this income is the starting point for setting a budget.

Another crucial component is expenses. A budget has to indicate where our money is getting spent, therefore enabling us to allocate it appropriately. In this sense, there are variable and discretionary expenses classified per individual needs. For example, utilities, food expenses, and other daily costs are classified as variable expenses (Tyson, Eric, & Tony, 2018). These are given priority when allocating our funds since they are the essentials for which we need to budget. We should, of course, streamline these expenses to fit within our means. If we earn $1000 per month and our rent is $950, we are seeking to live beyond our means. We can change their spending habits to ensure they attain their financial goals (Fedosov et al., 2021). Consequently, individuals can cut costs to ensure that their spending conciliates with their income and financial needs.

Discretionary expenses are those that individuals can do without. They include entertainment and meals at restaurants; while they are fundamental in enhancing their quality of life, individuals do not depend on them for survival. Budgets have to account for these expenses since they are part of our spending.

The next part of a budget concerns our vision. Vision plays an important role in planning to accomplish our goals. Our vision is the focal point of the planning process and a crucial benchmark in determining whether our plan accomplishes our desired end goal.

Financial goals are integral components in the budgeting process. They determine the length and extent of the budget coupled with priorities in the allocation of finances (Fedosov et al., 2021). Without well laid out financial goals, developing feasible budgets becomes a daunting task because we have no precise idea of the objective we are seeking to accomplish. With clearly spelled out financial goals, developing an accurate budget is more easily accomplished. Our budgeting process should be tailored around our set financial goals (Tyson, Eric, & Tony, 2018). They give direction to our budget while providing us with benchmarks to review our budget's efficacy over time.

Having understood the most important components in a budget, we can begin to investigate our actual budget-making process. The first step involves collecting financial information, including financial statements and paperwork. This entails gathering up banking statements, utility bills, credit card bills, receipts from the past three months, and mortgage or auto loan statements. In cases of employed individuals, pay slips provide our income details. The most feasible approach to this is recording our monthly income (Jones et al., 2017). Of course, many of us these days work in the gig economy, with variable contracts and income. In this case, we should use as our baseline **income from the lowest-earning month**. The next step in this first phase is listing all the expenses in order of priority.

Categorizing fixed and variable expenses is important in ensuring that those costs that require immediate attention come first. It is also advisable to use information from past receipts to develop accurate estimates of the expenses (Tyson, Eric, & Tony, 2018). We should include surprise expenses in our budget; this helps to ensure that emergencies do not derail our budget. Of course, we need to ensure that our expenses are not greater than our income. This seems an obvious requirement, but is easily missed, especially when we are inexperienced budgeters.

Where income is greater than our expenses, one is off to a good start since one can use the extra income to save, invest or pay off debts. In other cases, if expenses are greater than income, developing an alternative approach to spending is the most feasible approach (Jones et al., 2017). In other words, we either have to cut costs or increase our income. Of the two, the former is the more easily achieved. More on this shortly.

The second phase of the budgeting process entails bringing financial goals into play. During this process, significant decisions need to be made regarding our allocation of expenses to meet our future goals. This is an important part of the budgeting processes since we must match our income and spending with our set objectives (Tyson, Eric, & Tony, 2018). The decisions we make here will determine whether we meet our goals.

In situations where the expenses outweigh income, we need to make sure our budgeting process is feasible. Cutting variable expenses is a viable solution to this situation. It entails eliminating discretionary expenses such as cutting out a gym membership, eating out less often, going for fewer holidays, or reducing spending on entertainment (Jones et al., 2017). Trimming fixed expenses is also highly advisable in a bid to reduce expenses – this might seem impossible but is often achievable. For example, if we have a two bedroomed apartment which we rent, could we sub-let the second room, thus sharing the rental costs and reducing expenses? Other approaches aimed at reducing expenses, can include optimizing energy and resource usage. For example, reducing food, water, and electricity wastage can help cut fixed costs by about 40 % (Tyson, Eric, & Tony, 2018).

Another approach here involves increasing income to help cover the budget's needs. Can we increase our hours at work? Is there a promotion in the offing? Should we take a short term second job?

Once we have listed our income, outlined our expenses, and planned to deliver our long-term goals, it is time to implement our budget. Implementation needs to be as rigorous as our budget-making process. One should make the budget work for them and not the other way round; that is, we should use this tool to help achieve our financial goals. Continuous tracking and monitoring of our spending helps achieve this outcome. It ensures that we keep our expenses to our budget and achieve our set financial objectives (Tyson, Eric, & Tony, 2018). Tracking expenses prevents us from overspending. The budget implementation process helps with the identification of problematic spending patterns or unnecessary expenses.

The envelope system is a good solution when we have issues tracking our expenses or following our budget outline. This entails putting money for different expenses in different envelopes. Once a particular envelope is empty; one must stop spending in that category (Jones et al., 2017). Taking funds from one expense category to help cover additional expenses can also work in an emergency. Keeping an eye on our spending ensures that we do not end up overdrawn at the end of the month or spend too heavily using expensive credit or store cards.

If we're in an area of the world that doesn't accept cash, then the envelope strategy may not be feasible. Online payment platforms globally track expenses and allocate expenses to different categories. If our bank doesn't have it, we can call them and see if they can help us set up expense tracking. Or we could look up other banks/credit cards to see if they do it. While this may involve a little loss of privacy, it does make it a lot easier to track our expenses. Implement email/text reminders with our bank to notify us when we spend over our allocated amount in a particular category.

Ensuring that a budget is highly flexible is also important. The shifts fueled by the volatile business environments require a budget that can align with changing circumstances or shifts in priorities. It is, therefore, useful to carry out periodic reviews to ensure that our budget is working both towards our goals and in line with our day-to-day requirements. An inflexible budget cannot account for life changes, for example, job changes, relocation, having additional children, or sickness (Tyson, Eric, & Tony, 2018). It is, then, less effective in helping us to reach their financial goals. Constant budget review is vital to help us keep up with our current circumstances. It is another foundation of an effective budget. We should also adjust our budgets periodically to correct any underestimated or overestimated expenses.

. It helps to carry out a benchmarking activity which, in most cases, will cross-reference spending against financial deliverables within a specific period (Jones et al., 2017). Continuous review ensures that our budget helps us to reach our desired future financial position.

One of the best budgeting approaches is the **50/30/20 technique**. It is simple to understand and easy to use. The 50/30/20 approach has been recommended as one of the most suitable financing approaches for individuals looking to develop personal budgets (Tyson, Eric, & Tony, 2018). It enables people to develop a viable approach to meeting expenses and saving part of their income to meet financial goals. It is also a good method to help us to repay debts and enjoy a more balanced approach when we align income with spending. This budgeting plan assumes that 50% of total income goes into covering expenses. This 50% should meet personal needs, including our fixed and variable expenses. 30% of the income should cover our discretional expenses, such as entertainment plus it can be used as an emergency fund should this be needed. Budgets should help individuals enjoy life, and accounting for every penny is helpful in achieving this. Setting aside money for our wants is pivotal in ensuring that we let our money work for us (Fedosov et al., 2021). Finally, 20% of total income should go towards saving, with elements like retirement funds, stocks, fixed deposit accounts, and investment schemes taking center stage. The 20% that goes into saving is crucial in meeting future financial goals.

Teens and young adults have an advantage over people of other age groups in understanding budgeting. When they develop budgeting skills at a young age, they can continually enhance their competence and become experts in the long run (Generation, 2021). They can experiment with different budgeting techniques and develop frameworks to augment their ability to achieve their financial goals. They embrace financial literacy and foster a better quality of life in the long run (Tyson, Eric, & Tony, 2018). Budgets teach teenagers responsibility; they help them adopt a culture of spending money wisely. A budget is a crucial tool for instilling discipline when it comes to spending money optimally. Embracing its efficacy at a young age helps teens and young adults identify their spending patterns and eliminate poor financial behavior. It also enables young people to develop insights on the most appropriate budget plan to accomplish their different financial goals. Apart from enabling teens and young adults to spend money wisely and develop financial responsibility, budgets play an integral role in augmenting effective decision-making (Garg & Singh, 2018). Young people with practical budgeting skills make financial decisions that align with their goals in life.

So, it's clear that we should spend some time learning to become an effective budget setter!

Indeed, having the ability to develop a budget is a fundamental financial skill vital for lifetime financial success. It helps us make wise decisions when spending money and live within our means. It is a helpful tool in ensuring that we do not get into debt. It is also an important concept in money management since it has ripple implications for young adults and increases their wealth-making abilities later in life (Garg & Singh, 2018). During teenage years making mistakes when creating budgets is understandable. We can quickly correct these mistakes, identify poor spending habits, and perfect our personal financial skills. Furthermore, developing budgeting skills at an early age helps teenagers commit to saving. We are all influenced by the success of milestones we achieve at an early age (Tyson, Eric, & Tony, 2018). Budgets play a central role in planning for holidays, buying the gadgets we need, and fostering financial freedom. Teens and young adults can therefore use budgets as their gateway to financial success over their lifetime.

Most young adults are also tech-savvy. Statistics indicate that technology adaptation among individuals in this age group is over 88%. Using budgeting tools that capitalize on innovation plays a central role in supporting financial management among young individuals (Garg & Singh, 2018). Spreadsheets are good for this; they are simple to use and help us to develop accurate budgets. Using spreadsheets, we can record our income, expenses, goals, and track our spending. A spreadsheet is a virtual platform that enhances the feasibility of budgeting among young people. The use of applications for mobile devices and software is also encouraged to underpin budgeting (Tyson, Eric, & Tony, 2018). The applications are vital in automating the budgeting processes and storing data that is helpful in analyzing budgeting trends. They assist us to manage spending, monitor financial goals, and keep track of our budget's efficacy.

Budgeting using technology platforms can also help us by setting up reminders and countering barriers that hinder budgeting processes.

With technology-based budgeting, managing finances wherever we are and keeping accurate records is an easier task. Furthermore, it helps us compare prices, track investments, and avoid financial mistakes that might derail an individual from their financial goals (Tyson, Eric, & Tony, 2018). Therefore, young people should capitalize on technology to develop their budgeting competencies and augment their financial management skills. It will play a crucial role in helping them make better financial decisions and put their budgets into practice. Additionally, technology-based budgeting is more accurate, helping us keep better track of our income, expenses, and spending patterns. We can also use it as a point of reference in benchmarking our progress towards our set financial goals.

Strategies to Increase Income

If you don't find a way to make money while you sleep, you will work until you die.

- Warren Buffett

Increasing income is important in reaching financial goals and enhancing our quality of life. With increased income, individuals can spend or invest more, have a better quality of life, and improve their ability to create wealth.

i. Earning a Raise

One of the most common ways people increase their income is by achieving a pay rise. This technique is applicable for employed individuals with a regular monthly income. Asking for a pay rise increases the salary paid by a certain percentage thus, increasing disposable income (Lazear, 2018).

We can tend to think as a raise as a reward for contribution to our firm. However, this kind of salary increase is not always easy to achieve. Our firm, like us, needs to stick to its budget. That means controlling expenses, and one of the biggest of these is its staff pay roll.

But there are other ways of achieving a raise. A pay increase could come in the form of more overtime or working hours. Frequently, overtime has a higher rate than regular working hours. To balance productivity, some firms prefer increasing regular working hours and overtime to augment pay increases. The pay rise, in this case, is influenced by the employee's productivity. Simply, the more we make for our company, the more they pay us to do so.

In other instances, one can ask for a pay rise due to the company's growth over time. For example, with increased profitability, employees can ask for an increase in their salary to motivate them to sustain their revenue generation ability (Ali & Ahmad, 2017).

While asking for a pay rise sounds like a walk in the park, it's a delicate undertaking that requires good timing and a careful approach. It is crucial to note that companies will periodically review their employees' salaries to determine to whom they will give a pay increase (Ali & Ahmad, 2017). For this reason, taking the incentive to ask for a salary increase is a daunting task. It requires efficient preparation beforehand coupled with discretion. Dressing to look the part is vital in approaching the boss for a salary increase. It is advisable to ask for a raise after an accomplishment is made.

When we approach the boss to ask for an increase, it is wise to have read the firm's human resource management policies. An idea of our employer's current financial state is also a good idea. We might not be able to see their precise figures, but we will have an idea how busy they are.

Having a valid reason for needing a raise can also help us to achieve our goals. For example, we might have a new baby, or need to undertake some training (Lazear, 2018). Even if we do not achieve a monetary increase, we may be able find an alternative way to increase our actual monthly surplus. For example, we can ask to work from home, thus saving on commuting costs. The Covid 19 pandemic has led to this becoming a much more commonplace way of working. We can ask to attend a specific conference or get new computing devices to enhance productivity. These alternatives should help us to increase performance, and this can be especially helpful to individuals paid via commission.

ii. Promotion

Promotions offer a variety of platforms to increase income. Increasing education, skills, and competencies call for a promotion (Ali

& Ahmad, 2017). Different organizations have different methods of promoting their staff. For example, an appraisal approach determines the probability of an individual being promoted based on their performance. Or we can ask for a promotion if we feel qualified for a particular position, one that is more senior than our current role. When organizations change, positions are bound to come up, creating room for promotions (Ali & Ahmad, 2017). Promotions offer a chance to work in a higher position and handle more responsibilities. With these responsibilities come more power and authority and, thus, an increased salary, perks and benefits. These might include elements such as a sitting allowance, overtime, transport allowances, housing allowances, and medical insurance. In most cases, promotions are automatically accompanied by an increase in income, while the perks play an integral role in increasing disposable income (Ali & Ahmad, 2017). The perks help in reducing the expenses and hence increase our income indirectly.

Promotions also comes through searching for a different job in another company if there are no promotions available within our own organization.

Although, we must be aware of the 'grass is always greener' problem. Once a person feels qualified for a higher position in another firm, they can opt to apply for such a post to promote their career. In most cases, individuals change their working environment when they feel another firm offers better rewards than their current firm or has a better working environment. This is not always the case, i.e., the grass is not always greener. When we look to move firms, we should do some research into our potential new employer to make sure that we will fit well. This is especially true if we are moving for monetary reasons rather than because we are unhappy in our current role. For example, perhaps our current employer gives us a free rein to do our job. Our new manager may not, instead operate a close monitoring approach. Not everybody can thrive in that kind of environment,

However, job promotions are often an indication that a firm understands the employee's market value (Lazear, 2018). Finally, in some cases, promotions come without a pay rise, and therefore individuals must negotiate with their employers to increase their salaries. In such cases, a 10% to 20% salary increase is a reasonable request.

Promotions also play a central role in career advancement and personal development.

iii. Side Business

While employment is a reliable source of income, it is highly rigid and guarantees limited extra opportunity to multiply our income. We cannot ask for a pay rise every week!

However, having a side business can increase our income. It can help individuals optimize their time usage and resourcefulness, which is critical in adding to productivity (Cosenz & Noto, 2018). Some side businesses flourish and later become the primary source of income. The most common side businesses are those that stem from hobbies. People use their interest and expertise to earn a little extra money. Examples can include gardening, painting, playing musical instruments, flower design, cooking, and photography. In recent years Do It Yourself (DIY) crafts, gaming, blogging, and vlogging have emerged as worthwhile hobbies (Cosenz & Noto, 2018). Jewelry making, hiking, dancing, woodwork and even comedy also provide opportunities to increase income.

Apart from hobbies, we can setup side businesses with the aim of making some extra money. One of the most common side businesses is driving for rideshare companies since this job offers flexibility, and one can create time to pursue it. It also has few set up costs since the same car we've use for personal transport can be turned into a taxi to help them generate extra revenue. However, there is a warning here, which we should consider whenever we look to set up a side business, in any field. We cannot just decide to offer a taxi service. We need to consider matters such as insurance and local and even national legislation. For example, to use our car as a taxi will almost certainly require us to take out new insurance and register ourselves. The same is true for other side businesses. We have to calculate whether the costs of starting and running a small side business will outweigh any money we make from it.

Other side businesses have more requirements with those in charge having to employ others to take charge when they are not present. A person can set up a side business leaving a trusted person to run it on their behalf. For example, despite being employed, a person can start a café, fast food restaurant, or retail store to generate more income (Cosenz & Noto, 2018). In other cases, a car wash, saloon, barbershop, or massage parlor are efficient side businesses. Such ventures have the potential for growth provided the owner keeps constant control and employs a qualified and faithful workforce. The businesses generate extra income by adding more revenue on top of what they earn.

For those with tech-savvy skills, the internet offers a wide array of side businesses. In many cases, there is the element of freelancing that fits with our ability to work during free time. Online side businesses require less capital investment and hence are highly attractive to many individuals. They should not, though, impact on our ability to perform our main job.

Selling goods online is a viable side-business as well. Individuals have numerous sites to sell products online, with Amazon, Craigslist and eBay being the most prominent (Cosenz & Noto, 2018). Selling collectibles, old furniture, clothes, sneakers, or household appliances can make an extra buck. In most cases, people get these items for free, clean, and sell them, making supernormal profits. Recycling electronics, including computer parts, old phones, or electronic components, is also viable for those with the talent to do so. These items are quickly sold through websites like Gazelle (Cosenz & Noto, 2018). Even holding a garage sale is a side business – a small one, but it can still generate more revenue for us. What is considered to be of no value to one person may be of high value to others, and hence a garage sale is always an option to generate some money.

We could offer services and amenities online such as renting a house or part of the house through Airbnb. Another side business is providing online services such as tutoring via Skype, creating YouTube tutorials, or managing social media accounts for small businesses. One can also sell freelance services via Upwork and Fiverr (Cosenz & Noto, 2018). Creative individuals might create a side business of designing logos, advertisements, or websites. Becoming a personal shopper is also a practical opportunity, as is dog walking. There are surprisingly big markets here. Similarly, we might offer ourselves as baby-sitters. By starting with friends, neighbors, and family we can earn a good reputation which makes us more attractive to customers who do not know us personally. Everybody likes a recommendation if they are to trust a stranger with their child.

The feasibility of a side business lies in its ability to provide extra income without disrupting the day job. Babysitting is perfect in this sense. Similarly, a primary advantage with online side businesses is flexibility; they also offer a perfect opportunity to perfect skills while earning extra income.

iv. Strategies for Teens and High Schoolers

As we grow older, our expenses increase. Thus, our need for extra income. By developing a continuous learning mindset young people can increase their knowledge, skills, and competencies and augment career growth when they move into the job market. It is also necessary to work on our traits and attributes, with employee training programs and boot camps playing a central role in this. While teens and high schoolers might not be eligible for promotions at a young age, maintaining the right mindset will set them up well for later in life.

Young people looking to make extra income could consider venturing into business at an early age. Apart from developing the right mindset, required character traits, and enhancing their skills and abilities, getting into activities that generate income offers valuable experiences.

Although, any side business a young person creates should not interrupt their schoolwork or family life. A part-time job is a more common way of earning a little extra pocket money. After school hours or summer holidays offer a perfect time to explore new job opportunities, and teenagers can learn and gain significant experience through such programs. It also helps them make money and therefore improve their financial independence at an early age. For those looking to become self-employed, babysitting, as mentioned earlier, is a popular side business. Babysitting requires a lot of responsibility and demonstrating this at an early age can impress later employers when looking for their first full-time job. It also enables young individuals to generate income while balancing their school and social life. Pet grooming and dog walking are also feasible side businesses for teenagers; they enable them to make money during their free time. Additionally, these side businesses require minimal financial investments or skills. Teenagers and high schoolers can also tap into the digital space with social media platforms such as Instagram, Tiktok, Facebook, and YouTube to generate income. Selling on these platforms or becoming influencers can help young people make money during their free time.

Strategies to Reduce Debt Burden

Never spend your money before you have earned it.

- Thomas Jefferson

Student loan debt, home loans, credit card loans and personal loans are the drivers of the global economy. People either get into a lot of debt for the essentials; or to increase their standard of life. Some people make a lot of money off other people's debts. So, being able to navigate debt is essential to thriving in the modern economy.

The best solution, of course, is to never get into debt to achieve what you need to get done. I know several people who live their lives debt-free and still enjoy a high standard of living. However, what if you have already taken on a lot of debt? Sometimes, it's your fault. Sometimes, it's not. But we still need to act and fix it. This chapter is for those who are in debt and want to get their lives on track.

i. What is Debt and Why People Take on Debt? What to Avoid?

When people spend more than they earn, they get into a financial crisis and require extra income (Greene, Greene, & Greene, 2021). White this is true, sometimes debt is necessary to help us to realize our financial goals. In such instances, we borrow to deal with our immediate need, then repay later. Debts can be used to finance emergencies, unforeseen expenses, or capital investments requiring more finances than our income can provide. A typical example might be buying a car. We need the car for work, perhaps, and want one to enhance our quality of life. But we may not be able to afford to buy one from our savings. We therefore take on debt to purchase the car, gaining its benefits straight away, and pay off the debt gradually, usually through monthly payments.

Although we will have to pay back more than we have borrowed, remember this increase is offset to some extent by inflation. If we waited until we had saved enough money to buy the car outright, it would be more expensive to purchase. Plus, we would not have enjoyed the benefit of having it in the meantime.

When anyone borrows money, they make agreements on the repayment schedule, and in most cases, the debt incurs an interest. It is important that we keep up to date with payments. In a forfeit, i.e., a failure to repay the debt as agreed, individuals are liable for litigations and punishments such as fines and a damaged credit score.

Among the most common types of debts are mortgages and student loans. These may be good debts, implying that they helped individuals create wealth, increase income, improve the quality of life, or get out of a financial crisis. For example, student loans help individuals learn and increase their earning potential (Greene, Greene, & Greene, 2021). On the other hand, bad debts have no return on investments or benefits to the person's financial life (Greene, Greene, & Greene, 2021). Home loans help us to buy houses and therefore eliminate the need for renting. Auto loans are also good debts since they help individuals to make capital investments and augment their movement.

As mentioned earlier, bad debts have adverse implications on people's financial lives. They offer no benefit to our quality of life or financial health. People that get into and stay in bad debts often have poor spending habits. They live beyond their means. Avoiding destructive spending patterns is critical to mitigating debts. It is also advisable to avoid buying things one cannot afford, relying on credit cards, and focusing on wants instead of needs. Spending without a budget is also a recipe for disaster when it comes to borrowing money. Avoid impulse buying, interest-free financing (businesses are making their money by increasing the price of the goods we are buying) and buy now pay later arrangements. While getting into debt may sometimes be necessary for capital investments, sinking into bad borrowing and becoming dependent on loans is a dangerous habit. Debts drive people into bad credit scores; and lead to depression and mental health issues. Therefore, avoiding bad debts at all costs is highly advisable for individuals looking to increase their financial health (Greene, Greene, & Greene, 2021).

Of course, such conclusions are obvious. Nobody sets out to get into bad or unaffordable debt. But we are all different and some people find it extremely hard to avoid addictive behaviors.

While debts can help us create more wealth and improve our quality of life, they can also be a source of misery and financial strain. There is nothing wrong, and much that is right, with borrowing. But we must do it in a healthy and sustainable way.

ii. Strategy 1 - Debt Snowball Method

The process of debt repayment is often daunting due to the financial strain it places on the borrower. Let us be honest, our motivation and willingness to repay a loan are not usually strong, especially when the debt did not achieve its set objectives. How many times do we take out a loan to pay for something we thought we really wanted, but by the time we are halfway through paying it back, we want to update the item we have bought? However, debt repayment is obligated by law and failure to stick to an agreement has significant implications on the borrower's credit score. In cases where one has several debts, repaying them at once is a tall order.

The debt snowball method comes in handy in such instances, enabling the borrower to reduce their debt burden procedurally (Gathergood et al., 2019). This technique entails repaying debts starting from the smallest to the largest. It capitalizes on the momentum augmented by repaying the small debts to completion. The accomplishment associated with repaying these debts motivates the borrower to repay their larger debts. It capitalizes on the momentum gathered from eliminating the smaller debts. The debt snowball method helps the borrower stay motivated to the cause.

The technique replicates the movement of a snowball on the ground. It gathers speed as it moves along. Young adults looking to use the snowball method should list their debts from the smallest to the largest regardless of their interest rates. The next phase is making minimum payments on all loans. They should then pay the highest amount they can on the smallest loan (Gathergood et al., 2019). The snowball approach entails repeating these steps until all the debts are paid. The technique helps reduce the debt burden progressively while ensuring that the borrower repays their loans and interests to the fullest.

Once more, this is not a panacea. Repaying debt using the snowball method is financially painful and can have an adverse impact on our quality of life over the short term. Simply put, we will not have any spare money for a while, because any we have will be used to accelerate the payment of our debts.

However, by capitalizing on the achievements of completing the smaller loans, the borrower pays their obligations until they become debt-free. It is a good method if we have made a mistake and find ourselves with an uncomfortable amount of debt to service.

To understand this concept, let's use the example of an individual with several credit card loans. The primary goal of using the snowball technique is reducing the debt burden by capitalizing on progressive success (Ottaviani & Vandone, 2018). An individual has credit card loan balances of $4000, $2000, $1000, and $3000. Irrespective of the interest rates incurred by each loan, the debt with the lowest minimum payment should take priority. In this example, the minimum payment for the $1000 debt is $50, $2000 debt is $65, $3000 debt is $75, and $4000 debt is $100. If the person allocates $1000 towards debt repayment each month, they first need to clear the minimum balances for each debt. Therefore, during the first month, they pay the minimum amount for every debt, which amounts to $290.

The snowball method requires that the borrowers repay the smallest debt first, and therefore the remaining 710 dollars should go towards repaying the 1000-dollar loan. Having paid $760 in the first month, the second month will see the borrower clear the $1000 debt and remain with $520. This amount will go towards the $2000 loan and repay $650 within the first two months. Having cleared the $1000 debt and cleared 33% of the $2000 debt within two months, the borrower will drastically reduce their debt burden. In the third month, they should pay the minimum balances for all loans, and the remainder should go towards repaying the $2000 debt. They should repeat this process until all debts are repaid.

iii. Strategy 1 - Refinance at a lower interest rate.

Reducing our debt burden is a critical process in augmenting our financial health and freedom. As earlier indicated, debts can either assist in making life better or play a central role in making it miserable. Rather than living through life with negativity due to the burden of debts, developing strategies to repay them less painfully is important. Because repay them we must.

One of the most effective methods of repaying loans is debt refinancing. This helps reduce the debt burden by ensuring that the debtor has a more suitable loan repayment plan. Debt refinancing is used to change loan repayment terms, making it less strenuous for the debtor (Ottaviani & Vandone, 2018). A bad loan harms our budget. It limits our ability to meet expenses and achieve our financial goals. In some cases, the debts have implications for our quality of life. The obligation towards repayment takes up most of the income we would use for other necessities. Refinancing helps us pay up the loan with less strain. On the other hand, it assures the lender that the debtor will repay the loan without default. It, therefore, creates a win-win situation for both parties.

It is not a panacea, however. Although debt refinancing helps ease our day-to-day financial burden, it will cost us more in the long run. Better still to take out only sensible debt we can afford.

Debt refinancing involves taking up a new loan to repay existing debt. Therefore, the debtor is left paying a new loan under a different repayment schedule and new interest rates. Several factors influence the debt refinancing process (Spader, 2021). The terms and conditions are subject to the state or country debt policies or a nation's credit rating. The borrower's creditworthiness, banking regulations, and level of financial distress also affect the refinancing process. Economic factors such as political environments, currency stability, and the projected inherent risks can also influence the refinancing process significantly. These elements play a pivotal role in developing the debt refinancing plan and the consequent repayment options. While many providers offer refinancing options, providing us with more favorable terms also aligns with a lender's profit-generating abilities (Ottaviani & Vandone, 2018).

In other words, while we are smiling because our monthly outgoings on debt are reduced, so is the lender because they are making more money from the deal. Sadly, refinancing is not an escape plan, rather a way of prolonging the debt repayment processes to give the borrower more breathing room.

There are advantages associated with debt refinancing. One of the most significant benefits is debt repayment with a lower interest rate. For example, we may be able to shift a credit card balance onto a new, 0% or very low interest rate. However, reduction of the interest rates in most cases comes with an increase in the debt repayment period. The new debt helps clear the old loan, and the repayment period is prolonged to reduce the monthly installments and the interest rates (Spader, 2021). Therefore, the debtor ends up paying less for a more extended period and clearing their debt with time. The new arrangement is more favorable since it does not take up a large portion of our monthly net income. In other instances, refinancing enables the borrower to avoid the penalties associated with defaulted repayments. Refinancing is also used to consolidate numerous debts into one loan, enabling the borrower to develop a more workable repayment plan. It, hence, makes the debt more affordable and therefore reduces the immediate debt burden on the borrower. It develops a more convenient repayment structure (Spader, 2021). However, we should emphasize that it will cost us more in the long run. If we can, sticking to our initial arrangements will allow us to repay our debts faster. We can then avoid the overall extra costs of more extended repayments and accrued interests.

Young adults who are burdened with student loans should consider searching for a lower interest rate loan. This approach has more benefits than limitations. For example, they can use the technique to refinance their student loans by consolidating the debts into one package. Therefore, instead of repaying the different student loans with different interest rates, they pay a consolidated debt with one lower interest rate. The approach makes student loans less of a financial burden in the early years of their career life. Another application of this approach is repaying credit card loans. It is important to point out that credit card loans accrue monthly interests, which are expensive in the long run (Ottaviani & Vandone, 2018). Many credit card users take up personal loans to pay up the credit card loans, reducing the costs associated with monthly interests. This type of refinancing can reduce loan costs. A credit card is a handy tool when we need to buy something quickly, but it is easy to lose track of how much we are spending on them.

Mortgages, auto, and business loans might also require refinancing to enable the borrower to pay the debt in more favorable terms. Understanding these aspects is crucial in enabling young adults to get out of debt and ensure that loan repayment has minimal implications on their future financial health. We say again, though, because it is important to stress the point. Refinancing is, in most cases, a viable resort, but the best option **is not getting into the debt problem in the first place**.

iv. Strategy 3 – Cut credit cards for those who have bad habits

Credit card expenditure can sink individuals into debt. Teenagers and young adults should avoid impulse buying using credit cards or buying stuff for personal gratification. Additionally, depending on credit cards to maintain a lifestyle will sink anyone into a financial crisis. If we find it hard to use our credit cards minimally, we should adopt a cash-only, or debit card approach to spending. We should also consider having one or two credit cards only.

In fact, having a credit card improves our credit rating, so it can be wise to have one. Just, keep our credit limit low to avoid over-spending. We should also pay more than the minimum amount on credit cards since that leads to the accumulation of debts (Murugiah & Mohd Rashid, 2017). Shopping as per our budget is wise as it helps in reducing the probability of using credit cards and getting into debt. It ensures that we only buy what we need, or can afford as a want, thus helping us develop good spending habits. Rather than using credit cards, it is better to use debit cards since they do not incur debts. For those of us without financial discipline, steering clear of credit cards will go a long way in reducing their debt burden.

How Much Cash Should We Have In our Portfolio?

If cash comes with fame, come fame; if cash comes without fame, come cash.

- Jack London

i. **Depends on how stable the economy is/ risk of inflation**

A good knowledge of how the economy works and market forces influence our assets is a good initial step towards safeguarding our financial status. Following financial news through the various media sources is a good way of achieving this.,

One of the most negative influences on our money is inflation. Following the financial news will help us learn more about this. Inflation affects investments as well as the value of cash. For investments with annual returns, such as ordinary bonds, inflation harms our earnings. On the other hand, inflation affects stocks differently. When the economy is stable firms do more trade, raising their share price. However, firms must pay more for their own resources and to pay their workers, which reduces their returns. The impact of inflation on a stock relies on the performance of the organization. On the other hand, precious metals such as gold perform relatively well during high inflation. When the value of the dollar declines, it costs more to purchase the same amount of gold.

How can we plan for inflation? Inflation is one of the primary reasons most individuals do not store money in banks due to reduction in value of their savings. As a result, some people favor putting their cash in higher-growth investments, such as stocks since they are less affected by inflation. Here, an individual must consider having a portfolio that reduces the impact of inflation, such as with fixed investments. Although inflation is impossible to avoid, planning for it and enacting a strong investment approach can help reduce the effect on our financial plans. Another strategy is to rethink our emergency fund. It is difficult to keep a lot of money in a savings account when its value may decline quickly. Consequently, many financial experts recommend moving our money when inflation is increasing. In addition, one can choose to review debt balances. One can repay their debt with cash that is worth less than the amount they borrowed. Put simply, if the value of the interest we are earning on savings is less than the interest we are paying on a debt, it makes financial sense to use the money to pay off the debt.

However, we need to check that we will not incur penalties for taking our money out of a savings plan. If we do, again we simply calculate the cost of this against the benefit of paying off the debt. It is not quite the same if we have invested in stocks and shares. Here, the value we gain fluctuates, and we would need to consider whether the short-term gain of taking out the money from our portfolio is worthwhile if it prevents us from getting future benefits when the markets pick up.

We can also get ready for inflation by de-risking our portfolio while continuing to invest, adjusting our emergency fund approach as required, and moving away from variable-rate debt.

ii. Depends on our personal situation

Everyone must have a safety net to fall back when the unanticipated occurs. However, we are all different. This means that the amount of money one should keep depends on their personal circumstances and lifestyle. Financial advice is not a one-size-fits-all, and any individual who offers us a standard plan of how much we should have is selling us short. Hence, when individuals ask how much money one should hold, it should not surprise us that there is no single answer. However, we need to keep cash to cater for regular bills, discretionary spending, and an emergency fund. Half of the world's population utilizes only cash. Cash is predictable, reliable… and boring. Nevertheless, it should be readily accessed when one needs it.

Even though we are all different, many of us still seek a rough guide to how much cash we should keep available. A cash reserve of around $2-3000 (in the United States) will help us cater for unexpected expenses and prevent us from being caught off guard (Long, 2016). Extra cash beyond this should be allocated to short and long-term goals.

Another way to look at this is more focused to the individual. Some say between six and twelve months of essential expenditure, while others recommend three months of fixed expenses. Financial experts recommend keeping the emergency fund in the bank to gather interests and other benefits, especially high-yield savings. We should be aware, though, that to get the best interest rates sometimes means tying up our funds. Since they are there for emergencies, we do need to ensure we have ready and rapid access to them. While such a fund will be affected by inflation in the long run, it is not something that requires us to keep adding unless our fixed expenses change. The goal is to survive tough times and gather money for savings and investments.

As a useful rule of thumb, money set aside for our short-term goals needs to be readily accessible, while that for the longer term is best invested in something offering the promise of good returns, such a mixed stocks and shares portfolio with mixed risk, but one that might suffer short term fluctuation. Therefore, if our goals go beyond five years, the money should be invested in the stock market, such as stocks, bonds, or mutual funds. The aim is to ensure that we can sell without consequence when it is time to fund our goal.

iii. General Recommendation is 6 Months of Living Expenses

The first step is to formulate our expenses. We need to check our actual spending and what we are spending on. Once we identify this, we decide which expenses should be catered for in case of a crisis, such as a job loss. Let's divide the spending into three sections as shown below in Figure 2.

Figure 2: *Break down of spending in sections*

Essential	Comfortable	Non-essential
Rent/mortgage	Internet	Eating out/takeaway
Food	Education costs	Gym membership
Utility bills & council tax	Clothing	General shopping
Medicines/healthcare	Transport costs	Holidays
Insurance	Mobile phone	Pension/savings
		Alcohol
		Entertainment

Source: (Long, 2016)

We are all different. The decision over which bills to cater for will rely on the compromises we are willing to endure during tough times. It depends on the savings goal we are seeking to realize. Most of the us will aim for a minimum of three to six months' worth of expenses when working (although this increases substantially when we reach retirement and have less opportunity to boost our income.)

Budgeting is a great way to determine how much cash we need. There are several ways to plan for a budget; and we looked at the

50/30/20 rule plan earlier. Another budget formulation strategy is Dave Ramsey`s Method.

According to Ramsey, 10% of our income should be for savings. From the above strategy, the cash for the fund should come from the part of the budget dedicated to savings: around 20% from the "50/30/20" Rule or Ramsey`s 10%. However, everyone has a different opinion for the amount of money one should keep in this fund. According to Nofsinger (2017), one should keep eight-month emergency funds since it takes a lengthy period for an ordinary person to get work if they lose their job.

The primary concern when dealing with the emergency fund is whether the fund should be kept in the bank. Some professionals suggest keeping huge emergency funds in an investment account with fairly safe shares. This would earn more interest than one would get in a savings account. On the other hand, some are concerned with the safety of the fund. The primary issue is that the money should be immediately accessible when one requires it.

Hence, one should create an emergency fund before committing their savings towards retirement and other financial goals. Once our fund is established, further savings should go towards retirement and other investments to deliver our financial goals. If we use our emergency fund, we switch priorities to rebuilding it until it is, once more, complete.

How Much Risk Should We Take?

Take calculated risks. That is quite different from being rash.

- George S. Patton

Risk tolerance is the degree of unpredictability in investment returns that an investor is ready to take to achieve their financial goals. Risk tolerance is a fundamental aspect of investing. Individuals should have a practical comprehension of their capacity and readiness to endure huge swings in the value of their investments. If one undertakes a lot of risks, one might panic and dispose of them at the wrong time. Risk tolerance is frequently linked to age. Young individuals have a lengthier time horizon and are frequently asked to undertake larger risks than older people. However, this is not the only determining force. In addition, greater risk tolerance is frequently equated to equities and equity funds and ETFs, while our preparedness to take lower risk is linked to bonds and bond funds. Age, life goals and financial goals influence the amount of risk an individual can tolerate. Other factors include the time horizon one has in which to invest, future earning ability and the presence of other assets like a pension or inheritance. So, there are several factors to consider when we decide on where to invest our spare income.

There are three types of investors when it comes to risk tolerance: aggressive, moderate, and conservative. Effective aggressive investors are market-savvy individuals with an extended comprehension of securities and their value. As such, this enables these people and institutions to buy highly volatile assets, like small-firm stocks that can crash to zero or options contracts that can terminate worthless. While keeping a foundation of riskless securities, aggressive investors attain maximum returns with maximum risk.

But we do need to be aware of our own limitations. As amateurs, we may feel we understand the markets and are prepared to take a high risk. Probably, our knowledge is less than we think. If we do take a high-risk strategy, it is wise to keep a backup of lower risk investments in case anything goes wrong.

On the other hand, moderate investors tolerate some risk to their principal investments but implement a balanced strategy with intermediate-risk time horizons of between five to ten years. Moderate investors frequently utilize the 50/50 arrangement which entails combining large-firm mutual funds with less unstable bonds and riskless securities. A common approach entails investing 50% of the portfolio in a dividend-paying, growth fund. Additionally, conservative investors are ready to tolerate little or no instability in their investments.

For examples, those seeking to build a pension fund spend a lot of time establishing a portfolio that is not ready to facilitate any kind of risk to their pot. These individuals target instruments that are guaranteed and highly liquid.

i. Depends On Age and Life Goals

Our relationship with money starts at an early age when we see close ones exchanging cash for products and services we like. The power of money grows when we receive our first allowance or paid tasks. These childhood and adolescence activities foster our habits and beliefs that can last throughout our entire lives. The challenges increase as we head to adulthood and we are encouraged to take loans to purchase things, such as cars. Our parents and guardians set the pace for investment objectives early in our lives, teaching us to postpone satisfaction until we can fill the piggy bank, enabling the money to be used to purchase clothes and electronic gadgets. This close relationship between investment and lifestyle becomes more complex with age.

Investment goals can be seen as spread into three divisions: age, income, and perspective. Age can further be split into three parts:

young, middle-aged, and old. However, these categorizations are extremely broad and generalized.

Income is the starting point for any investment strategy. We cannot invest what we do not have. Investment starts young. Saving for a new piece of music or item of fashion, for example. It is normal to experience challenges during these earliest times. Many of us get stuck in a costly rental or a car loan that is larger than we can afford to pay. We can recover if we are willing to learn from bad experiences.

Perspective refers to the playing field in which we live our lives. For many young couples, family planning is their topmost priority. It is normal to focus on the number of children they want, their neighborhood preference, and the income required to realize those goals. Career expectations also play a vital role in these calculations, with highly educated individuals embracing increased earning power while others are trapped in jobs where they cannot advance, mandating them to cut back to meet their living expenses.

Investment goals are moving targets for most people, with carefully formulated plans encountering challenges of layoffs, unanticipated pregnancies, and health problems as well as benefitting from unexpected upturns in our lives. A windfall or a job promotion.

Fortunately, it is never too late to become an investor. Although fear can influence us when we are older, we can still add a sense of urgency to wealth management. All investments begin with a little cash set aside regardless of our age, income, or perspective. However, investing for the long term allows us to enjoy the fruits of decades of good behaviors.

At the start of one's professional journey, we should create a budget and adhere to it. At this stage, our investment appetite can be low since young people are filled with the eagerness to enjoy their newly found income. Some of the needs we have then might include higher education and renting a home. Most prefer credit solutions to create assets over time. At the same time, we should also seek wealth protection and insurance schemes.

The conventional wisdom holds that individuals in their 20s and 30s can embark on risk since they have a lot of time to handle and address the inevitable rough patches. Many financial experts suggest all-stock portfolios for these individuals. However, not every young investor can handle the markets. For instance, many millennials are particularly wary of stocks. Hence, young investors should get into stocks and take early risks to overcome this irrational fear. Some nervous investors in this demographic could embark on an 50% stock allocation with the remainder in bonds and maintain this combination throughout the market cycle. Young investors can then experience the euphoria of bull markets and the desolation of bear markets.

As we enter lower middle age, we may find our priorities shift towards preparing for retirement and managing our families.

Individuals in their 40s and 50s are probably hitting their peak earning years. Similarly, their financial expenses are also at peak, such as college tuition for their kids. Some investors are comfortable with more equities, but others prefer the extra stability offered by bonds. For those who have excellent saving habits, investing in low-risk ventures is the best approach. Nonetheless, individuals who wait until they reach their 40s must increase their risk levels. Financial experts recommend a portfolio of 60% in stocks and 40% in bonds. However, given the current near record-low interest rates, an investor should embark on shorter maturities for bonds and invest in high-yield bonds since they are less sensitive to rate hikes. Furthermore, asset allocation changes over time, hence, we should look for areas that are undervalued and allocate more of our funds there.

As we become older, and wiser, and approach retirement we still like to invest, but rely much less on credit. A comprehensive investment plan will allow older people to reinvest in investment returns to increase their retirement funds. Here, financial experts recommend a 50/50 portfolio of stocks and bonds. However, individuals playing catch-up should lean more on stocks to power their savings. At the same time, individuals need to balance their need for growth and stability.

In our 70s, we hopefully may be retired and adjusting to a new normal with a hobby or spending time with grandchildren. Some people find it difficult to change from an "accumulating assets" mindset to spending their retirement funds. On the other hand, it is tempting to think that our asset-allocations decisions are done now that we have retired. However, the need for growth is important even in retirement. Our portfolio must last until we are dead. Hence, one requires stability. In addition, financial gurus suggest a bucker approach. Here, we set aside a few years of required income in temporary bonds to cover our expenses.

The rest can be invested for growth, and we can replenish the expenses bucket when the markets are performing well. When the markers are down, we have enough money to weather the storm.

ii. What's Your Personal Outlook for Next 5/10 Years?

It is conventional wisdom that younger individuals have a long-term time horizon when planning on investment and taking more risks. When it comes to how much risks one should take, one must consider the investment. When will the funds be required? If the time horizon is fairly short, risk-taking should reduce. On the other hand, for long-term investments, there is adequate space for aggressive investing. However, with life expectancies increasing and advancing medical science, a 60-year-old individual may still have a 30-year-old time horizon to enjoy during their retirement. That enjoyment is enhanced if we have enough money to live comfortably.

Moreover, net worth and available capital must be taken into consideration when determining the amount of risk to take. Our net worth is assets minus liabilities. Risk capital is the funds available for investment or trade that will not impact our lifestyle if lost. Individuals with high net worth have a higher risk capital. Unfortunately, investors with little or no net worth and restricted risk capital are frequently drawn to riskier investments, such as options, because of the appeal of quick, easy, and huge returns.

Another thing to consider is the risk is calculating how much uncertainty can be tolerated. Here, just because an individual can embark on riskier investments does not mean that they should. For instance, if capital preservation is the aim and we are a new investor, we should be cautious of undertaking too much risk. Our level of investment experience plays a major role in our investment endeavors. Start with caution and gather experience before committing too much money. Remember, spreading our risk reduces our overall exposure to reliance on any single investment. With correct diversification, the likelihood of total loss is significantly minimized. However, understanding one's risk tolerance is a sophisticated process that involves striking a balance between our real-life financial situation and our financial goals.

The Importance of Portfolio Construction

The difference between success and failure is not which stock you buy or which piece of real estate you buy, it's asset allocation.

- Tony Robbins

Portfolio construction is all about finding the perfect combination of assets that serve as an investment solution for us as investors. Creating a portfolio encompasses comprehending various kinds of investments and combining them to fulfil set investment goals and objectives.

There are four primary aims of portfolio construction which include: controlling risk, matching an investment approach with needs and objectives, creating a level of expectation for portfolio performance from the selected investment strategy, and guiding the expected volatility linked with the investment approach.

A good portfolio should contain multiple objectives and realize a sound balance among them. Firstly, once investment security is assured, the portfolio should generate a stable current income. The current yields should at least equal the opportunity cost of the funds invested. In other words, our investment should not see a reduction in purchasing power. Secondly, we have marketability. An excellent portfolio encompasses investments that can easily be marketed. When there are numerous inactive shares in the portfolio, one may encounter hurdles in disposing of them or moving from one investment to another. It is advisable to invest in firms whose shares are actively traded. Thirdly, since tax regulation is a fundamental element in planning, an effective portfolio must consider income tax, capital gains, tax, and gift tax during its construction. As a result, it will help us in tax planning. Four, a good portfolio should appreciate in the long term, safeguarding the investor from losing their buying power because of inflation. Here, a balanced portfolio should have specific investments that have a strong real rate of return. In addition, a portfolio guarantees that there is adequate money on short notice for the investor to cater to liquidity needs. Hence, it is advisable to have a line of credit from the bank for use in case of an emergency. Finally, a portfolio guarantees that our investment is secure (*Invest blue*).

i. Diversification and Stability

Diversification increases our chance of securing a winning return. Therefore, portfolio diversification is the act of investing funds in varying assets and securities to reduce the overall risk. Imagine what would happen if we put all our funds in a single asset. It would be like gambling our house on the winner of a horse race – great returns if our bet comes up, but disaster is far more likely given the chances of the horse losing are greater than it winning. In other words, things would be good as long as the asset performed well. However, in case of a sudden crash, we would lose our entire savings in a single moment.

A diversified approach is intended to help minimize the volatility of the portfolio with time and to maximize returns by investing in varying areas that react differently. The key to successful investing is learning how to balance our investment against our time horizon. Invest in our retirement conservatively at a young age, and we will run the danger of having an investment growth rate that cannot keep pace with inflation (Fabozzi & Markowitz, 2011). On the other hand, if we invest aggressively in the later stages of our life, we can leave our savings unprotected from market unpredictability, which can reduce the value of our investments at a time when we have fewer chances to recover our losses.

One of the primary ways to balance risk and rewards in our portfolio is through diversification. It can help lessen the risk and volatility in our portfolio, possibly minimizing the effects of unpredictability. Most financial experts agree that, although diversification does not protect absolutely from loss, it is the most essential aspect of realizing long-term financial goals while minimizing risks. How does diversification work? Imagine our portfolio comprises airline stocks. Here, share prices may decline after a bad incident, such as an unspecified pilot strike that might lead to the cancelation of flights. As a result, our portfolio will undergo a significant drop in value. However, because we have diversified, we can counterbalance the airline stocks with some railway stocks, meaning that only a section of our portfolio will be impacted. There is also a high chance that the railway stocks will increase in value since more passengers will be seeking substitute means of transportation. In addition, we should diversify our portfolio across varying industries and organizations. The more uncorrelated investments we have, the better.

Diversification helps reduced exposure to risk, which improves the stability and potential yields of an investment portfolio. It helps investors to create a strong portfolio. Although some may prefer higher risk for greater returns, most investors want a stable and reliable way to secure their financial goals. It is essential to have clear investment goals since an individual who is saving for retirement may have a completely different risk tolerance and time horizon than an individual investing for short-term goals.

Since risk mitigation is a primary principle in portfolio diversification, we need to know which types of risk diversification can minimize, and how a decline in those risks can affect a portfolio`s efficiency. Unsystematic risk, also called diversifiable risk, is a portfolio risk that applies to a particular asset class (*Invest blue*). It comprises dangers that are distinct to a firm, industry, market or other segments within the financial system (Fabozzi & Markowitz, 2011). The vulnerability emanating from unsystematic risk can be reduced via a portfolio management approach that diversifies investments across different industries that do not share the same unsystematic risk. Consequently, **creating a diversified investment portfolio with little or no correlation** can mitigate the effect of any losses from a specific firm, asset class, sector, or region.

Systematic risk is the risk intrinsic to the financial structure as a whole. It includes trends that affect the entire global financial system, like rising inflation and interest rates. Although it is impossible to eradicate exposure to the danger of an economic downturn, it is possible to diversify into ventures that minimize the loss in case of such events, particularly in the long run. For instance, when interest rates rise, purchasing fixed-income assets with the capacity of realizing high returns, like bonds, could offset losses. Furthermore, putting our money into hard assets, like commercial real estate, can help protect against inflation increases and lead to better long-term yields.

Diversification leads to lower risk and higher portfolio return potential. When the risk is correctly lessened via diversification, it is less susceptible to volatility. The portfolio is more stable, and its yield potential is more anticipated. Although diversification cannot do away with risk, a well-structured diversified portfolio can lead to improved risk-adjusted earnings. Financial experts use mean-variance analysis to calculate a portfolio`s risk. In addition, the effect of diversification is visible in the long-term time horizon and monetary objectives. For instance, if we are saving for retirement, an efficient diversified approach should enhance its value over the years.

How do we diversify our portfolio?

We can explore other investment avenues for our portfolio. Here, we can consider bonds, real estate, mutual funds, and pension initiatives. Generally, bonds and equity markets have opposing movements. Hence, by venturing into both markets, we can counterbalance any harmful results in one of those markets. In addition, adding bond funds to the portfolio can provide much-required stability. At the same time, investing in index funds is a highly cost-effective strategy since its charge are relatively low compared to actively managed funds (Guerard Jr, 2009). Similarly, putting money in bond funds safeguards the portfolio from markets unpredictability and prevents gains from being reduced to zero during markets volatility.

Another portfolio diversification approach is to keep building it. Implementing this strategy can allow us to better mitigate volatility and remain invested across market cycles (Guerard Jr, 2009). In addition, portfolio diversification involves knowing when to exit our investments. If the asset category we have been investing in has not performed as expected for a long time, we should consider an exit. This is the same for any fundamental changes to the portfolio that do not align with our goals and risk appetite. However, we should not exit after short-term unpredictability. Another factor to consider is commission. For those using the investment services of a professional, they must check out the fees they are incurring. This helps to prevent commissions from taking too great a toll on our end yields.

Let us consider the four main components of a diversified portfolio: domestic stocks, bonds, short-term investments, and international stocks. Stocks are the most aggressive part of the portfolio and offer the chance for greater growth. Nonetheless, their higher probability for growth carries a greater risk, especially in the short term. This is because stocks are typically more volatile than other kinds of assets. International stocks are issued by international companies and often perform differently than domestic firms, offering exposure to opportunities not provided by US securities. Those of us looking for investments with asymmetric yields and higher risks should add foreign stocks to our portfolios.

Most bonds offer consistent interest income and are typically regarded as less unpredictable than stocks. Bonds can also serve as cushions against volatility since they behave differently from stocks. Investors who prefer safety to growth favor bonds, while minimizing their exposure to stocks. These individuals understand that bonds offer lower returns than stocks in the long term. Nonetheless, some fixed-income investments, such as high-yield bonds and specific global bonds, can provide greater returns, albeit accompanied by more risk. On the other hand, short-term investments include money funds and short-term CDs (certificates of deposit) (Guerard Jr, 2009). Money market funds are perfect for those seeking to preserve our principal investment since they are conservative ventures that provide stability and easy access to funds. In return for safety, money markets typically offer lower yields than bonds. Although money markets are seen as secure, they are not insured by the FDIC like CD's are.

Sector stocks concentrate on a specific section of the economy. They can be vital instruments for investors looking for opportunities in varying stages of the economic cycle. Although only the most knowledgeable investors should invest in commodities, adding equity funds that concentrate on commodity-intensive sectors to our portfolio, like mining and gas, can offer a hedge against inflation. In addition, real estate funds can play a part in portfolio diversification and offer some safeguards against inflation. For individuals who lack the time or knowledge to create a diversified portfolio, asset allocation funds can act as an effective single-fund approach.

How does diversification help minimize the impact of market volatility? If there was a period that illustrates the effectiveness of creating a diversified portfolio, it would be now.

Since the start of the Covid-19 pandemic, stock prices have been all over the place, as investors unsuccessfully react to the effect of the global health pandemic on the global economy and the stock markets. It is unsuccessful since it is an evolving scenario and the extent of its effect on stability is still uncertain. Although the effect is not easily measurable, the economy is facing a recession. To support businesses during these uncertain times, various Central Banks around the planet have reduced interest rates. As a result, bond prices have increased. Currently, although equity prices have been volatile, bond prices keep on going up. Today, investors with well-diversified portfolios that are spread across equity and fixed income tools are likely to come out fairly unscratched from the existing turmoil. This illustrates the significance of portfolio diversification.

ii. Emotions in Investing

It is a sad fact, but close to 40% of individuals that win the lottery go into bankruptcy within five years. Lottery winners on average lack the adequate emotional intelligence to sensibly manage their money (Gutkevych & Vikhliaiev, 2021). Emotions play a dangerous role in investing. Awareness of our emotional triggers can prevent us from taking unnecessary risks on a 'hunch' or gamble.

Emotional Intelligence (EQ) is a broad field. One aspect of emotional intelligence entails comprehending your capacity to discriminate between emotions and rational decision-making. It is about understanding your inner belief system and creating a successful relationship between you and your money. Reflect on your character and its impact on your relationship with cash. Are you a conservative individual who misses put on higher yields because of adversity to risk? No matter who you are, your personality has a profound impact on how you approach money, investments, and your portfolio. Based on your personality, your relationship will vary dramatically.

Based on your emotional personality, you will approach investing differently from an individual with a different character. Your emotional personality plays a vital role when it comes to dealing with externalities. No portfolio is immune to unanticipated externalities, such as recessions, stock crashes, or unexpected health expenses. Wealth accumulation is typically a boring process that emanates from deliberate steps. Only a handful of individuals become rich from hair-triggered, emotional decisions. Therefore, comprehending your personality is essential to correctly manage external situations. The other option is to fall victim to hot-headed emotions, which generally leads to disposing of or purchasing at a bad time.

The two most prevalent strategies to investing are dollar-cost averaging and diversification. These strategies allow investors to eliminate the guesswork in investment decisions and minimize the danger of poor timing due to emotional investing. The most effective approach of the two is the dollar-cost averaging. This is an approach where an equal amount of dollars is invested at an ordered, predetermined interval. It can be used in any market situation. In a downward trending market, investors buy shares at reduced prices. On the other hand, during an upward trend, the shares held in the portfolio are generating capital gains. Similarly, since the dollar investment is a static amount, fewer shares are bought when the share price is higher.

The most essential aspect of the dollar-cost averaging approach is to stay on course. Here, you should formulate a strategy and do not interfere with it unless a major alteration mandates re-examination and reorganization of the original course. This approach is more effective in plans with matching benefits since a static dollar amount is deducted from the salary and the employer offers extra contributions.

How to Construct a Portfolio

The difference between success and failure is not which stock you buy or which piece of real estate you buy, it's asset allocation.

- Tony Robbins

A lot of modern investment advice focuses on generating as much yield as possible in the least amount of time. What about accepting the probability of risk and actively looking to establish a high-risk investment portfolio? Such a portfolio may contain significant prospects for higher returns, but investors must have proper knowledge when approaching this type of investment.

i. High Risk Portfolio

The best way to think about risk is in terms of the probability of an investment underperforming or even resulting in a considerable loss of capital. A high-risk investment is where the chances of underperformance, or losing all the investment, are greater than average (Hunjra, 2020). These investment ventures provide investors the prospect for bigger yield for accepting the associated degree of risk. Many high-risk ventures are categorized as alternative investments and are utilized to balance a portfolio and introduce investment opportunities that have little or no market correlation.

There is a definite relationship between risk and potential reward. Hence, investors after huge returns in relatively short time must accept a disproportional higher degree of risk than those seeking steadier returns. In addition, the connection between risk and reward is not always predictable, but there is a time-tested correlation between the two. If investors wish for greater returns, they must accept to undertake more risk (Russo, 2013). However, this kind of investor can fall victim to a dangerous pair of conditions. These are false superiority and optimism bias. In other words, a sense that we understand the markets better than we do, and the unjustified feeling that we are bound to win out. These two cognitive preconceptions combine to make us believe that we will thrive where others have failed.

Another primary element of high-risk portfolios is volatility (Royal, 2021). Some financial experts and market participants do not consider volatility as a substitution for risk. Some stocks can experience considerable swings but also generate significant returns for investors. Especially over the longer term.

A fundamental aspect to note when creating a high-risk portfolio is that not all risk is the same. This means that investors should only pursue smart risks, which they get rewarded for taking. For example, investing in the shares of bankrupt businesses is always a bad option. Even if the business survives, the bankruptcy process almost wipes out equity for investors and there is no sufficient room left to validate their risk. In addition, investor must guard against idleness and complacency. High-risk investing requires awareness and attention to detail. Hence, creating a portfolio without thorough due diligence and taking one's eye off it, it is high-risk investing that is unlikely to deliver rewards.

There are various types of high-risk portfolios. We can build one without altering investment strategies. Investing heavily in a single industry can definitely increase risk along with potential yield. For example, investors who invested significantly in technology stocks in the later 1990s received handsome returns, right up until the dot.com bubble burst. Similarly, those who effectively participate in cyclical commodity runs can do very well. Concentrating on a single sector is an approach that is grounded on a good understanding of the industry, however. Similarly, it is vital to comprehend market psychology and mood. Concentrating on an unpopular industry is likely not to ramp up yields. Unless, of course, one gets in just as the industry is about to grow.

Another high-risk investing strategy for our portfolio is momentum investing. The concept behind this is to put our money in stocks that are displaying strong price action. The risk associated with this strategy is linked to the above-average valuations that these stocks carry, but costly stocks can frequently trade up before fading fast. So, the risk is that we will get our timing wrong, invest at the top of the market and then see our investment fall in value. Momentum investing requires selling self-restraint. Here, investors can seek a diversified portfolio to reduce their risk, but a comprehensive market decline will hit the growth of their portfolio hard. A willingness to go short can help offset any losses, but that is a tricky business. Here, we sell our stocks and shares early with the intention of buying them back when their price falls. We are then gambling on these values rising in the future, thereby increasing our returns.

Another approach we could adopt if we are to become a high-risk investor is to put our money emerging technology companies. Such ventures provide investors with opportunities in new technologies and commodities (Russo, 2013). With this strategy, diversification is vital. We need to be patient and ready to endure returns since most emerging technology companies fail. Therefore, investors should seek out firms that have access to capital.

Futures and options often require leverage allowing a handful of capital to have influence over a larger amount of capital. Along with currency these require a combination of patience, confidence, and agility in the investor. Futures are different from stocks because an investor has to make the right decision, but the expected move has to occur before the contract expires. On the other hand, options and option approaches can be used to achieve higher yields while protecting against downside. Both options and futures are complex topics that requires a lot of study and testing before one emerges on them. The various complexities are beyond the scope of this book.

Another high-risk investment area lies with cryptocurrencies. These are digital currencies that operate independently from central banks. Although there are investors who have made huge returns from their markets, they are extremely volatile, and many have lost considerable funds.

Another possibility for the high risk investors is to seek angel investing. Here, we invest like the rich people on The Shark Tank or Dragons' Den. We put our money into innovative start-ups in return for a share of the company. Most start-ups fail, but some make it big and will therefore offer a good return on our investment. Again, due diligence can mitigate our risk.

An ideal high-risk portfolio should comprise of 50% Speculative, 10% Cash, 30% Income (Dividend Stocks/Real Estate), and 10% Gold/Bonds as shown in figure 5. All the above-mentioned investments should be in the **Speculative** portion of the portfolio; while the rest of the portfolio is in more stable assets.

Figure 5: *Example of a High-risk Portfolio*

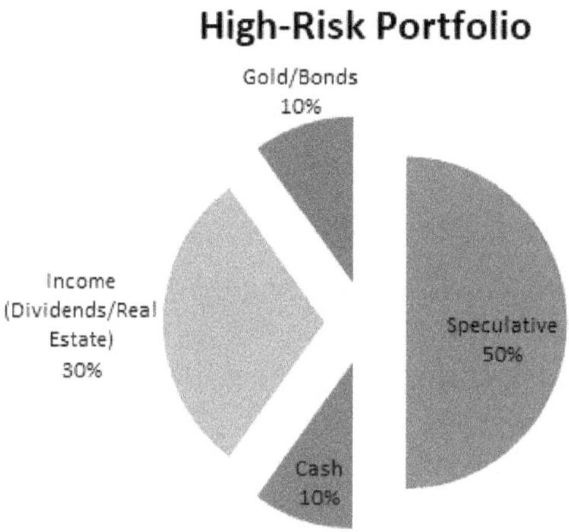

For investors with enough money and a long enough time horizon, an aggressive / high-risk portfolio is something to explore. With time, intelligence and discipline the investor can generate considerable and above-average yields.

Mid Risk / Moderate Portfolio

A mid risk portfolio is also known as a moderate portfolio where the investor wants to protect most of the portfolio`s value but is ready to tolerate some risk to counter inflation. It is a portfolio where an investor has a time limit longer than five years. Investors are ready to endure some market volatility in exchange for yields that surpass inflation. A standard mid-risk portfolio includes something like 20% speculative assets, 20% cash, 50% income, and 10% gold or bonds as depicted in Figure 6.

A common approach when choosing this portfolio structure involves current income. Here, we select securities that pay a higher degree of dividends. For example, one can choose to invest 40% in large-cap stocks, 10% in small-cap stock, 15% in foreign stock fund, 30% in intermediate-term bonds, and 5% in money market fund. From this portfolio, an investor can get an average yearly return of 7-8%, with its best annual yield being around 20-30%, and its largest annual decline ranging from 20-25%. The majority of investors fall into the low-risk investment category.

Figure 6: *Example of a Mid-risk Portfolio*

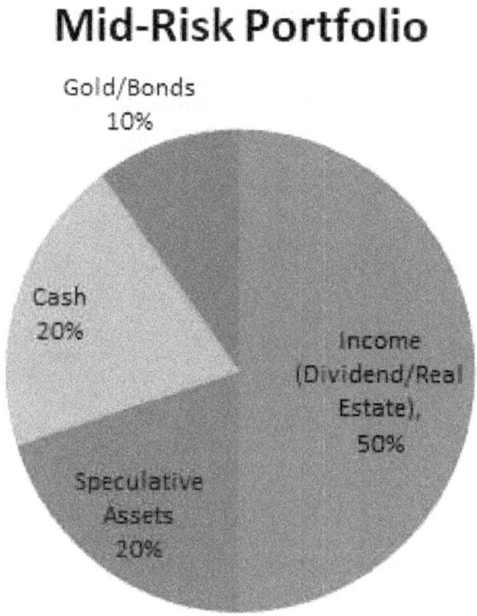

Low Risk Portfolio

A low-risk or conservative portfolio has a primary aim to protect its principal investment. A low-risk strategy typically allocates a huge portion of the funds to lower-risk securities, like money markets and fixed income securities. Even if we are extremely conservative and seek to avoid the stock market completely, some exposure to stocks can help counterbalance inflation.

For low-risk portfolio investors, an extended time horizon is important. This is because conservative investors are not ready to tolerate periods of extreme market volatility and look for returns that match or surpass inflation (Royal, 2021). An ideal low risk portfolio should comprise of 5% speculative assets, 30% cash, 50% income, and 15% gold or bonds as illustrated in figure 7.

Figure 7: *Example of a Low-risk Portfolio*

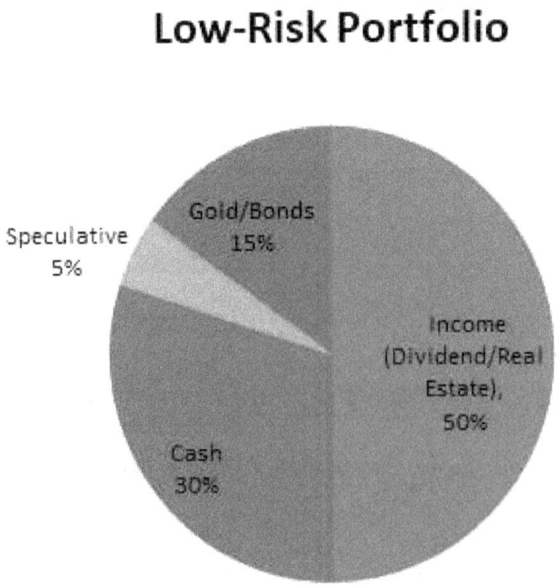

Although not technically an investment, savings accounts provide modest return on our money. A savings account is entirely safe, and most accounts are government-insured, meaning one will be compensated if the financial institution fails. The only drawback of a saving account is that inflation can erode the purchasing power of money. Certificates of deposit (CDs) offer low-risk investment since they are loss-proof in a government-backed account. Certificates of deposits are ideal for conservative investors because when they leave them untouched until they expire, the bank pledges to pay a set rate of interest over the specified term. However, if money is removed from CDs early, then some of the interested earned is lost. Similarly, some banks will also hit the investor with a loss of a portion of their principal as well. Furthermore, money market funds offer liquidity and are relatively safe. Investors could also invest in corporate bonds, such as high-yield bonds.

Below is a comparison of the different portfolio types.

The low risk portfolio has a higher concentration in bonds, gold and cash; while the higher risk portfolio has a higher concentration in speculative assets and income producing assets.

b) ***Figure 8: High, Mid and Low Risk Portfolios Comparisons***

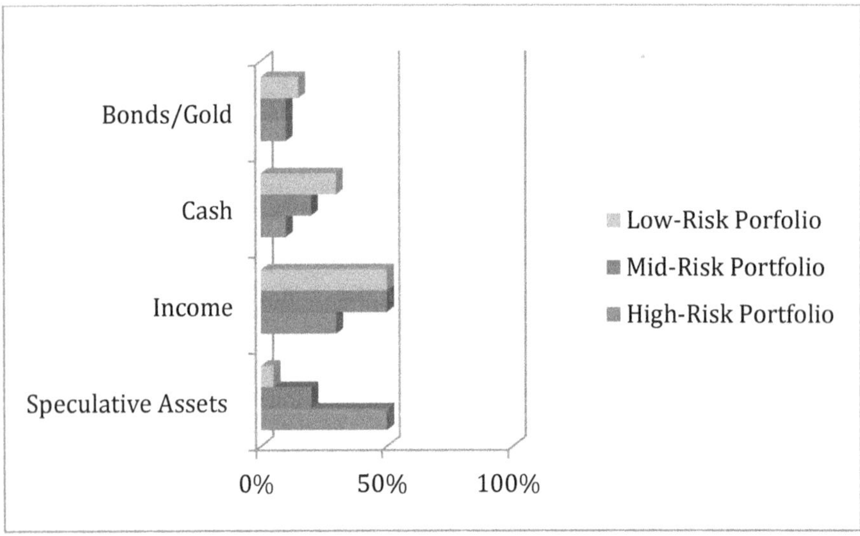

These portfolio models and strategies offer only a guideline. We can alter proportions to fit our investment goals. The best approach depends on what type of an investor we are as well as our financial requirements. For example, we can divide our equity portions into subclasses. This will allow us to realize a specialized risk-yield potential within a percentage of our portfolio. At the same time, the proportion of the portfolio dedicated to money market tools will rely on the amount of liquidity and protection we require (Hunjra, 2020). Hence, if we require investments that we can liquidate swiftly, we can consider placing a bigger percentage of the portfolio in money markets or temporary fixed-income securities. On the other hand, investors who do not prefer liquidity and have greater risk endurance will have a tiny percentage of their portfolio within these tools.

As we construct our portfolio, we might select one of the many basic allocation strategies available. Each approach provides varying benefits grounded on the investor`s time limit, objectives, and risk endurance (Royal, 2021). Hence, when the portfolio is active, it is important to perform periodic reviews. This entails a consideration of life and financial goals.

Asset allocation is an investment principle that aims to maximize returns while minimizing risk. The varying asset allocation approaches discussed above cover many investment methods, accommodating different risk endurance, time frames, and objectives

(Hunjra, 2020). Therefore, when selecting an asset allocation strategy that fits our needs, we should remember to reexamine our portfolio periodically to make sure that we are still on track to achieve our long-term financial goals.

Speculative Assets

Not every investor is happy with the prospect of patient long-term returns. For some, home run trade is better; a move that can alter their fortunes overnight. Such a procedure is called speculation and it comes with considerable risk. Speculation is the act of purchasing or selling assets where there is a chance of considerable gain, but also considerable loss. These gains act as compensation for the huge risk. Most of these investors are active traders; they seek to beat the market average and have a better hand-on strategy, particularly during temporary swings in the market.

An investor who buys a speculative asset is likely concentrated on price fluctuations. Although the risk linked with the asset is high, speculators are normally concerned with generating a profit grounded on market value changes for that asset rather than long-term investing. Speculative investing also encompasses the purchase of foreign currency, which is called currency speculation. In such a situation, a speculator purchases a currency seeking to sell it later when it appreciates.

However, without the prospect of considerable returns, there would be little incentive to participate in speculation.

For some, investment decisions can be grounded on social media groups and memes. This was the main force behind the surge in stock prices for firms such as GameStop and AMC Theaters. Another example is Dogecoin, a cryptocurrency that experienced enormous spikes at the start of 2021 when famous personalities, such as Elon Musk, discussed it on Twitter. After Elon Musk's appearance on Saturday Night Live, Dogecoin fell more than 30% (Philavong & Phomvongsa, 2021). In addition, a sequence of tweets from Musk was to blame for the volatility of Bitcoin after Tesla stated that it would not accept Bitcoin as a form of payment.

In April 2021, the price of Bitcoin was around $65,300, but it fell to $33,000 after Tesla`s announcement (Philavong & Phomvongsa, 2021). On the other hand, some speculators base their decisions on a hunch during market volatility. For the wise investor, such a hunch is based around some information. This might include information that demonstrates the potential to them and risks to other individuals. There are plenty of opportunities for the speculative investor; almost all markets have a corner which caters for this.

Speculation is most likely to succeed when investors have a strong understanding of an industry. They generally identify a facilitator or event likely to trigger a considerable movement toward their goal. When an investor feels that the event is probable, they will purchase assets they believe will gather most returns once their prediction occurs. A primary example is the 2020 election cycle. At the time, the majority believed that if Joe Biden won the presidency, that cannabis would be legalized by the national government. As a result, firms, such as Tilray (TLRY) and Aurora Cannabis, were ground zero for speculators (Apergis, Hayat & Saeed, 2021).

Speculation is common among penny stocks and over-the-counter investments. Firms that deal in the OTC markets are inexpensive but highly risky since they lack oversight and have a shaky monetary history.

For instance, real estate can blur the line between investment and speculation when purchasing property to rent it out. Although this can be termed as investing, purchasing many properties with minimal down payments for the aim of reselling swiftly at a profit is regarded as speculation. Hence, speculators can manipulate markets during periods of high volatility, making it high risk. In addition, speculative short selling can keep bullishness in check and prevent the creation of asset price bubbles via hedging against successful results.

Mutual and hedge funds frequently participate in speculation in the foreign exchange, bonds, and stock markets.

Foreign exchange is a highly speculative market where investors trade currencies, such as the Japanese Yen and the British Pound, without a centralized exchange. The primary purpose of these markets is to take advantage of short-term price fluctuations between currencies. Up to $6.6 trillion exchanges hands every day in foreign market speculation (Apergis, Hayat & Saeed, 2021). So, it can be seen, speculation is big, if risky, business. Transactions in these markets often feature spot deals to purchase and sell currency pairs. The market is dominated by asset managers and hedge funds with portfolios worth billions of dollars. However, speculation in foreign exchange markets can be difficult to differentiate from normal hedging actions, which take place when a firm purchases or sells a currency to hedge against markets cycles. For instance, a sale of foreign currency associated with a bond purchase can be seen as a hedge of the bond`s value or normal speculation.

In some circles, speculation and investment seem interchangeable. However, there is a huge difference between investing and speculating. Investors and traders make calculated risks as they seek to get returns from transactions they make in the markets. The degree of risk incurred in these transactions and the types of financial instruments used are the primary difference between investing and speculating. When an individual buys an asset with the expectation of returning a dividend long term, they are investing. Here analysis shows that the venture has a good probability of success. However, what if the same individual puts money in a venture that illustrates a high chance of failure? Here, they are speculating since their success or failure relies mainly on probability or uncontrollable factors. High-risk speculation is linked to gambling, while lower risk investing utilizes a basis of fundamentals and analysis.

The word `speculative` has a negative connotation to it, implying the asset in question is in a bubble and the spectator is not well informed. Speculative assets, which can include such varied commodities as land, gold and cryptocurrency, are difficult to value at any given time because there are no future returns to utilize to determine their value. Naturally, every asset has some speculative aspect to it – nothing can be guaranteed in life, even taxes and death - but this typically makes up only a small part of the returns of the asset in the long term. When we have a speculative asset, the speculative element dominates the yields, even in the long run.

Speculative stocks are clustered in industries, such as mining, energy, technology, and biotechnology. Although there is significant risk involved in investing in the early-stage firms in these industries, the tiny possibility that a small company will find a colossal mineral deposit, invent a popular app, or discover a cure for an illness provides adequate motivation for speculators to invest in them (Apergis, Hayat & Saeed, 2021). While most of the speculative stocks occur in early-stage firms, a blue-chip company can occasionally become a speculative stock if it encounters challenging events that reduce its prospects. Such a stock is called a fallen angel.

Another speculative asset is cryptocurrency. The best aspect of cryptocurrency investment is that yields could be incredible. As technology advances, cryptocurrency has become an increasingly significant way of transacting and storing value. Currently, there are thousands of cryptocurrencies throughout the world but the most famous include Bitcoin, Ethereum, and Dogecoin (Philavong & Phomvongsa, 2021). Although cryptocurrency is not centralized or controlled by governments, it has become a primary investment venture for some people because of its capabilities. It gives an individual autonomy and cuts out the middleman in most transactions. If the cryptocurrency in which we invest takes off in the future our returns will be astonishing. Further, the probability is that we started with only a small investment that cannot impact our financial situation. This is what happened to Bitcoin in the last few years. Developed at the start of the last decade, the value of Bitcoin skyrocketed as individuals and businesses started using cryptocurrency to trade. Consequently, those who won this lottery have inspired many individuals to add cryptocurrency to their portfolios. A small, speculative investment may well be worthwhile. The only problem is that many are suggesting the cryptocurrency bubble is bursting, and maybe the boat has left the port.

However, cryptocurrency could be part of our portfolio. One of the advantages of cryptocurrency is that it is flexible and exists only in the ether, rather than physical form. However, there are several drawbacks to having cryptocurrency as an investment. It can be lost, and new ones are invented regularly. The market cannot sustain too many types of cryptocurrency, it is believed, and indeed a part of the appeal of Bitcoin was that it was a single currency which could be used to trade globally, a huge advantage over traditional fiat currencies such as the dollar, euro and sterling where exchange rates impact on value. If too many cryptocurrencies emerge, the same exchange rate problem will surface with this digital currency. Furthermore, cryptocurrency is extremely volatile, which means that its future returns are highly unpredictable. Hence, we should look for ones that can stand the test of time and that increase in value with time. Since the oldest of these is still pre-teen (at the time of writing) such longevity is impossible to predict.

High-end art falls in the speculative asset category. Art is a favored speculative asset, especially for the wealthy. The most expensive art tends to appreciate at a higher rate than normal art since the returns often range between 5.3% and 7.5%. As the purchaser of some top-quality art, we also have the pleasure of ownership. Although, admittedly, some investors look to store these assets securely out of sight. The cost of insurance can also offset some of the gains we hope to make.

. Speculative investors are often interested in initial public offerings (IPOs) or stocks that are alleged to be annexation targets. Hence, technology or biotechnology companies on the verge of creating a single breakthrough product fall in this category. The wise investor, even if they are speculative, keeps to no more than 10% of their portfolio for these investments, so unpredictable are they.

Leveraged exchange-traded funds also represent speculation. However, while returns can once more be excellent, a good knowledge of the market is important to mitigate risk as much as possible. Such monitoring can be time consuming.

Speculation is not for the faint-hearted. Although the allure for huge profits exists, it is wise to seek advice from a financial expert to ensure that we are not taking on more than we can handle. If we decide speculation is for us, we should consider undertaking an extensive risk assessment to allow us to understand how we will respond to losses. Finally, we should see speculative investments as something separate from investments aiming to deliver short- and medium-term objectives. Basically, if they come up smelling of roses, that is an excellent bonus, but we should not rely on the size of our returns. If we decide to hedge our portfolio utilizing speculative assets, we can restrict how much we invest in these. Although 1% is regarded as a small investment rather than a hedge, spending 5-10% of our portfolio on assets that do not generate profit, interest, or rent can leave us working longer than we want to while still having to manage a sophisticated and costly portfolio along the way.

Note:

1. **Importance of Timing: Buying speculative assets that have value does contain a lot of risk. One way of reducing the risk is to buy when the asset is at a lower valuation. For example, buying Bitcoin at a value of $10000 after a crash is a different scenario than buying it when it has just risen to $100000. Try to**

avoid investing during emotional frenzies in the market

2. **Dollar Cost Averaging: Dollar Cost Averaging is the process of investing a fixed amount of money over a fixed period of time into a fixed asset. If you have an asset you're interested in investing in and are unsure of whether it is expensive, investing a small amount monthly can be a good way to reduce risk. When the price is low, you get a higher number of shares with the same amount. When it's high, you get a lower number of shares.**

How to Value Companies

Determining the fair value of a company can be a sophisticated task. After all, there are numerous factors to consider. How do financial experts evaluate assets? During valuation, all elements of a business are assessed to determine its current worth. The evaluation encompasses gathering and assessing several aspects, such as revenue, profits, losses, risks, and opportunities a business encounter. It also entails examining a company`s management, its capital structure, and future earnings prospects. Business valuation allows entrepreneurs and investors to make informed purchase, sale, or investment decisions (Vayas-Ortega et al., 2020). The tools utilized for valuation vary among financial experts, businesses, and industries. Valuation is also fundamental in tax reporting. Some tax-related activities like sale of shares will be taxable depending on a company`s valuation.

Nonetheless, the valuation process is not entirely scientific. There is a large amount of art involved since it will depend on some subjective inputs. The estimates and assumptions made during the process makes valuation an educated guess at best. Valuations helps financial experts calculate the intrinsic value of an asset, which is often disconnected from its existing trading market price. Intrinsic value is objective and is also less impacted by temporary market cycles. The valuation process is, though, largely technical: the individual performing the assessment must have adequate financial knowledge. Hence, the evaluator must be conversant with the company`s business model, its strategy, and have an extensive understanding of the industry.

There are various factors to consider in the evaluation process. Many considerations during evaluation fall into two main categories: profitability and risk. This is because investors examine the opportunity cost of making their investment, and if a venture is profitable and carries less risk, it is more likely to be an investment option. We should also be aware that emotional and non-financial forces may influence the valuation process's outcome. Furthermore, the value of a company can depend on external factors and market forces. The more comprehensive and detailed the information one has about a business, the better quality the results of any assessment will be.

i. Discounted Free Cash Flow method (DCF)

Discounted cash flow (DCF) is a valuation method utilized to estimate the value of an investment grounded on its anticipated future cash flows. It seeks to calculate the value of an investment today grounded on the predictions of future earnings. This method applies to the decisions of investors in companies or securities, like acquiring a firm, investing in a technology startup, or purchasing a stock.

Using DCF Method

There are several steps in the DCF method of valuation. First, take the average of the last three years free cash flow (FCF) of the firm. Then, multiply this FCF with the anticipated growth rate to estimate the FCF of the future. Next, calculate the net present value of this cash flow by dividing it by the discount factor. Repeat the same process for the next 10 years to find the net present value (NPV) of the future free cash flows. Add the NPV's of the FCF for all the ten years. After, find the terminal value of the stock by multiplying the final year FCF with a terminal multiple factor. Finally, divide the calculated number in previous step by the total number of outstanding shares to arrive at the intrinsic value per share of the company.

For us to understand our DCF analysis, we must see how it is calculated. For instance, let's say we want to see if Apple stock was fairly valued at a specific point in time. In June 2008, Apple had a market capitalization of $150 billion. The firm was generating operating cash flow of close to $7 billion per year. We will assign a WACC (weighted average cost of capital) of 7% to Apple since it is financially stable and can raise equity and debt capital economically. Similarly, we will assume that the company can expand its operating cash flow by 15% per annum in the next decade. From here, DCF would value Apple at a market cap of $106.3 billion, 30% below its stock market price at the time. Here, DCF offers an indication that the market may be paying too high for Apple`s common stock.

The purpose of DCF is to estimate the funds an investor would get from an investment, adjusted for the time value of money. The value of money assumes that a dollar today is worth more than a dollar in the future since it can be invested and, thus, grow. DCF assessment is therefore suitable in any scenario where an individual is paying cash in the present with the anticipation of getting returns in the future. It identifies the present value of expected future cash flow utilizing a discount rate. Investors can use this to gauge if the future cash flows of an investment are identical or greater than the value of the initial investment (Vayas-Ortega et al., 2020). When the results of DCF are higher than the existing cost of investment, the opportunity cost should be taken into consideration. When the investors cannot access the relevant information or the investment is extremely sophisticated, DCF will not be efficient and substitute methods should be used.

When employing the DCF method special attention should be given to the factors that might impact financial projections. In addition, market analysis and competition should be considered during the evaluation. A complete analysis involves the five forces of Porter: competitors, supplier power, buyer power, threat of substitution and threat of new entry. Comprehending the impacts of the five forces identified by Porter will enable investors to predict future demand, measure the negotiation power of customers and suppliers, and understand a company`s vulnerability in the industry (Vayas-Ortega et al., 2020). Moreover, analyzing the positioning of competitors in the industry will influence the value of any investment.

The primary drawback of DCF is that it requires numerous assumptions. Hence, an investor must correctly estimate future cash flow from an investment. The future cash flow depends on various factors, like market demand, competition, technology, and unexpected risks and opportunities. In addition, estimating future cash flow incorrectly can result in selecting an investment that might not give returns in the future, affecting profits. Similarly, estimating cash flows to be too low can result in missed chances. Furthermore, selecting a discount rate for the framework relies on assumption and must be appropriate to make the model valuable.

ii. Margin of Safety Method

Margin of safety is a standard of investing in which an investor only buys securities when their market value is considerably lower than their intrinsic value. When the market price of a security is considerably below our estimation of its intrinsic value, the difference is the margin safety. Since many investors may put a margin of safety based on their own risk preferences, purchasing securities when this variation exists enables an investment to be undertaken with negligible risk. The margin of safety became a popular valuation method because of the famous British-American investor Benjamin Graham and his followers (Battisti et al., 2019). Here, investors use both qualitative and quantitative factors, including company management, industry performance, and assets, to determine a security's intrinsic value. The mark up price is utilized as a point of comparison to calculate the margin of safety.

Calculating Margin of Safety

The formula for the margin of safety is:

Margin of Safety = 1 – Stock`s Current Price/Stock`s Intrinsic Value

First, we must calculate the intrinsic value and apply a margin of safety to the number to determine at what point we can buy. The formula for finding the value is:

$$V* = \frac{EPS \times (8.5 + 2g) \times 4.4}{Y}$$

Where V* = Intrinsic Value,

g = Expected Growth rate,

EPS = Earnings per share and

Y = Current interest rate of 10-year US Treasury Notes

Expected growth rate (g) can be obtained on Yahoo Finance.

https://finance.yahoo.com/quote/MSFT/analysis?p=MSFT

Growth Estimates	MSFT	Industry	Sector(s)	S&P 500
Current Qtr.	13.70%	N/A	N/A	N/A
Next Qtr.	9.40%	N/A	N/A	N/A
Current Year	9.30%	N/A	N/A	N/A
Next Year	14.70%	N/A	N/A	N/A
Next 5 Years (per annum)	15.25%	N/A	N/A	N/A
Past 5 Years (per annum)	18.17%	N/A	N/A	N/A

Current EPS is also obtained on Yahoo Finance.

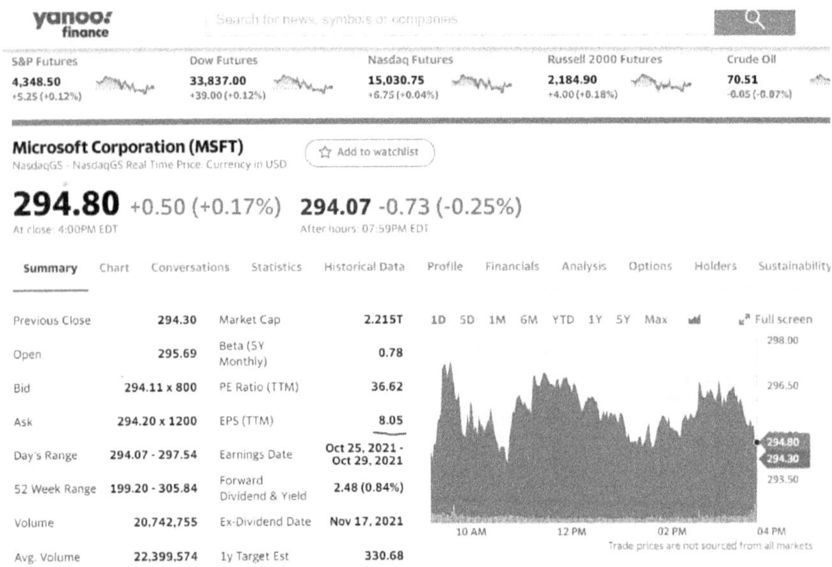

Let's say that we have Microsoft shares has the following characteristics: Current EPS $8.05, Growth 15.25%, and Yield at 4.28%. The calculated intrinsic value is **$322.7** (based on above formula), and the current price of Microsoft shares is $294.8.

Here, Microsoft stocks are trading above the intrinsic value of the company, which means we have no margin of safety if we buy at its current price. To create a margin of safety we want to purchase it below the intrinsic value. Hence, if we are looking for a 25% margin of safety, we would multiply the intrinsic value by 75%. In this case, it would mean $322.7 X 0.75 = **$242.06**. This is the price that we should look for in order to buy.

Considering the margin of safety when investing offers a cushion against errors in calculation. Nonetheless, it does not guarantee a successful investment since determining a company`s intrinsic value is extremely subjective.

An important part of investing is to make sure that there is a margin of safety with our investment. This means that we purchase a stock when its price in not only below or equal to our calculated fair price, but that it is considerably lower. This gives us a cushion where the assumptions regarding the company might be incorrect and the investment will be safe in the long run (Battisti et al., 2019). The margin of safety means that our assumptions would have to be considerably wrong for the investment to fail. However, by diversifying our portfolio, once more we add an additional layer of protection to our investment.

Figure 9: *Description of Fair Value Vs. Stock Price.*

Source: (Dividend Monk).

In the chart above, the best time to purchase would be when the stock price falls below the fair value. However, we must bear in mind that this figure is based largely on estimations.

For us to purchase at an undervalued price, we must know the fair price first. This requires a mixture of science and art. Science is used to determine company estimates and our expected rate of return, vital in calculating the objective fair value of the business. Art is used to handle the imperfect estimates which are based on historical growth rates and future trends. Here, a Discounted Cash Flow Analysis can be utilized since this is a fundamental stock evaluation method for any asset or company that produces cash flows.

Value investing is often seen as a conservative investing technique. However, the primary aim of a margin of safety is to protect our return. When we purchase a stock for lower than the estimated fair value, the expectation is that the stock price will revert back to fair value, given a rational market. When growth expectations turn out to be correct and we purchased at an undervalued price, we will end up with a higher rate of return. On the other hand, the longer the stock remains undervalued, the more benefits shareholders get since their reinvested dividend continue to accumulate undervalued shares. An excellent example an individual who uses the margin of safety method is Warren Buffet. In his early days, Buffet did not invest in businesses expanding rapidly. Instead, he invested in companies that were profoundly undervalued. As his capital base expanded, he made the decision to purchase either entire companies or invest primarily in huge caps.

There are two primary reasons for purchasing with a margin of safety. First, it makes our portfolio more conservative since our growth estimates might be a little bit off without preventing our investment from achieving success (Battisti et al., 2019). Second, if the estimates are accurate, the rate of return will be higher since over time the growth rate of investment will be enhanced by the fact that it was purchased at an undervalued price.

iii. Avoid Dividend Traps

When searching for dividend stocks, it's tempting to head towards securities with the highest yields. This is not always the best approach; there's a lot more to a good dividend stock than a high yield. Dividends are frequently given by established firms, but dividends can also be utilized by troubled companies attempting to attract investors. A dividend trap, also known as a value trap, occurs when investors are lured by a high dividend return, only to discover that the investment was not great in the end.

Dividends are the income component of shareholder returns. Dividend yield is one of the oldest valuation methods. As such, dividend-paying stocks are frequently regarded as higher quality and more stable than non-dividend stocks. However, there is a point at which these stocks become riskier than normal stocks. Some deals are also too good to be true. Consider a second-hand car dealer offering a huge discount on a vehicle you are interested in (Price, 2012). If the discount is too large, we begin to question the motives of the dealer. Although there are many stocks poised to offer a great return to investors, a large dividend yield mandates further investigation.

The first sign of a dividend trap is when a company is paying a much higher dividend return than its peers. When we come across such a scenario, we should not just accept it at face value. Instead, assess the company`s and its management's capacity to meet its obligations. If the stock continually drops or the firm is unable to pay the dividend as pledged, it is a value trap (Price, 2012). Here, we should assess the company`s payout ratio, which is the amount of income going to dividend payments. A business that is paying out most of what it makes will be unable to sustain the dividend for long and may be heading toward financial problems. A payout ratio of more than 40% is a big red flag. Therefore, we should establish if a stock has a high, low, or average dividend yield before investing.

The Importance of Precious Metals

Gold is money. Everything else is credit.

- J. P. Morgan

Throughout history, precious metals have played an essential role in the global economy. Although the universal landscape has considerably changed since the commencement of the Gold Standard, precious metals still play a vital role in our financial future. Investors seeking a reliable investment can consider an investment in precious metal. Unlike any other elements on earth, their distinct combination of brilliance, scarcity, durability, and utility infuse them with many economic purposes. Similarly, precious metals, such as gold, silver, platinum, and palladium, act as money, industrial products, and investment instruments throughout the global market (Shahid et.al, 2019). Consequently, this makes them a unique and practical investment option. Throughout the centuries, precious metals have been valued for their permanent value and a worldwide medium of exchange. At the same time, they have played a fundamental part in art and industry.

Precious metals are rare metals that have a high economic value because of the multiple factors listed above. The most popular precious metals for investors include gold, silver, and platinum. In the past, precious metals played a primary part in the global economy since numerous currencies were either minted utilizing these metals or backed by them. Nonetheless, the situation has changed in the contemporary world and individuals can buy precious metals as financial assets. As an investment, precious metals are primarily used to diversify portfolios and as a store of value, specifically to hedge against volatility. For commercial purchases, precious metals are a vital component for commodities like electronics or jewelry.

Other metals often utilized in industrial activities include iridium, which is used in forte alloys, and palladium, which is utilized in chemical processes and electronics. Which precious metal is best for investment?

Gold is distinct because of its durability, malleability, and capacity to conduct both heat and electricity. Although it is primarily known as a store of value and for making jewelry, it has several industrial applications in electronics and dentistry. It is one of the most secure stores of value in any asset that one can invest in. Furthermore, the gold market is not affected by the supply and demand of other assets, which makes the metal a good investment during economic downturns.

Gold prices have remained relatively stable despite the numerous crises that other markets across the world have had to endure (Shahid et.al, 2019). This is one of the primary reasons why individuals invest in gold and other metals.

A gold investment allows the investor to have considerable control over their asset, especially in times of market volatility.

Figure 10: *Historical prices of gold*

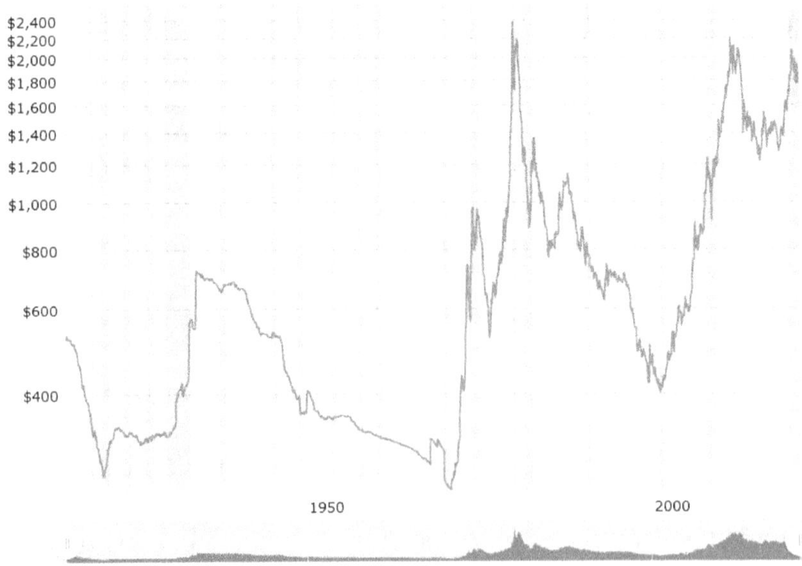

Source (Precious Metals Charts and Data | MacroTrends, n.d.)

The value of gold is determined by the market and are less impacted by the forces of supply and demand than other commodities because the new mine supply is massively overshadowed by the amount of hoarded gold. This means that when hoarders want to sell, the price drops, and when they want to purchase, a new supply is absorbed and gold prices increase (Hammoudeh, Malik & McAleer, 2011). Various factors increase the value of gold. First, we have systemic financial apprehensions. When the financial institutions are seen as unstable or the political climate is uncertain, people seek gold as a store of value. Second, we have inflation. When real estate markets are suffering, investors may seek gold as it will retain its value. Finally, war and political instability often send individuals into a gold-hoarding mode (Hammoudeh, Malik & McAleer, 2011). A person can store their entire life savings on gold and trade it off for products and services.

Silver is frequently seen as the poor cousin of gold, though its price often broadly follows that of gold. Unlike gold, the price of silver fluctuates between its apparent role as a store of value and as an industrial component. As a result, the price fluctuations of silver are volatile than gold. In the last year, most financial experts stipulate that silver has outperformed gold (Hammoudeh, Malik & McAleer, 2011). Although most people see silver as less desirable than gold, it can also be more reliant in a prosperous economy, where the demand for metal is high. Irrespective of silver`s higher volatility, it is viewed as a hedge against inflation.

Figure 11: *Historical prices for silver*

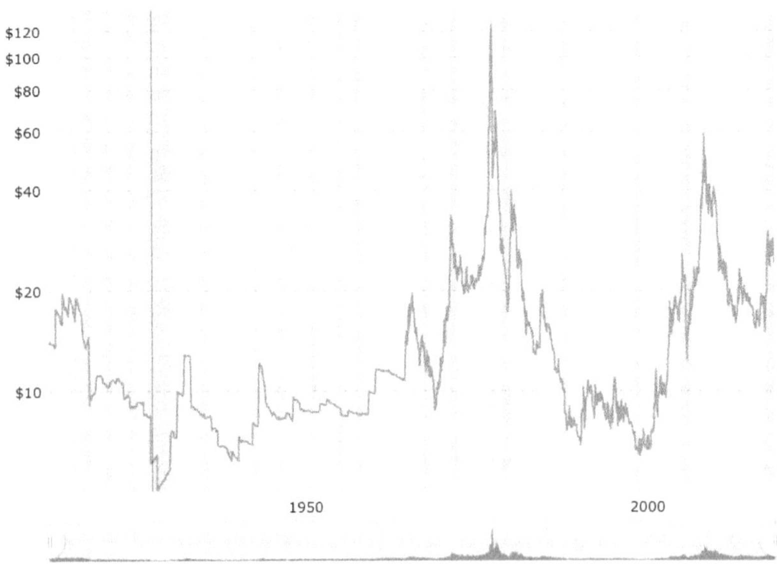

Source (Precious Metals Charts and Data | MacroTrends, n.d.)

Although silver trades in line with gold as a precious commodity, its industrial use exerts an equally strong effect on its price.

Silver is used in various industries including the photography sector to make silver-based photographic film. Furthermore, the rise of a huge middle class in developing countries in the East and Africa has created an escalated demand for electrical gadgets, medical equipment, and other products that require silver as a raw material (Hammoudeh, Malik & McAleer, 2011). Similarly, silver is used in superconductor applications and microcircuit markers. Currently, it is not clear if, or the degree to which these innovations will impact the overall non-investment demand for silver.

Apart from gold and silver, another precious metal in which it is ideal to invest is platinum. This is traded in the global commodities market. It tends to have a greater price than gold during normal times and when there is political stability since it is rarer. Only a small amount of platinum is mined annually. Despite having higher prices than gold, platinum is not as prevalent among investors due to its scarcity.

Figure 12: *Historical Prices of Platinum*

Source (Precious Metals Charts and Data | MacroTrends, n.d.)

Various factors affect platinum`s price. Platinum is an industrial component, and its greatest demand comes from the automotive sector. The metal is a fundamental constitute in catalytic converters, which are used to minimize destructive emissions. Jewelry follows, and then the petroleum and computer industries come after that. Due to the automobile's heavy dependence on platinum, its prices are influenced primarily by vehicle sales and production. Another factor that affects platinum`s demand is the fact that platinum mines are concentrated in only two nations: South Africa and Russia (Hammoudeh, Malik &

McAleer, 2011). As a result, this creates a greater likelihood for cartel-like behavior that can both back and artificially increase platinum prices. Therefore, platinum`s rarity combine with its vast industrial use, makes it an appealing investment alternative to competing assets such as stocks, bonds, and currencies.

One of the lesser-known and underrated precious metals is palladium, which also has industrial uses. Palladium is a shiny, silvery metal utilized in numerous manufacturing processes, especially in electronic and industrial commodities. The metal can also be utilized in medicine, chemical processes, jewelry, and groundwater treatment. The supply of palladium is limited, and it is mined in the United States, Canada, Russia, and South Africa. Close to 50% of the planet`s supply of palladium comes from Russia (Hammoudeh, Malik & McAleer, 2011). Palladium was first incorporated into jewelry in 1939. Here, palladium was mixed with yellow gold to form an alloy stronger than white gold. The metal can create thin sheets up to one-two hundredth fifty-thousandths of an inch. It is malleable but becomes stronger and harder when worked at room temperature. These sheets are utilized to make fuel cells and solar energy Palladium is much harder than platinum, making the element more durable than platinum.

Having completed that brief background into some precious metals, the question now emerges as to how we can invest in them. Investors looking to add precious metals to their portfolios have various ways of realizing that. Those who prefer to hold these metals directly can buy physical bullion, like bars or minted coins, and store them in safety deposit boxes. For individuals anticipating the worst in terms of global and national economic stability, bullion is the best choice while for those with a wider time horizon, bullion is illiquid and hard to maintain (Shahid et.al, 2019). Bullion represents a direct approach towards ownership that minimizes risk but incurs more costs because of insurance and storage. Another approach is to purchase future contracts for the specific metal or to purchase shares in publicly traded firms involved in the exploration or production of these metals. In addition, mutual funds and exchange-traded funds provide many alternatives, such as money backed by bullion and leveraged exposure. However, exchange-traded funds do not provide us access to the physical product, which means that we do not have a claim on the metal in the fund.

Another method is through future and option markets which offer liquidity and leverage to investors who wish to place huge bets on precious metals (Shahid et.al, 2019). Finally, certificates give investors all the advantages of physical ownership of the metal without the trouble of mobility and storage. For those looking for insurance during a crisis, certificates are an ideal approach.

Every investment carries unique risks. Despite leveraging some level of security, investing in precious metals is a risk. Prices can plummet during recessions, forcing investors to liquidate their assets to cover their expenses. At the same time, physical assets can be hard to dispose of at reasonable prices, especially during periods of increased volatility. Finally, precious metals have an extra risk of being stolen when stored in the house. However, during economic uncertainty, the prices of precious metals are reliable. This makes them popular, which increases prices thus benefitting sellers.

Like other natural resources, the mining of these metals will decline until they are depleted. They are not infinite. At the same time, the demand for precious metals continues to increase as consumer applications increase. Therefore, acquiring gold and silver bullion today will augment our chances of having extremely valuable resources in the future. Another reason for investing in precious metals is liquidity. The problem with having a house is that we cannot dispose of it when in need of quick cash. Although most assets have value, the complete process of disposing of them is cumbersome, making it difficult for people to sell them. However, precious metals are easy to trade.

Investing in precious metals diversifies a portfolio and helps keep a healthy balance between physical and stock assets. In 2008, many people in the United States lost their investments and assets because of the financial recession. In such times, precious metal investment becomes vital in holding a stable financial portfolio. If individuals had invested in these metals, they could have mitigated some of their losses during that financial crisis. Therefore, it is wise to be prepared for an economic crisis by investing in precious metals. Furthermore, precious metals are a haven against the dollar. The US dollar is continually losing value because of inflation, while precious metals increase in value. As of 2019, the US owes China more than $22 trillion (Shahid et.al, 2019). Since the value of the dollar is based on the fact that the US has pledged to pay back its debt, this means that in case of another crisis, the value of the dollar could potentially be obliterated, and people would require a backup to maintain financial protection. The haven is precious metals. That is clearly a worst-case scenario but demonstrates the importance of holding something secure like gold, silver, or platinum in our portfolio.

Additionally, precious metals are easily purchased from bullion traders, market dealers, and banks. Apart from their easy access, these metals are relatively easy to acquire in the markets, despite their global scarcity. The range of precious metals available means that, for example, investors with a difficulty investing in a full ounce gold can still opt for other more affordable precious metal such as silver. Furthermore, the demand for precious metals, like gold and silver has surged in the previous year. Regardless of the numerous economic uncertainties and market volatilities of the current, pandemic influenced, times, the demand for silver and gold has continued to increase compared to other precious metals.

Precious metals provide distinct inflationary safety because they have inherent value, carry no credit risk, and cannot be inflated. In addition, they provide genuine insurance against financial or political turmoil. From an investment perspective, precious metals offer low or negative correlation to the performance of other asset categories such as bonds and stocks. As such, even a tiny portion of these metals in our portfolio will minimize volatility and risk. This shows that precious metals offer a practical way of diversifying a portfolio.

As ever, however, our primary requirement is to understand our financial goals and risk profile before investing. That way, gold, silver, platinum, palladium, or another precious metal can really earn money for us on our journey towards achieving those financial goals.

References

A Guide to High-risk Investments. (n.d.). SyndicateRoom. https://www.syndicateroom.com/alternative-investments/high-risk-investments

Apergis, N., Hayat, T., & Saeed, T. (2021). US partisan conflict uncertainty and oil prices. *Energy Policy*, *150*, 112118.

Armantier, O., Koşar, G., Pomerantz, R., Skandalis, D., Smith, K., Topa, G., & Van der Klaauw, W. (2021). How economic crises affect inflation beliefs: Evidence from the Covid-19 pandemic. Journal of Economic Behavior & Organization, 189, 443-469.

Battisti, E., Miglietta, N., Salvi, A., & Creta, F. (2019). Strategic approaches to value investing: a systematic literature review of international studies. Review of International Business and Strategy.

Brittney. (2021). Dave Ramsey Budget Percentages. Retrieved from https://makesavespendgive.com/dave-ramsey-budget-percentages/

How to use a Margin of Safety when Investing. (n.d). Dividend Monk. Retrieved from https://www.dividendmonk.com/margin-of-safety/

Fabozzi, F. J., & Markowitz, H. M. (Eds.). (2011). The theory and practice of investment management: Asset allocation, valuation, portfolio construction, and strategies (Vol. 198). John Wiley & Sons.

Guerard Jr, J. B. (Ed.). (2009). Handbook of portfolio construction: contemporary applications of Markowitz techniques. Springer Science & Business Media.

Gutkevych, S., & Vikhliaiev, M. (2021). Risks In Investing. Baltic Journal of Economic Studies, 7(3), 82-87.

Hammoudeh, S., Malik, F., & McAleer, M. (2011). Risk management of precious metals. The Quarterly Review of Economics and Finance, 51(4), 435-441.

Hardyman, R. (2017). Understanding Stocks and Investing. The Rosen Publishing Group, Inc.

Hillier, D., Draper, P., & Faff, R. (2006). Do precious metals shine? An investment perspective. Financial Analysts Journal, 62(2), 98-106.

Hunjra, A. I., Alawi, S. M., Colombage, S., Sahito, U., & Hanif, M. (2020). Portfolio Construction by Using Different Risk Models: A Comparison among Diverse Economic Scenarios. Risks, 8(4), 126.

Lee, S. C., & Eid, W. (2018). Portfolio construction and risk management: theory versus practice. RAUSP Management Journal, 53, 345-365.

Long, T. (2016). Serving up a budgeting pie will help youth stay financially healthy. Retrieved from https://www.canr.msu.edu/news/serving_up_a_budgeting_pie_will_help_youth_stay_financially_healthy

Nguyen, L., Gallery, G., & Newton, C. (2019). The joint influence of financial risk perception and risk tolerance on individual investment decision-making. Accounting & Finance, 59, 747-771.

Nofsinger, J. R. (2017). The psychology of investing. Routledge.

Philavong, M., & Phomvongsa, S. (2021). Cryptocurrency Business Covers the Psychological Impact of the Business Market on the Youth Segment. *Journal of Asian Multicultural Research for Economy and Management Study*, *2*(2), 35-39.

Portfolio Construction. (n.d). Invest Blue. Retrieved from https://www.investblue.com.au/belief-5-portfolio-construction

Price, J. (2012). Return on equity traps and how to avoid them. Equity, 26(3), 4-6.

Royal, J. (2021, August 1). 8 Best Low-Risk Investments in March 2020. Bankrate. https://www.bankrate.com/investing/low-risk-investments/

Russo, A. (2013). Low risk equity Investments: Empirical evidence, theories, and the Amundi experience." (pp. 1-32). Amundi Working Paper WP-033-2013.

Shahid, M. N., Jehanzeb, M., Abbas, A., Zubair, A., & Akbar, M. A. H. (2019). Predictability of precious metals and adaptive market hypothesis. International Journal of Emerging Markets.

Vayas-Ortega, G., Soguero-Ruiz, C., Rojo-Álvarez, J. L., & Gimeno-Blanes, F. J. (2020). On the differential analysis of enterprise valuation methods as a guideline for unlisted companies' assessment (I): Empowering discounted cash flow valuation. Applied Sciences, 10(17), 5875.

Starving Billionaires

The History of Inflation and Hyperinflation

Introduction

Introduction

Imagine the price of a loaf of bread doubling in a matter of hours. This is a possible reality of hyperinflation, where prices rise exponentially, and money becomes worthless. Inflation has become a prominent subject of discussion in the United States and across the world. Despite current concerns regarding the impact of a devalued dollar on the economy, history reveals how past inflations have been much worse than today. In 2008, Steve Hanke, a professor at Johns Hopkins University, researched the Zimbabwean hyperinflation to see how it compared to historical instances of the same (Toscano, 2014). The study revealed that hyperinflation typically coincides with wars and a set of ill-advised and uninformed fiscal policies. However, the primary cause is a quick increase in the money supply without economic growth. The first recorded hyperinflation in modern times occurred during the French

Revolution, where monthly inflation rose to 143% (Toscano, 2014). This kind of inflation only appeared again in the 20th century.

This book discusses several great inflations and hyperinflations throughout the history of civilizations, from Ancient Rome to the current problems in Venezuela. In the 20th century, seventeen hyperinflations occurred in Europe and Central Asia, including five in Latin America, four in Western Europe, one in Asia, and one in Africa. A look at the United States reveals that the country had never experienced hyperinflation but came close twice during the Revolutionary War and the Civil War when the national government printed money to cater to its war initiatives. Nonetheless, in the American cases, inflation never surpassed a 50% monthly rate, which is significantly lower than history`s hysterics cases.

Scholars assert that hyperinflations had never happened when commodity acted as money or when paper currency converts to a hard asset (such as gold or silver). Hyperinflation mainly occurs when the money supply had no natural constraints and was controlled by a discretionary paper money standard. Although hyperinflation mandates a series of extreme political and social events, we see that fiat currency is vulnerable to rampant inflation. The economic costs of hyperinflation include a fall in the value of savings, unemployment, lack of confidence in the finance sector, and lack of investment and economic growth.

The most devastating hyperinflation happened in Hungary in July 1946, when prices surged by 4.19 quintillion percent. Another severe hyperinflation was in Germany from 1922 to 1923, when prices doubled every two days. The most recent hyperinflation episode is happening in Venezuela since 2016 (Toscano, 2014). This book looks at ten different hyperinflations across history, starting with the fall of Ancient Rome and ending in the Venezuelan disaster.

What are Inflation and Hyperinflation?

Inflation is a sustained increase in the aggregate price level; and measures the growth rate in prices for a diversified range of products and services. It is the decline of purchasing power of a particular currency over time. The first thing to comprehend regarding hyperinflation is that it is not just high inflation. High inflation refers to the general rise in prices and wages. High inflation can be disruptive. For instance, during the 1970s, the UK point prices rose by more than 20% annually, ushering in a decade of civil unrest and financial turmoil (Amadeo, 2020).

Hyperinflation is a completely different ball game. Hyperinflation occurs when prices rise at a rate of more than 50% per month (Amadeo, 2020). At this rate, an item worth $1 in January would cost at least $130 at the end of the year. It means that a loaf of bread would cost higher in the afternoon than in the morning. It represents the point at which faith in a nation`s currency and economy are dead. As a result, the currency is effectively worthless. Hyperinflation is widely a 20th-century phenomenon. The most explored hyperinflation happened in Germany after World War I when the country experienced a monthly inflation rate of 322% (Salemi, 2021). On average, prices quadrupled every month during the sixteen months of hyperinflation.

What causes hyperinflation? No single shock, no matter how devastating, can explain sustained, consistent, quick growth of prices. The two world wars did not cause hyperinflation in Germany and

Hungary. Hyperinflation has two primary causes: increased money supply and demand-pull inflation (Salemi, 2021). An increase in money supply happens when the monetary and fiscal authorities start printing money to pay for a large stream of government expenditures. As the money supply increases, so do the prices.

On the other hand, demand-pull inflations occur when a surge in demand surpasses supply, sending prices up. This scenario occurs when consumer spending increases because of a growing economy, an instant rise in exports, or increased government spending. The two factors go hand-in-hand. Rather than restricting the money supply to reduce inflation, the state continues to print more money. Consequently, prices surge since there is too much money circulating. Here, the consumers expect inflation to continue rising; thus, they purchase more in the present to avoid paying a greater price in the future. Excessive demand worsens inflation.

What are the effects of hyperinflation?

One of the primary effects of hyperinflation is the relocation of wealth. Hyperinflations transfer wealth from the public, which holds money, to the state, which issues money. It leads to shortages as individuals begin to hoard both durable and perishable goods. As a result, daily commodities become scarce, and the economy crashes. Additionally, life savings become worthless, and financial institutions collapse as their loans lose value and people stop making deposits.

Hyperinflation severely diminishes the value of a currency in foreign exchange markets, making it hard for importers to buy foreign commodities. Unemployment rises as businesses close and government tax revenue declines. In most cases, the state prints more money as a response to pay its bills, worsening the hyperinflation. However, there are two primary winners in hyperinflation. Those who have loans benefit as the higher prices make their debt worthless. Exporters win big since their exports are cheaper than foreign competitors.

US Revolutionary War Great Inflation

Like many other nations, the United States started as a colony and had to fight for its independence. From 1775 to 1783, the country fought an all-out war with its colonial master Great Britain. This became known as the US revolutionary war since it changed the region's history. Following the war, economic turmoil and inflation hit the nation, leading to financial hardships. It was the foundation of the American civil war entailing infighting among American citizens. Now, let us look into the revolutionary war period, emphasizing its implications on the country's economic downturn. The chapter articulates events leading up to the war and the consequent significant inflation that hit the United States. It also investigates elements surrounding the inflation years and how ordinary citizens fared during this period. Also discussed in the chapter are the efforts taken by the leaders to salvage the situation with economic policies used to stir up growth taking center stage. The US revolutionary war is a viable example of the role of war in destabilizing the economy and disrupting currency circulation.

The Leadup to the Great Inflation

Towards the second half of the 18th century, Great Britain continued to reign supreme over other nations, managing colonies in nearly all continents around the globe. Its far-reaching power had considerable implications on its territories and their economic capabilities. Following the French and Indian wars, also known as the Seven Year Wars, Great Britain had drained its revenue and ability to support its vast military. By 1763, when these wars ended, Britain was gasping for an economic revamp and looking for new revenue sources (Bezanson, 2016). Its national debt had skyrocketed, and hence it looked for adopted taxation policies aimed at changing the situation. Maintaining and populating the British troops in the colonies they had conquered was subject to the funds they would obtain from these frontiers. Therefore, they imposed the Stamp and Townshend Acts targeting the British American colonies (Ferraro, 2021). These policies looked to impose direct taxes on the colonies and enforce higher taxation policies. These acts also increased the Britain legislature's power over colonies for tax and control of economic policies.

It is vital to point out that the Townshend and Stamp acts came in between 1767 and 1768. Other policies looking to increase taxation, such as the Sugar Act and Tea Act, also came in the following years. These were not well received in the colonies. They provoked colonial opposition and unrest whereby the British American colonies' inhabitants resisted the heavy taxation (Ferraro, 2021). They claimed that they would not agree to taxation without representation in the British legislature. On March 5th 1770, the Boston massacre was the tipping point of this resistance. An angry mob confronted British soldiers in Boston leading to a massacre (Hamilton, 1977). The Boston tea party followed the Boston massacre in 1773. Patriots and merchants resisted and burnt up a British ship bringing in tax free tea from China. Great Britain responded by instilling punitive measures known as the Intolerable Acts of 1774 (Taskinsoy, 2020). These policies were meant to punish the colony for the Boston tea party and resistance towards the

Tea acts. In response, Americans took up arms, and an all-out battle broke out in 1775 led by George Washington.

Figure 1. *The Boston tea party 1773*

Source: (Hamilton, 1977)

The American War of Independence marked the start of events that led to an inflationary period like no other. To get into war with Great Britain meant that the United States had to amass significant resources for the campaign. One of the most critical elements in this war would be financing to recruit and pay soldiers. It is crucial to indicate that Americans were highly opposed to taxation. Therefore, the leaders opted to raise revenue through means other than tax. They printed more currency to increase monetary circulation, and laws were put in place to ensure people exchanged goods and services in paper currency or specie (Bredin & Fountas, 2018). The increase in the circulation of the continental dollar was vital in increasing the revenue available for military spending.

The American leaders also opted to print bills of credit redeemable for future taxes. The continental congress was digging a pit that would later lead the United States into economic turmoil. The country suffered inflation at the expense of independence, and it took decades to recover from this predicament fully.

Figure 2. *American Revolutionary War*

Source: (Bredin & Fountas, 2018)

The First Signs

The first signs of inflation showed when the young republic struggled to develop economic freedom. Having cut ties with its primary trade partner and provider of manufactured goods, the United States had to restructure its economic policies to augment its liberty (Ferraro, 2021). Britain had also barred the United States from trading with the sugar colonies in the Caribbean, leaving the region to develop internal trade. Additionally, Britain's naval force blockaded all trade routes and left the United States to fend for itself. With the situation at hand, the country had to deal with a looming economic crisis. They had to discover new ways to generate revenue, given that taxation was not possible. It struggled to settle the debts incurred while the continental dollar lost value in favor of silver coins (Taskinsoy, 2020). There was excessive currency in circulation, leading to an exponential increase in the price of goods and services.

Figure 3. *Continental currency printed to support the revolutionary war*

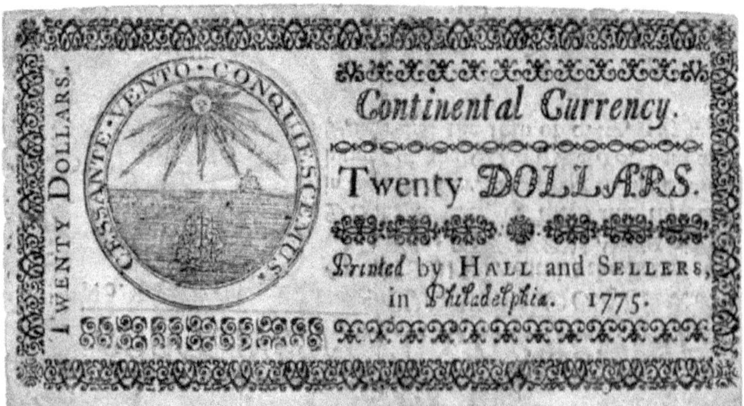

Source: (Bezanson, 2016)

A significant aspect to point out is that every state had the ability to print continental dollars in addition to the federal government. Thus, the rates of inflation in each state were different. For example, in Virginia, hyperinflation kicked in by 1779, with inflation increasing more than 50% monthly (Bezanson, 2016). While some other states barely experienced any inflation.

Other early signs of inflation appeared when the amount of currency flowing in the region increased despite shortages in goods and services. Individuals had hoarded currency earlier during the war, spending little due to uncertainty. However, towards the end of the war, individuals started spending, but there was not much to purchase. There was, therefore, excessive circulation of continental dollars, which in many senses reduced its value. Other early signs included the government's increased spending despite the ever-increasing national debt (Taskinsoy, 2020). Furthermore, inclination towards taxation and price controls to limit the ever-increasing costs of goods indicated that the government had realized that inflation would continue destabilizing the region's economy.

The Inflationary Years

The populace felt most of the inflation after the end of the war. As indicated earlier, the troops incurred much of the expenses, promoting the continental congress to develop ingenious means to increase revenue generation. By 1780, the United States had issued about 400 million dollars to its army. Congress put up a spirited fight to counter the runaway inflation, but its tactics only devalued the continental dollar further. From 1775 there was an average annual inflation rate of 4.5% over the next decade (Hamilton, 1977). The worst year was 1778 when inflation reached an all-time high of 29%. This spelt economic doom for the region, unless the leaders implemented drastic control measures (Hamilton, 1977). This inflation was followed by disloyalty towards the new government, outright resistance, and protests with significant civil unrest. Discontent over rising prices increased rapidly, spreading from state to state, and people started taking up arms to counter the continental congress's agenda. Numerous food riots were the order of the day during this period, with large plantation owners inciting the peasants to hold the government to account for the economic downturn.

Figure 4. *Inflation during and after the American War for Independence*

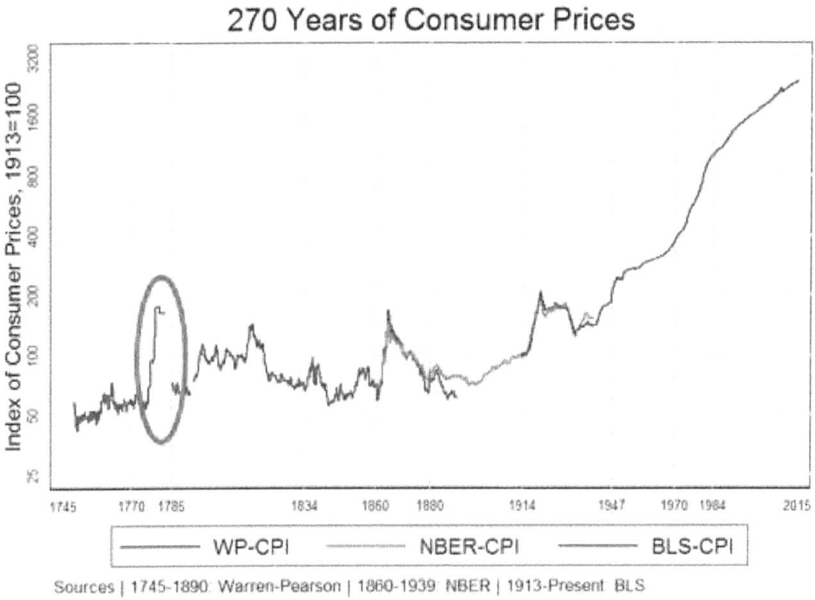

Source: (Hamilton, 1977)

The continental congress responded by printing even more dollars thereby devaluing the continental dollar. With the devaluation of the currency came an increase in prices of goods and services, causing further unease among ordinary citizens. Congress also faced another critical issue with counterfeit continental dollars in circulation. It was

Britain that primarily spread the counterfeit currency to derail America's recovery process. Great Britain counted on the counterfeit continental dollars to help them win the war and increase America's dependence on them (Bredin & Fountas, 2018). This increased inflation rates significantly and sabotaged the region's economic progress. However, America's road towards independence accelerated with the development of a constitution and the growth of political institutions. The inhabitants held liberty in high regard, and therefore despite economic turmoil, they wanted nothing to do with their former colonizers. In many senses, the hardships experienced during the inflationary years helped shape the United States. The resilience of the United States lasted far beyond this period and is one of the reasons they became a long-term superpower.

The troops played a significant role in increasing inflation during and after the American revolutionary war. Late into the war, the continental congress decided on each state's role in supporting its troops. It is important to point out that there was no national or central bank during this period, and therefore monetary control remained elusive (Aizenman & Marion, 2011). In the wake of these policies, the states went overboard in equipping and servicing their troops. To pay for the soldiers' upkeep, the states printed more continental currencies while imposing taxation on their citizens. This further made controlling inflation an uphill task since each state had its own methods, policies, and consequent inflation rates. By the time the war ended, the United States federal government had spent about 37 million dollars while the states had spent about 114 million dollars (Hildebrand, 2018). The states had to negotiate with the continental congress to reduce the money supply and counter inflation in respective regions. These efforts put the young republic in jeopardy, further halting economic progress with runaway inflation. The debts incurred in maintaining troops and the closure of trade routes caused the post-war economic slump.

There was also the flooding of British goods at cheaper prices and increased money supply. This fueled rampant inflation reducing American quality of life and ability to trade. Many traders and merchants preferred barter with increasing debts calling for new means of currency exchange. One such method was the exchange of tobacco for notes redeemable in shops.

Currency debts were issued in the form of currency notes which were to be paid back later (Baack, 2008). These debts eliminated a standard currency value and consequent outright currency power. It led to economic issues that prompted the continental congress to develop policies to loosen laws governing debt repayment. Relaxation of prison terms, repossession, and public shaming were strategies adopted to force those in debt to pay their dues. This, however, angered the conservatives and those who looked to get paid, further putting the currency system at risk. The inflationary years became a battle between those with and those without, hence forming the Republican and Democrat factions.

Figure 5. *Credit notes*

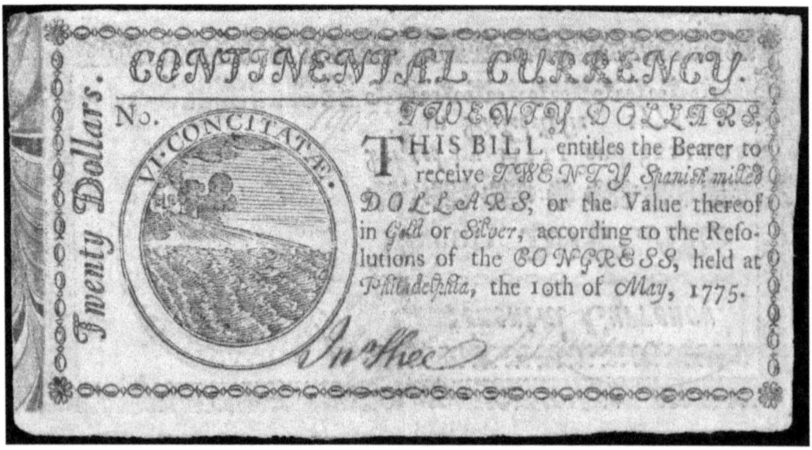

Source: (Baack, 2008)

How the Common Man Fared During the Inflationary Period

During the inflationary period, the citizens had a hard time surviving the ongoing economic crisis. There was paper money that continued to become worthless, combined with a lack of quality goods due to the closure of trade between the US and Great Britain. Additionally, limited exports meant that many ordinary citizens had little or no means of livelihood and hence suffered dearly (Hildebrand, 2018).

The Britain loyalists faced it rough due to castigation for supporting Britain. They were attacked and their estates were repossessed by the patriots who felt entitled to their wealth. The soldiers who had participated in the revolutionary war also had a rough time integrating into society. Despite compensation in land, they could only practice subsistence farming for barter trade (Berg, 2021). They, therefore, had limited economic prosperity as earlier promised by the state. They became ordinary citizens who were at the mercy of the government's policies in reversing inflation and increasing the region's economic growth.

It is essential to note that the continental government did not have the powers to impose taxation to generate revenue. It, therefore, continued to print paper money while borrowing domestically. Towards the end of the war, those that lent to the government were paid with obligations to pay (IOU notes) and therefore had minimal revenue to spend (Hildebrand, 2018). Life got harder for ordinary citizens, but it was much worse for the slaves. The slaves that participated in the war with the promise of liberty found themselves back into the shackles of slavery. They did not enjoy the promised freedom and instead continued under their masters as before the war. Women were also disregarded post-war despite their critical role during the war. Equality was out of the equation, and they went back to their role of being housewives (Bredin & Fountas, 2018). These aspects indicate that the common man had a tough life, but this was the situation across the board. All social classes were suffering, and the government had to develop drastic measures to salvage the situation.

Figure 6. *Women during the revolutionary war*

Source: (Bredin & Fountas, 2018).

The government implemented measures to control prices, which did not augur well with ordinary citizens and merchants. Many hoarded goods and were later robbed as the government looked to repossesses their property. Soldiers were also notorious for taking what was not theirs, raiding farmlands, taking grain, wine and animals for their supplies (Hildebrand, 2018). They were bad news to peasant farmers since they saw it as their right to take whatever was in their path to help sustain their ability to fight. Free speech also suffered during this period, given that dissent was strongly squashed. The army procurement officers started seizing whatever supplies were needed and providing certificates of debts in return. They, therefore, oppressed the common man for war.

To make matters worse, they did not allow complaints or grievances. The policy antagonized the ordinary citizens making their lives difficult (Bezanson, 2016). Many hid their horses and dismantled their wagons to keep them away from the soldiers. In other cases, they snuck behind the soldiers' lines to take back what was theirs. Therefore, it is accurate to conclude that the inflationary years caused strife between the common man, the army, and the government.

The Deleveraging

Economic reforms aimed at reducing inflation bore fruits about five decades later after the end of the revolutionary war. The continental congress realized that despite the convenience of the specie, the region needed a paper currency to enhance its economic dominance. They, therefore, continued to issue the continental dollar at a controlled rate while developing policies to limit barter trade. The continental congress also set up the Bank of America as a national reserve to lend loans to the government. According to Berg (2021), it imposed Gresham's law which looked to ensure that the region did away with specie in favor of paper currency. Individuals had hoarded large sums of coin currency flowing in from trade with Havana and the French troops. However, this law ensured that it was eliminated from circulation and used for imports. The United States now had depreciated paper currency as the primary medium of exchange. It imposed taxes, opened up trade, and increased government expenditure to open up the region's economy. Towards 1840, the region's economic growth picked up pace, increasing the dollar's value and balancing money circulation in the economy (Berg, 2021). The United States eventually overcame the inflation and has been on an upward economic trend ever since.

Hyperinflation during the US Civil War

The southern states experienced a classic case of hyperinflation during the US Civil War (1861-1865). When the war ended, the confederate currency was worthless. The North also faced significant financial hardship but had a thriving economy centered on railroads and factories. The South was solely dependent on farming, and the abolition of slave labor brought the entire economy to its knees.

The tension between the Northern and Southern states had been brewing years earlier. Slave labor was the leading cause of the conflict. The Southern states thrived on agricultural exports thanks to the expansive lands and the use of slaves in the farms. The slaves were deemed assets in the South (Historical Statistics, 1949). Most of the Northern population felt that slave labor was inhumane and wrong. The southern farmers and the elite, on the other hand, felt threatened because slavery was the backbone of their economy. As illustrated in Figure 1, slaves formed a large part of the economy. Slave labor brought Southern prosperity. All interventions to end the simmering tensions were futile, and the war began in 1861.

War boils down to money. When the first onslaught happened at Fort Sumter, the South and North quickly found ways to fund the war. The North had a diversified economy, and the government gradually increased taxes. In addition, they floated in war bonds which complimented the expanded tax base (Doyle, 2001). The Confederate States, on the other hand, had announced an embargo of their products which meant that they did not have enough income to tax (Doyle, 2001). Even though the South accounted for close to a third of United States assets, they lacked liquid assets. The Confederacy then began to print money in a bid to get supplies for the war. The eleven Confederate States introduced the Confederate Dollar in 1861 and started using it as legal tender. The currency was not backed by any hard assets) such as gold), meaning that the currency was simply a credit promissory note. The Confederacy also lacked sufficient printing equipment and technical knowledge, making simple currency that could easily be duplicated. Counterfeiters took full advantage of the situation (Doyle, 2001). While the North also printed money, their diversified economy was able to absorb the shock of inflation.

Figure 1

This image shows the flag of the Confederate flying above Fort Sumter in April 1861 when the war began.

Source: Library of Congress, *(reproduction no.LC-DIG-ppmsca-32284)*

At the start of the Civil War, one confederate dollar had a value of one gold dollar. Four months into the war, inflation had risen by 5% (Lerner, 1955). The Confederate Government's money to support the war was mainly from printed cash and borrowed funds from outside the Confederate. Bond sales and taxes were relatively small. When the Union armies conquered Southern territories, the Confederate notes were banned. As a result, the defeated Confederates sent large amounts of money to other confederates. The increased stock of funds prompted the Confederate Government to raise taxes and introduce a holding tax for those in possession of the currency (Lerner, 1955). The population promptly spent the money to avoid the tax, which increased the prices of commodities. The North further isolated the defeated confederates, stifling output and foreign trade. The increased cash flow, reduced production, and diminished foreign trade resulted in unprecedented inflation. As illustrated in Figure 2, the price of shoes spiked over the course of the civil war. A year after the war started, prices had more than doubled. Between 1863 and 1865, prices continued to rise extraordinarily. When the war ended, the Confederate currency was worthless. The populace had begun engaging in barter trade or even using Union currency to purchase commodities.

Figure 2

The prices of shoes during the War.

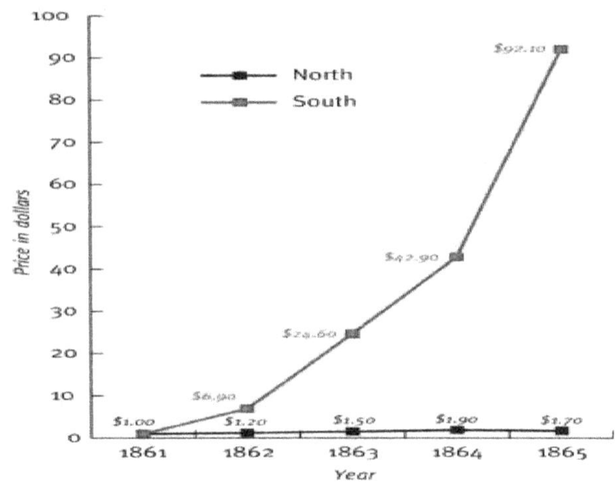

Source:

While the Confederate government mismanaged the inflation crisis, partly because of the economy's structure, the Union economy seemed to have reinvented itself. The Union economy expanded and improved during the war. The Union government introduced a raft of measures to win the war and stabilize the economy. The confederate government, before the war, had adopted a constitution that emphasized the autonomy of the different member states (Lerner, 1955). The institution of slavery was also unequivocally protected.

Conversely, the Union government adopted Acts such as the National Banking Act, Homestead Act, and the Railroad Act (Lerner, 1955). The Acts revolutionized tax, land, education, and financial systems. The National Banking Act embraced a national currency that banks backed. This way, the Union could effectively fund the war through government bonds, new taxes, and printing money. The Confederate financed the war by printing money, contributions such as horses and food, bonds, and taxes.

Figure 3

How the North and the South financed the War.

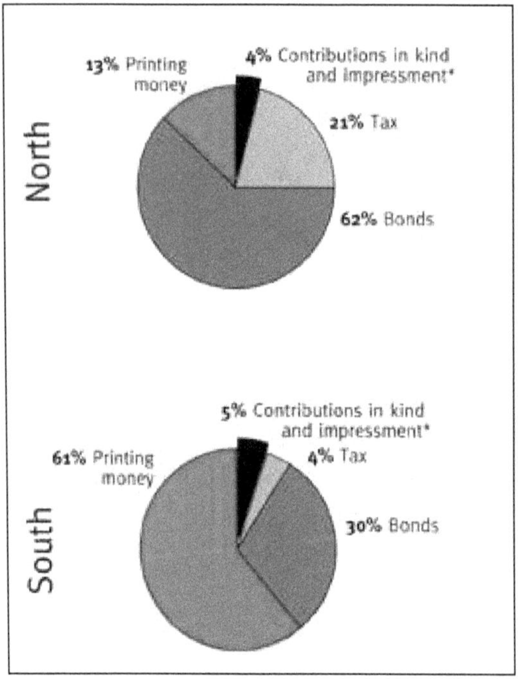

Source: Doyle (2001).

Inflation happens all over the world. How a government handles it is what makes the difference. The US Civil War (1861-1865) gives a unique case study of inflation and hyperinflation. The Confederate government did not only lose the war but also ended up with a crippled economy. Both opponents were formidable, and it was expected that they would have similar approaches to fund the war as the decision-makers had worked together in the past. However, this was not the case. The Union government pursued a long-term strategy, introducing taxes on previously zero-rated commodities, licenses, and income. Government credibility paved the way for a dynamic bond market. The union further slashed non-interest-bearing notes that became instrumental in stifling inflation.

On the other hand, the Confederate government adopted a more short-term approach. The regime relied heavily on non-interest-bearing notes. Taxes introduced by the Southerners were unpopular among the masses, making it challenging to collect. In a bid to mask the unpopular taxes, the Confederacy put more emphasis on printing money and bonds. The majority of the banks in the South encouraged speculation by being lenient. The banks issued reckless loans to customers. In the end, the currency became redundant and was declared worthless. As a result, inflation was a significant problem throughout the war, eventually leading to a total collapse of the southern economy.

A Short message from the Author:

Hey, are you enjoying the book? I'd love to hear your thoughts!

Many readers do not know how hard reviews are to come by, and how much they help an author.

I would be incredibly thankful if you could take just 60 seconds to write a brief review on Amazon, even if it's just a few sentences!

Thank you for taking the time to share your thoughts!

Your review will genuinely make a difference for me and help gain exposure for my work.

Weimar Republic Hyperinflation

Another significant example of hyperinflation was during the early 1920s in the Weimar Republic (Germany). In the era following the end of World War I, Germany witnessed its worst hyperinflation in history. For several months, citizens fought price inflation so bad that entire people's life savings were reduced to the cost of an apple. The state`s strategy of financing the war by borrowing heavily and printing vast amounts of unsupported currency started the inflationary spiral. Germany suffered the loss of resources and reparations as mandated by the Treaty of Versailles and political conflict.

During World War I, the supply of German currency had increased fourfold. By 1923, it had risen by billions. Between 1914 and 1923, the German currency fell from around four marks to the USD to one trillion marks to 1 USD, as shown in Figure 1 (Amadeo, 2020). Initially, the government`s fiscal policy lowered the cost of exports had increased economic growth. After the war, the Allied Forces mandated

Germany to pay 132 billion marks in war compensations. Production declined in Germany, causing a shortage of commodities. Because of increased money circulation, the prices of essential commodities doubled every four days. In 1923, the inflation rate was 20.9% a day (Amadeo, 2020). It eroded the cash savings of the middle class and caused foreign exchange rates to rise steeply, disrupting commercial activity. By November, the German economy had collapsed completely. Foreign loans and the issuing of a completely new currency called the Rentenmark eventually reinstated confidence and ended the crisis (The Weimar Republic, 2021).

Figure 1. Value of German currency against the US Dollar

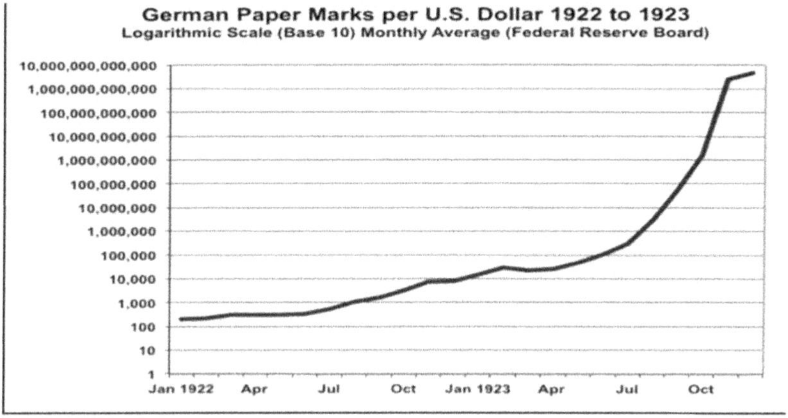

(Source: Economics Help, 2019)

Background

There are various reasons why Germany entered hyperinflation in the early 1920s. One of the primary reasons is the elimination of goods in the international economy. Before World War I, the global monetary structure was on the gold standard, with the value of major currencies fixed to gold. The Weimar Republic got rid of the gold standard at the onset of the war in 1914 to provide additional financial flexibility during the crisis. Before the war, a third of the banknotes issued were backed by gold as per the central bank`s regulations, limiting the money supply.

However, when Germany eliminated the gold standard, the amount of paper money increased considerably, from 2 billion marks in 1913 to 45 billion in 1919, ushering in inflation. During World War I, the cost of living increased threefold.

Another factor that led up to the inflation was the Treaty of Versailles. Under the agreement, the Weimar Republic lost a lot of population and territory. The country was forced to pay considerable reparations, estimated at 6.6 billion pounds. Germany was mandated to pay annual installments of 100 million pounds (Pettinger, 2021). However, collecting this money proved to be a continuous struggle for the state and undermined the currency.

Political instability also played a pivotal role in facilitating hyperinflation. After World War I, Germany experienced close to 400 political murders between 1919 and 1922 (Amadeo, 2020). This escalated political risk and facilitated surging inflation.

As World War I came to an end, Germany entered a period of economic crisis. In November 1918, masses of Germans took control of Germany`s cities, angry at the living conditions and demanding an end to the war (Haffert, Redeker & Rommel, 2019). They toppled Kaiser Wilhelm II`s monarchy. When millions of German soldiers returned from the Western Front, they joined an ever-increasing class of unemployed citizens in the country. Some turned into troops for the revolutionary far left, some supporting the new liberal government, and some joining the far right. In February 1919, more than one million Germans were unemployed, and the number continued to escalate.

The nation experienced an escalation in street violence as the revolutionary and the counter-revolutionary factions clashed. In addition to the internal disputes, the country was severely affected by the 1919 Treaty of Versailles that mandated it to pay an unprecedented amount of war debt (Haffert, Redeker & Rommel, 2019). Germany was to pay reparations equivalent to half a trillion USD to the allies. As a result, products, livestock, and raw resources like iron and coal started to be confiscated from Germany as compensation. As a response to the loss of physical and financial resources, the Weimar government constantly printed banknotes with nothing to back them. This approach started to devalue the German currency. After making its first repayments, the value of the German currency declined drastically, ushering in hyperinflation. In February 1922, 160 German marks equaled one USD, and by November 1923, the value had depreciated to 4,200,000,000,000 German marks to one USD (Amadeo, 2020).

First Signs of Hyperinflation

The journey from inflation to hyperinflation accelerated in 1921. In July 1921, Germany experienced a 505% increase in official food prices. Between 1914 and 1922, egg prices increased 180x, while a liter of milk increased from 7 marks in April 1922 to 26 marks in September 1922. In July 1922, prices increased by 50% per month (*Lessons from the past*, 2021). In 1923, prices were rising every few hours.

Barter became a prevalent method of trade, using products such as brass and fuel. For instance, a movie ticket could be traded for a lump of coal (*Lessons from the past*, 2021). Similarly, there were narratives of individuals ordering meals in hotels and being charged more when the bill came. During this period, the German currency collapsed as its supply rose drastically. Between November 1918 and November 1923, the currency value fell from 7.4 Marks per USD to 2.5 trillion Marks per USD (*Lessons from the past*, 2021).

Hyperinflation Years

At the start of August 1921, Germany started purchasing foreign currency with its devalued Mark currency. However, the move only increased the rate of breakdown in the value of the Mark. In early 1921, the German currency stabilized at around 320 marks per USD (Lessons from the *past*, 2021). Global reparations conferences complemented this. However, these conferences failed to establish a workable solution, causing inflation to become hyperinflation as the German currency fell to 8,000 Marks per USD in December 1922, as depicted in Figure 2 (Salemi, n.d). The result was the currency losing its real money balance index, as shown in Figure 2. The real money balance below is an indication of the quantity of goods and services in the economy.

Figure 2. Fall of the real money balance and an increase in inflation.

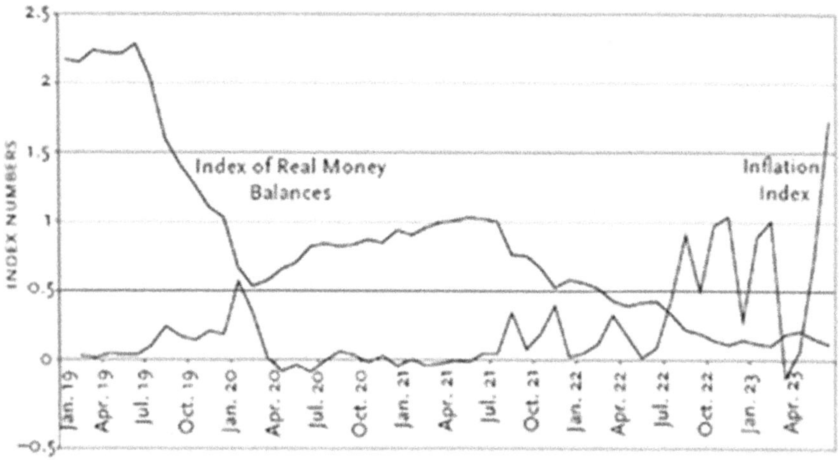

Source: (Econlib)

In January 1923, the Mark was further weakened by the French occupation of the Ruhr in reaction to non-payment of reparations. French and Belgian soldiers occupied the Ruhr and the industrial region of Germany in the Ruhr valley. This was to ensure that the nation paid reparations with commodities like coal since the Mark was worthless (Salemi, n.d). The decrease in state revenue caused further strain on state finances, encouraging the German government to print more currency to continue paying off its reparations, sparking off hyperinflation.

We can follow the hyperinflation using banknote denominations. Immediately after the occupation of the Ruhr in 1923, the 100,000- and 1-million-mark notes were printed. By July the same year, a 50-million mark was issued, and by September, a 500-million note had been issued. In October, the entire value of banknotes in circulation amounted to 2,490,833,908,038,000,000 marks (Hanke, 2007). By November, the central bank printed a 100-million-mark note, marking the peak of hyperinflation. Throughout the hyperinflation era, the printers worked day and night.

Consequently, the German currency became worthless. The hyperinflation continued because of a lack of political will to stop it. The fear of extreme poverty caused higher unemployment and increased political conflict. In October 1922, share prices hit rock bottom as the stock market had declined by 97% from its 1913 level (Hanke, 2007).

As the economy collapsed, Germany started to fall apart. Riots and theft broke out around the nation, with unemployment rising to over 24% in October 1923 (Hanke, 2007). Revolts against central authority erupted in Bavaria and Saxony, leading to the launch of separate currencies by cities that threatened the country's long-term existence. The existential danger to the German state eventually stimulated politicians to act. In October 1923, an enabling law was enacted, allowing the government to legislate without Reichstag`s permission, making Germany a temporary dictatorship. On 17th October 1923, a new central bank called the Rentenbank was established (Hanke, 2007). In November, they introduced a new currency at an exchange rate of 1-trillion old paper marks to one new Rentenmark. They halted the printing of old Marks and controlled the supply of the new currency and state expenditures. By September 1924, the country had a stable currency, ushering in the end of the hyperinflation.

Consumer Behavior during Hyperinflation

The hyperinflation significantly lowered the quality of life for Germans since most of them previously worked stable jobs in factories. It led to food shortages, rioting, poverty, and political instability. It intensified corruption, tax evasion, currency speculation, and anti-foreign lobbying. The exponential rise in prices made it hard for ordinary people to acquire essential commodities, such as bread and meat. There are many instances of Germans rushing to the bakery during their lunch breaks because their money would depreciate by the end of the day to a point where they could not afford essential commodities (Goodell, 2018). By September 1923, Germans required enormous amounts of paper money for essential goods. It was a common occurrence to see people carrying buckets or wheelbarrows full of banknotes. Banknotes became worthless to the point that some Germans started using them as wall papers and as toilet paper (Goodell, 2018).

Figure 3. A German Carrying Stacks of Money with a Wheelbarrow

Source: (Keripardon, 2013)

The hyperinflation led to a significant redistribution of wealth in Germany. Those dependent on fixed salaries or pensions witnessed a collapse in income, and those with local savings lost everything. At the same time, rents fell close to zero, diminishing the income of landlords. Urban centers starved as farmers refused to accept paper currency in payment and deferred selling their produce, expecting better prices and causing disputes between cities and the nation. Two million individuals emigrated from towns and cities to the countryside during the inflationary era.

Hyperinflation led to an enormous trade in physical assets. At the start of the hyperinflation, many foreigners took advantage of the collapse of the German Mark to purchase German goods in foreign currency. The middle class was mandated to dispose of their possessions when incomes collapsed. However, any individual with debt benefitted as debts were inflated to nothing. For instance, a German landowner who took a loan to buy a property in March 1922 could manage to repay it during the autumn with the sale of less than half a carrot (*Lessons from the past*, 2021). Similarly, the government benefitted since its debts were inflated away.

The Deleveraging

The hyperinflation era continued until 1924, when the coalition government introduced a new temporary currency, renegotiated debt payment to the Allies, and secured new American loans to fund state institutions (*Lessons from the past*, 2021). After introducing the new currency, the Rentenmark, to replace the worthless Reichsbank marks in November 1923, prices in the new currency across Germany remained stable. The move to introduce a new currency was seen as a miracle by Germans as previous intervention efforts only led to more inflation. The new currency was issued at a fixed amount and was backed by physical assets like agricultural land and industrial assets. In August 1923, Karl Helfferich suggested introducing a new currency backed by mortgage bonds indexed to market prices of rye grain (*Lessons from the past*, 2021). However, the proposal was rejected because of the fluctuating cost of rye with the German currency. Then, the agricultural ministry suggested a different proposal that substituted gold for rye. Gold could be traded with a new currency, the Rentenmark, backed by bonds connected to the market prices of gold. Gold bonds were made at a rate of 2,790 gold Marks per kilogram of gold. Here, the new currency was not redeemable in gold but only indexed to the gold bonds. The Rentemark proposal was implemented into the monetary reforms of October 1923 that established a new bank called the Rentebank (*Lessons from the past*, 2021).

From November 1923, the old central bank, the Reichsbank, was not permitted to discount any government treasury bills, thus stopping the printing of paper marks. The discounting of commercial trade bills was allowed, and the amount of Rentenmarks increased. However, the printing of the Rentenmark was firmly regulated to adhere to existing commercial and state transactions. The new central bank denied credit to the state and speculators who could not borrow Rentenmarks since Rentenmarks were not legal tender. By the end of November, there were 500 million Rentenmarks in circulation, which grew to 1000 million by the start of 1924 and 1800 million in July 1924 (*Hyperinflation in Weimar*, n.d).

Meanwhile, the old currency remained in circulation. By July 1924, the old German Mark has increased to 1211 quintillion and continued to decline in value to one-third of their conversion value in

Rentenmarks. In August 1924, a new monetary law allowed the exchange of the old 1 trillion Mark notes for one Rentenmark (*Hyperinflation in Weimar*, n.d).

Ultimately, some of the debts were restored to moderately reimburse those who had been creditors. In 1925, an order restored some mortgages at 25% of the face value of the new currency if they were held for more than four years. At the same time, some government bonds were restored at 2% of face value after reparations were made (*Hyperinflation in Weimar*, n.d). Here, the restoration of several debts, combined with the recommencement of effective taxation in the crippling economy, prompted a wave of company bankruptcies.

One of the most significant stabilization factors during hyperinflation is revaluation, which involves raising the exchange rate of one currency against other currencies. It also entails the restoration of the value of a currency depreciated by inflation. The German government had the option of either enacting a revaluation law to address the hyperinflation rapidly or to address sprawling and political violence on the streets. The state asserted that the interests of creditors and debtors had to be just and balanced. As such, neither the living standard price index nor the share price index were deemed viable inflation measures. The conversion relation to the dollar index and wholesale price index was better used as a gauge. Here, the government adhered to market-orientated reasoning that the dollar and wholesale price indexes would offer the actual price level during the high inflation and hyperinflation era. The revaluation was grounded on the exchange rate between the Mark and the USD.

Despite the end of the inflation, Germany`s nightmare had only just begun. Although the hyperinflation did not usher Hitler to power, it provided a breeding ground for extremism. It would be ten years before Hitler came to power, but many scholars assert that hyperinflation nurtured the seed of Nazism.

North Korea Hyperinflation

In a meeting with the International Monetary Fund (IMF) delegates in 1997, North Korean representatives provided some data that showed that the GDP of their country had fallen by half in the preceding four years and that the condition of the economy were deteriorating. North Korea's request to join the IMF has never been approved because of the nation's political hurdles. The North Korean government has no practice releasing statistics often, and most of the economic data regarding the country has been grounded on third-party estimates.

For years, the North Korean economy had suffered due to low manufacturing production. In recent years, the country's crippling economy had been exacerbated by harsh, international economic sanctions because of North Korea's regime and nuclear programs (He, 2017). With the death of the supreme leader Kim Jong-Il in 2011, the international community hoped that his successor would launch constructive economic and political reforms. However, one year after taking power, the new leader had not delivered his promised economic reforms, and the country's economy continued to crumble. In the last decade, North Korea has faced international criticism because of its domestic nuclear program. However, this distracted the world from the nation's economic woes at the start of the decade.

For years, the North Korean currency, the Won, had been officially secured by the USD. Exchange controls and many connected regulations and punitive penalties have rendered the won inconvertible. A robust black market for foreign currency has risen in the country (Powell, 2009). This has resulted in severe inflationary consequences.

Background

The pertinent question is, how can hyperinflation happen in an economy where the government controls almost every aspect of the nation, from prices of goods to local and foreign trade? Ordinary individuals in North Korea are allocated essential supplies of food, health care, housing, and education for free but in limited quantities. Since the late 1990s, after an era of economic inaction and natural calamities that led to famine, North Korea relaxed government controls by allowing private business on a small scale while looking for a Stalinist-styled financial system. Numerous joint ventures with overseas companies from South Korea and other nations developed in North Korea in recent years. Tourism has become a crucial source of foreign exchange. Consequently, a shadow economy has been growing in the nation.

A state can exercise monetary policy as long as the nation's household sector holds a considerable amount of money. And this is what occurred in North Korea at the start of the 21st century. Just like South Korea, North Korea has used a currency system since the 1940s. From the 1940s, the nation has experienced four primary currency reforms in 1959, 1979, 1992, and 2009. In each reform, old notes were withdrawn quickly, and new notes with larger denominations were issued (Powell, 2009). The 1959 and 2009 reforms included redenomination as new notes replaced old notes at a rate of 100 to 1. As a result, these forms mandated the cancelation of excess currency held by its citizens and caused an expansionary monetary policy. Money stock in the country has been expanding at a faster rate than inhibited inflation.

In the late 1900s, as new international revenues started to flow into North Korea, the state attempted to rebuild the image of a socialist economy. In 2000, North Koreans held around $964 million in foreign exchange, with an average of $186 per household, of which 60% was in USD, and the rest was primarily in Chinese Renminbi (Powell, 2009). The foreign exchange reserves allowed the country to import luxury commodities or save money with stable value. There are stores in North Korea where one could only purchase using foreign currency like the USD, the Chinese Renminbi, and the Japanese Yen. The exchange rates on the black market differed significantly from the state's rates (Powell, 2009).

First Sign of Hyperinflation

However, these efforts mainly took the form of initiatives intended to strengthen central planning. In 2002, the state suddenly instituted a wide range of economic measures. Here, the government downsized official ration guarantees, increased wages and consumption prices drastically, and dramatically slashed the official exchange rate with the USD (Eberstadt, 2010). As a result, these initiatives increased the sanctioned function of currency and markets. In 2003, the North Korean regime undertook a public bond for an unstipulated amount. The bonds had a ten-year maturity with no fixed interest rate (Eberstadt, 2010). Bondholders were compensated with a lottery-grounded cash prize.

However, these economic measures failed to work as intended. Consequently, there was a lot of new money circulating in the economy, generating significant inflation. By November 2009, the North Korean won's black-market value in dollars was hardly 5% of the level when the 2002 measures were implemented, a depreciation averaging over 3% per month (Eberstadt, 2010). Here, the North Korean government attempted to tackle these problems with a single swift blow with the currency reform of 2009.

Hyperinflation Years

In November 2009, the North Korean government instituted a currency reform. There were two main reasons for the 2009 currency reform. First, North Korea was experiencing a widening gap between the rich and the poor due to relatively free markets (Powell, 2009). The state felt that the currency change would reduce inequality by making a broad swath of its population poorer. However, the gap continued to persist since the most prominent and wealthiest merchants, including state-owned companies, had long swapped the North Korean won and instead held the Chinese Yuan and the USD as a store of value. The black market value of the Won has been decreasing for years, and North Korean inflation has been accelerating.

Secondly, the government wanted control of the economy (Powell, 2009). The state had initially allowed the black market to grow out of desperation, but it had expanded to a point where the government felt threatened. Small merchants and black markets existed outside state control, and the regime could not allow this to continue. Hence, the reform was intended to deal a significant blow to black markets and enable the state to tighten its control of the economy.

The 2009 currency reform was a catastrophic initiative for North Korea. The state attempted to handle runaway inflation by instituting a deceptive currency initiative (He, 2017). In reality, the reform was a currency redenomination program that arbitrarily eliminated two zeros off every note. The residents were given less than two weeks to exchange all their won for new currency notes. The state set limits on the amount of won a household could exchange for new won. In December 2009, the government established the redenomination at a rate of 1 new note for 100 old notes (He, 2017). There were maximum restrictions for each household in the exchange.

The state extended upper limits to individuals` bank deposits. For those who had saved a lot of Won, the reform acted as an effective wealth tax initiative. Individuals with savings of more than the maximum allowed for exchange were at risk of losing their savings.

The government did not make a public announcement about the 2009 currency reform. Instead, it used internal channels, including cable radio and loudspeakers in local communities, to notify the people about the currency conversion. The state asserted that the purpose of the currency reform was to prevent inflation, limit the black markets, and readjust the economic system. However, this caused widespread panic and chaos in North Korea. As a result, people rushed to rural areas to purchase rice and corn, and others flooded the black market to buy foreign currency, which plummeted the Won, as shown in Figure 1. Individuals holding foreign currency lined at the doors of stores that sold goods in foreign exchange.

Figure 1. *The price of rice*

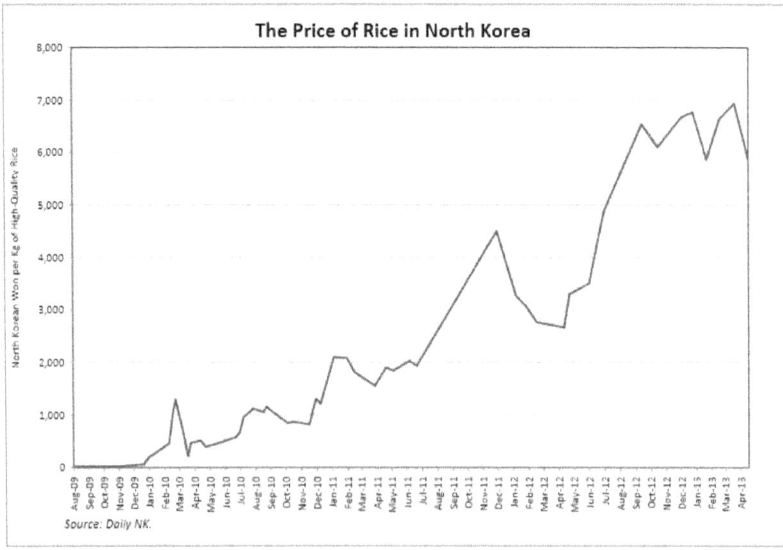

Source: (Hanke, S. (2013)

The state had to delay the currency conversion for a day, and it closed all stores and department stores for three days. It sent armed police to the streets to maintain order in cities. In February 2010, the state decided to relax the limitations to prevent more protests and revolts from the residents (He, 2017). Owing to redenomination, the value of the Won against the dollar collapsed, and the price of essential commodities skyrocketed. Within two months, prices of rice and corn soared in the countryside. Rice prices doubled within the first two weeks of December. As the Won plunged, inflation surged. North Korea officially entered hyperinflation in December 2009 as inflation exceeded 50% per month. The hyperinflation reached its peak in March 2010, when the monthly inflation rate reached 926%. At the same time, prices rose 28.5 times between December 2009 and March 2010 (He, 2017).

Figure 2. *The fall of the won.*

Source: (Hanke, S. (2013)

In March 2010, the North Korean government tried to stop inflation but bore little success. Hyperinflation gradually continued to affect the nation, as depicted in Figure 3. Black market exchange rates remained considerably higher than the state's rates. Due to the country's nuclear program, its trade flows were increasingly restricted by the United Nations. Consequently, North Korea remained isolated, which increased its foreign exchange scarcity, severely affecting its economy. To address the budget deficit that emerged because of a stagnant economy and isolation from the global economy, North Korea embarked on a loose monetary policy to sustain its economy. It was not until January 2011 that North Korea's hyperinflation came to an end (Hanke, 2013).

Figure 3. *Monthly inflation rate*

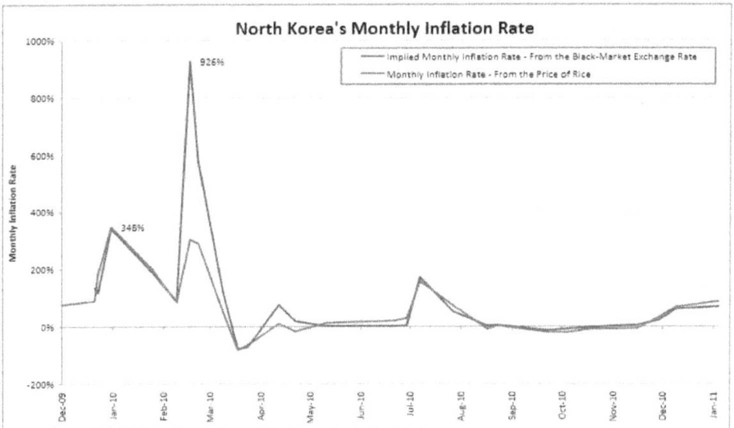

Source: (Hanke, 2013)

Consumer Impact

The reform sparked a panic in the country's underground markets for goods and services. The black markets, which emerged out of necessity during the famine of the 1990s, mainly existed to counteract shortages that emerged because of government control of agriculture

(Hanke, 2013). According to the United Nations, almost half of the food consumed by North Koreans were bought in these black markets. Due to the bungled currency reform, the demand for hard currency (USD and Chinese Yuan) skyrocketed as more and more traders in the black markets required transactions to occur in hard cash. Consequently, the value of the won tumbled on the black market. During the hyperinflation era, many North Koreans started to exchange their depreciating won for more stable foreign currencies like the USD and the Chinese Yuan to preserve their savings and purchasing power.

The Deleveraging

In 2011, Kim Jong-un assumed power to inherit an economy that looked like a disaster. The new leader instantaneously instituted policies to stabilize the currency, prices, and the entire economy. Instead of enacting another devastating currency reform, the new leader embarked on a two-pronged monetary approach. First, he changed the domestic monetary policy to shadow the USD on the black market (Hanke, 2013). The Won/USD exchange rate stability became the Nation's primary monetary goal. Second, the government introduced a policy of benign neglect that facilitated the spontaneous dollarization of the North Korean economy (Hanke, 2013). As a result, the Chinese Yuan and the USD became the economy's currency in practice, replacing the KPW.

The new leader also allowed the black market economy to thrive. He made it possible for vast parts of the economy to privatize impulsively. As the effects of the international sanctions started to affect North Korea, the state developed various squeeze-avoidance strategies.

North Korea embarked on a dollarization approach to address the hyperinflation, as the method has been used by other inflation-ravaged nations, like Zimbabwe and Venezuela. (In June *2008, Zimbabwe's hyperinflation reached a yearly rate of 89.7 sextillion percent (Hanke, 2013). As a result, the people abandoned the Zimbabwe dollar and exclusively utilized the USD and other stable currencies, like the South African Rand and the Mozambican metical. Zimbabwe's hyperinflation stopped instantaneously, and the inflation rates returned to single digits. Due to the dollarization of the economy, Zimbabwe's government was mandated to accept the end of the Zimbabwe dollar and legitimately dollarize the economy).*

Since 2011, the Chinese Yuan and the USD have been used more widely in North Korea than the Won. Based on recent statistics, North Korean markets along the Chinese border conduct about 80% of their transactions in the Chinese Yuan (Hanke, 2013). Similarly, merchants inside the country conducted about 50% of their transactions in USD. This trend was a result of spontaneous dollarization. The practice of dumping the local currency in favor of stable foreign currency became widespread despite the government criminalizing the circulation of foreign currencies on the black markets.

An excellent example is Kaesong Industrial Complex, which was jointly owned by North and South Korea (Hanke, 2013). Employees utilized a South Korean marshmallow cookie treat, called the ChocoPie, as an unofficial currency within the complex. The USD exchange rate for a ChocoPie reached close to $10 in Kaesong before the administration stopped providing its employees their bonuses in ChocoPies (Hanke, 2013).

Although the North Korean government did not allow foreign currency, spontaneous dollarization was and is a reality, especially along the Chinese border. There were calls for North Korea to Yuan-ize its economy since China accounts for more than 50% of North Korea's foreign trade and a vast share of its foreign direct investment (Hanke, 2013). Since the mid-2000s, China has continued to increase its trade and investments in North Korea, especially along the border. China is also working to build infrastructure, such as bridges, power links, and high-speed rail lines in the Northeast (Hanke, 2013). Therefore, the official adoption of the Yuan by North Korea would end the inflation woes and facilitate increased trade with China and neighboring nations.

Consequently, such action would counter the current US policy stance against North Korea. However, North Korea has shown it is not affected by the sanctions placed by the international community since it is willing to let its people starve while it pursues nuclear capabilities. For China, yuan-ization and economic reforms in North Korea would result in a much less combative and dangerous neighbor. This is why China is pushing for increased integration of China's Northeast region and North Korea.

Kim Jong-un's spontaneous dollarization and privatization strategies have worked in reducing inflation and stimulating the North Korean economy. Today, the won has stabilized against other currencies in the foreign exchange since 2012. Additionally, the prices of essential commodities, such as rice, have been stable since 2012. This shows that North Korea is not haunted by inflation anymore. Today, the black market has become the new normal. Kim Jong-Un's government has little choice but to continue its fledgling efforts at economic reforms that reflect market realities on the ground or risk losing its grip on power (Pearson, 2015).

Inflation in Ancient Rome

Regarded as one of the strongest empires in history, Rome ruled a quarter of the world at its peak. For three centuries, Rome stood as an indestructible force, with its large armies, stellar governance, and trade surpluses playing a central role in its growth. Therefore, its fall had a resounding impact on global economics, given that the empire was a critical trading partner with other nations. Today the alphabet, calendar, architecture, and languages are highly influenced by the Romans. Experts regard Rome's size and consequent administrative costs as one of the primary reasons for its downfall. Others consider rampant corruption, moral decay, and constant attacks from German barbarians as contributing factors to Rome's downfall. However, there is the economic aspect with taxation, trade, and currency exchange taking center stage. This chapter looks into the great inflation in ancient Rome as one of the primary contributing factors to its downfall.

Background

The Roman Empire enjoyed prosperity and expansion for over three centuries. The growth in size, armies, and economic development played a pivotal role in its establishment. Consequently, it was critical in the empire's downfall, given that when the expansion reached optimum levels, trade reduced, and scarcity of resources kicked in (Butcher, 2015). Inflation in the Roman Empire was subject to several elements, including fluctuations in labor supply and availability of precious metals. The empire's reliance on slave labor had critical implications when it slowed down conquests towards the third century.

The rise of the rival Germanic Barbarians, whose primary aim was freeing slaves, led to a reduced labor supply. Warfare and technological advancement were also central aspects affecting the Empire's ability to maintain its currency circulation and consequent economic stability (Bhardwaj, 2020). These elements had critical implications on pricing and later led to hyperinflation in the region.

It is vital to point out that the Roman Empire anchored its economy on a system of multiple currencies. They borrowed this system from the Greeks, with weights and measures playing a central role in currency valuation. The silver coins, also known as the Denarius, and gold coins, known as Aureus, were the primary currencies. Additionally, the empire used copper and bronze columns with less value and limited centralization when minting. According to Butcher (2015), the army was responsible for the minting of coins and consequent circulation. The soldiers were incentivized to increase their salaries with additional money supply. During the first and second centuries, the empire enjoyed relative peace and prosperity, which were critical for economic stability (Horesh, 2020). However, infighting, corruption, and a breakdown in moral values paved the way for the catastrophe that was about to befall the Roman empire.

Figure 1. *Rome's Denarius silver coins*

Source: (Butcher, 2015).

In the years leading to inflation, the Roman Empire experienced several notable events. Between 160 AD to 185 AD, the empire suffered one of the worst plagues in history, that significantly reduced its population size. Then came the frequent usurpations and the auction of the imperial seat in 193 AD (Horesh, 2020). These events had critical implications on political stability, which had ripple effects on the empire's agricultural economy and trade. As mentioned earlier, military setbacks, especially those orchestrated by Barbarian invasions, further weakened the kingdom limiting its conquests and ability to gain access to resources. There were also rising administrative costs, riots from citizens, and increased bread-dole costs, which further complicated the situation. These events led to the emperor's decision to debase the currency to increase currency volume. This was despite the loss of gold and silver from mines and conquests (Horesh, 2020). The currency debasement was the principal cause of inflation as the leaders looked to continue appeasing the armies, urban population and tackle fiscal deficits.

The First Signs

From 160 to 274 AD, the empire reduced its gold and silver coins significantly. The lack of the required raw materials coupled with the empire's political, social, and economic situation prompted its leaders to reduce the minting costs by reducing the purity of the currency coins. During this period, the silver coin decreased in purity from 95% to 2% (Andreu & Blanco-Pérez, 2019). With the drastic reduction came an increased circulation of worthless coins in the economy. Additionally, the government raised taxes to increase revenue, increasing the available revenue the government could spend. In retrospect, these aspects increased the amount of wealth held by the elite while increasingly oppressing the poor. This transfer of wealth and an increase in coins of poorer quality into the economy had adverse implications on prosperity (Stange, 2021). It meant that people paid more for the same products. These were the early signs of runaway inflation whereby more coins of poor quality caused higher costs for purchasing goods.

Figure 2. *The debasement of the silver coins 64AD to 288AD*

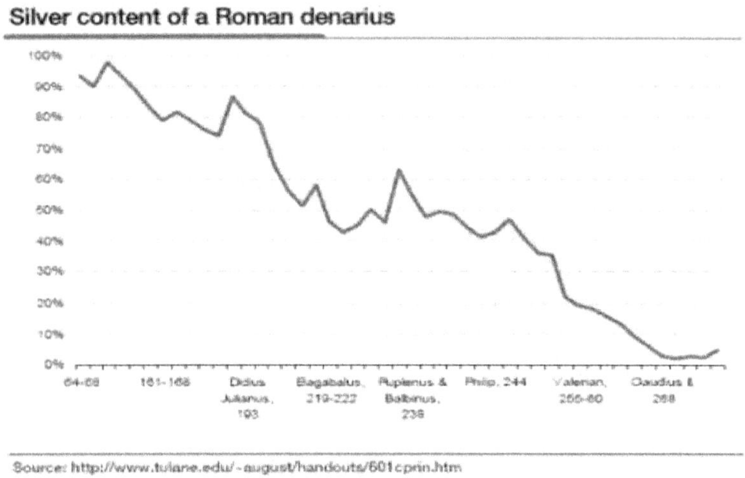

Source: (Stange, 2021).

Runaway inflation was also evident with the increase in wages and salaries. People and especially the soldiers, demanded more, given that the quality and value of the coins were decreasing. In 210 AD, Emperor Caracalla raised the soldiers' wages by 50% (Andreu & Blanco-Pérez, 2019). By 274 AD, only Barbarian mercenaries were paid using gold coins (whose purity was not debased like silver coins). Another critical problem was ineffective price controls, which further drove the economy into a freefall. Black market activity increased significantly, with barter taking center stage as the silver coins continued becoming worthless. Despite the emperors' attempts to salvage the situation,

Rome's toxic inflation cycle continued. For example, in 301 AD, Diocletian introduced a new coin equal to 50 Denarii (Stange, 2021). However, within a decade, the coin's value had plummeted, and it was now equal to 100 Denarii.

The Great Inflation Years

Runaway inflation played a significant role in Rome's downfall. The inflation started around 160 AD, and from then onward, it was an economic and political free fall. It is plausible to claim that these were the inflation years; they were characterized by rampant poverty for the lower classes and increasing wealth for the ruling elite. It is vital to point out that while the silver coin purity decreased drastically, gold coin purity remained strong. Despite using the gold coins to pay Barbarian mercenaries, the ruling elite hoarded gold coins keeping them away from ordinary citizens (Stange, 2021). They, therefore, lived opulent lifestyles while the ordinary citizens continued bearing the burden of hardships.

Additionally, during this period, the ruling elite moved away from exchanging goods through barter trade and adopting the currency system. Earlier, they exchanged goods in the form of land, horses, and slaves.

Their adoption of the currency system further increased money circulation in the economy, thereby fostering runaway inflation.

However, it is vital to indicate that loyalty to the emperor slowed the inflation process and made it last centuries. Despite the reduction in the purity of the silver coin, ordinary citizens trusted the government. They, therefore, did not devalue the currency as fast as the quality of the coins declined; this played a crucial role in prolonging the inflationary period and hindering the ability to salvage the situation. During the inflationary period, increased taxation was the order of the day. The government looked to continue with its development programs while supporting its vast army and ever-rising administrative costs. There was also a decline in resources due to an inability to expand the empire further (Parsons, 2010). In addition, there was significant political instability whereby leadership was free for all. The strong usurped the throne, killing leaders and eliminating the element of legitimacy when it came to leadership. Each emperor came with different tactics for tackling inflation, with many achieving little, if any. The deteriorating leadership eventually fueled hyperinflation rates with the devaluation of the currency reaching 1000% by the time Rome crumbled (Parsons, 2010).

Figure 3. *The debasement of Rome's currency system owing to a scarcity of resources*

Figure 1: Metallic content of Roman coins, 160-280 AD

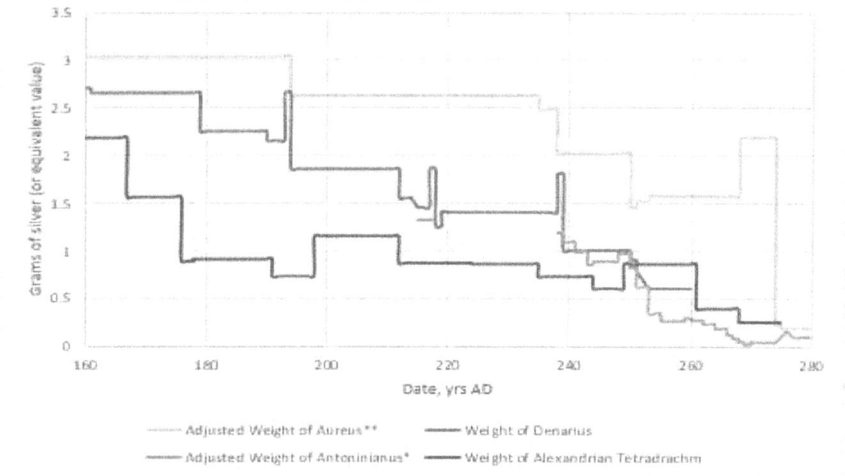

Source: (Parsons, 2010)

The inflationary years had a lasting implication on Rome's trade. Worthless currency, soaring taxes, and a significant increase in the price of goods and services led to the dissolution of the empire's economy (Heather, 2018). With trade decreasing at an alarming rate, the economy became paralyzed, and the empire began collapsing. With no meaningful medium of exchange, barter was the primary form of trade. By the 3rd century, decades of high inflation had reduced Rome to a lame duck, barely resembling the strong empire it was before. Many dove into the black market since engaging in free trade became a dangerous activity.

Trade networks disintegrated, and the exchange of goods and services remained local. Constant civil wars and uprisings further destabilized the empire. The empire split into three states. It was a free for all, given that political instability crippled the leadership. For example, from 234 to 284 AD, there were about 50 emperors, many of whom were killed in battle, assassinated, or murdered by usurpers (Heather, 2018). Therefore, the inflationary years brought about hardships that had significant implications on the fall of the ancient Roman Empire.

Figure 4. *The decline in the silver value of Denarii fueling hyperinflation*

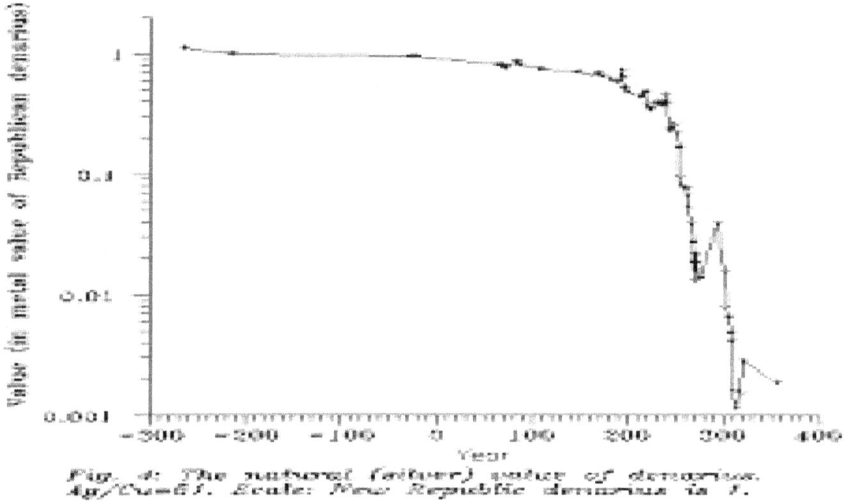

Source: (Andreu & Blanco-Pérez, 2019).

How the Common Man Fared During the Inflationary Period

As mentioned earlier, the common man suffered the most during the inflationary period. They had to deal with the rising prices of goods, limited resources, and ever-increasing taxation. The quality of life went on a sharp decline with the increase in the price of goods and services. To keep from paying more, people hoarded goods and therefore created shortages. Individuals had currency but few goods to purchase. Daily supplies such as wheat, wine, and milk also became scarce, throwing the economy into turmoil. It is important to point out is that the ruling elite felt extraordinarily little hardship during inflation. They continued increasing their wealth, especially with the gold coin's slow debasement, which was the primary medium of exchange for the ruling class (Butcher, 2015). As prosperity continued decreasing, the commoner struggled to survive, which led to a lack of trust towards the government and a consequent rise in crime.

During the inflationary period, lawlessness increased significantly. Apart from the hoarding of goods and consequent scarcity, there was the issue of government welfare programs. Bread-dole, the government's welfare program providing bread to its poorest citizens, became a tall order. Therefore, it had to do away with the program since government expenditure kept rising rapidly. This caused significant civil unrest and rioting as the common man started going hungry (Andreu & Blanco-Pérez, 2019). It led to internal strife, which had long lasting effects on the relationship between the government and its citizens.

Additionally, the disintegration of trade networks increased black market activity, which was only affordable to the wealthy. Therefore, the common man went through hardships that can only be termed as survival for the fittest. Soldiers became the gods of this era, given that they are the only ones that possessed currency. The government focused on soldiers and the ruling elite at the expense of ordinary citizens, further deteriorating Rome and its ordinary citizens.

Figure 4. *The nobles enjoyed life at the expense of ordinary citizens during the inflationary years*

Source: (He, 2017)

As indicated earlier, Rome was an agricultural economy, and once inflation hit, food production took a sharp downward turn. Large landowners would no longer export agrarian produce due to the breakdown of trade networks (Heather, 2018). They, therefore, delved into subsistence farming and developed sustainable households. Ordinary citizens started moving away from cities searching for food and security, which led to the adoption of a new system of slavery known as coloni. The common man gave away their civil rights and became half citizens owing their allegiance to large farm owners in exchange for farmlands and security. This formed the foundation of the feudal society and hereditary peasantry, which became common during the Middle Ages. It was also the beginning of self-sufficient societies, which later became a problem for the Roman Empire since they were hostile towards the tax collectors (He, 2017). Therefore, the changes brought about by the inflationary years had lifelong implications on the ordinary citizens' mannerisms and way of doing things.

The Deleveraging

Inflation in the Roman Empire remained a thorny issue until its downfall. Emperors tried salvaging the situation in many ways but to no avail. As highlighted earlier, Rome had numerous illegitimate rulers who had little knowledge of governance during this period. They, therefore, put ineffective laws and policies in place, further accelerating inflation. It is vital to point out that despite the measures put in place, the resource scarcity hindered efforts to control inflation (He, 2017). The main reason was the limited amount of silver and the consequent continuous debasement of the Denarii.

Additionally, many opted to increase government spending on armies to buy their loyalty and secure the throne. They increased taxation to increase revenue while eliminating government welfare programs. Additionally, they increased the soldier's salary to buy loyalty, thus failing to stir up economic growth. Dimitrijevic & Golubovic (2017) argue that by 275 AD, they abandoned the silver coin currency as worthless, introducing copper and bronze coins. These new currency systems did little to save the situation, and thus there was a further increase in inflation and deterioration of the economy. By that time, inflation was at 1000%, with the prices of goods and services increasing sharply.

In 284 AD, Diocletian rose to power and put in policies to counter runaway inflation. He first raised the weight of gold coins from 60 to 72 pounds to increase their value. He also introduced new currencies, introducing a silver coin equal to 50 Denarii and a bronze coin equal to 20 Denarii. However, less than a decade later, the coin's value was half the original value, meaning there was more than 100% inflation during this period.

From 312 AD, the new emperor Constantine also made several reforms to help counter inflation (He, 2017). He first introduced a new gold coin that was more debased than the previous one, helping solidify the gold standards. He also raided treasuries of other empires and took treasures from pagan temples. Constantine also introduced taxes on senator estates and merchant's capital. These elements played a pivotal role in increasing the empire's revenue. However, he faced the problem of counterfeit coins, given that by this time, the gold coin was the primary medium of exchange. Constantine accepted payment of taxes in the form of services or in-kind to limit the number of counterfeit coins circulating among soldiers and civil servants (Dimitrijevic & Golubovic, 2017). This did not last long, and inflation persisted until the fall of the Roman empire.

The Roman Empire faced hurdle after hurdle despite putting measures in place to counter inflation. The leaders had to deal with increasing administrative costs coupled with a reduction in the availability of resources. The debasement of the silver coin had long lasting implications on ordinary citizens, and currency exchange using gold coins was not a feasible idea. The elite continued to flourish at the expense of the ordinary citizens, causing erosion of liberty within the empire. People revolted against the government, creating internal strife, which did not help counter foreign invasion. Therefore, it is accurate to state that inflation crippled Rome's economy and social values, accelerating its downfall.

French Revolution Hyperinflation

When governments have been unable to continue raising taxes or borrowing funds, they have always looked at printing paper money to finance their expanding expenditures. The resulting inflations have frequently weakened the social fabric, ruined the economy, and ushered in revolutions and tyranny. France`s hyperinflation during the French Revolution is an excellent example of this. From an economic perspective, the French Revolution was a disastrous era since it ushered in the first hyperinflation in modern times. France also experienced a considerable decrease in output and severe disruption in its markets. Hyperinflation during the French Revolution left a lasting impact on world history since it led to momentous political and social changes.

Background

Before the French Revolution of 1789, France was a perfect example of mercantilism. No economic activity could occur without state approval and regulation. While the monarch controlled the economy, the royal court amassed national wealth. King Louis XVI`s military guard had 9,500 soldiers, and his civilian household had close to 4,000 individuals (Brezis & Crouzet, 1995). The king has 128 musicians, 75 religious leaders, and 198 individuals to take care of his body. The nobility and the clergy were exempt from paying taxes, mandating ordinary citizens to cater to the tax burden. In 1774, the state expenditure was 399 million livres, with tax accounting for only 373 million livres, leaving a deficit of around 27 million livres (Brezis & Crouzet, 1995). The loans and monetary expansions made by the king contributed to the eventual hyperinflation during the Revolution.

To address the problems with the state finances, the king appointed a brilliant economist, Anne-Robert-Jacques Turgot, to act as the finance minister. Turgot tried to use his authority to limit government spending and regulation, but he faced stiff opposition from privileged groups. He was eventually fired by the king in 1776 (Brezis & Crouzet, 1995). (Brezis & Crouzet, 1995).

Figure 1. *The chart on French government finances: 1789-1795.*

Expenditures, Deficit and Debt of the French Government: 1789-1795.

(current prices, millions of Livres)

Year	[1] Government Expenditures G	[2] Debt Services rB	[3] Taxes T	[4] Government Deficit G-T	[5] Debt Financing ΔB	[6] Money Financing ΔM	[7] Land Financing ΔL	[8] Total Debt B	[9] Gov. Deficit ratio of GNP G-T/Y
1789	656	230	396	260				4500	0.08
1790	657	281	160	497	-93	590			0.16
1791	823	241	234	589	-637	900	326		0.19
1792	1250	204	412	838	-200	760	278	4000	0.20
1793	3532		341	3191		2850	341		0.70
1794	3180		490	2690		2144	546		0.51
1795	16380		1416	14964		14309	655		0.12

Source: (Velde, 1992).

Subsequently, the chaos of the monarch`s finances led to the session of the Estates-Generals. This was followed by the start of the French Revolutions with the fall of Bastille in July 1789. However, the new revolutionary administration was extravagant in its spending, as shown in Figure 1. Vast amounts of money went to public works to create jobs, and 17 million livres were offered to the citizens in food subsidies. King Louis XVI faced the mammoth task of financing the budget deficit that emerged from its debts, which stood at 230 million livres in 1789 (Brezis & Crouzet, 1995). At that time, the public became reluctant to increase its debt holding, making it hard to finance France`s budget deficit by issuing further debt. The state also could not raise taxes because the citizens were convinced that they were being overtaxed. When the Third Estate entered the National Assembly after the political and social revolution, it faced the same economic predicament.

The new assembly stipulated that evading taxes was illegal and that there would be no rejection of debt. The primary recommendation to address the budgetary problem was to confiscate and sell church property. The rationale behind the confiscation of the church by the new government was to destroy a rival social authority that could check its moral and political power (Trask, 2020). It also appeased the powerful in Paris and overseas by offering a way to fund the enormous debt of the monarchy. Finally, it established a new group of landowners loyal to the state. Since the deficit was growing at an alarming rate and the sale of land could not occur in the short term, the state decided to address the problem by issuing a new financial tool, the assignats. In March 1790, the new government voted to issue a new paper currency called the **assignat**.

The government also realized that the sale of church land was not enough to get the financial results it wanted. The sale of all the properties would reduce their selling price (due to excessive supply), and France lacked enough capital to embark on large-scale purchases. As a final solution to its fiscal insolvency, the state issued a fiat paper currency (Trask, 2020). The government would finance its deficit by issuing the assignat, and after they sold the Church property, they withdrew the assignats. The assignats would be interest-bearing promissory notes secured by the church land (Trask, 2020). As a result, there was a lot of discussion about what form the assignat would take to solve the budget deficit. Some wanted assignats to become money, and some claimed that it was a political action used to manifest France`s national sovereignty. However, others opposed the introduction of the assignats based on economic principles. They asserted that the new currency would depreciate, and further depreciation would follow, leading to a financial crisis. These objections and warnings were overlooked since the state claimed that France had immense wealth in church property to provide security.

Hyperinflation Years

In December 1789, the government passed a decree to establish assignats as financial security to be exchanged for land, but not as a medium of exchange. The new currency issued in large denominations was interest-bearing but had no legal tender.

By April of that year, 400 million assignat were in circulation. In 1790, they lowered the interest rates on assignats, lowered the denominations, and made it legal tender. The Assembly sanctioned the printing of 400 million livres of paper assignats in denominations of 200, 300, and 1,000 livres, bearing three percent interest and receivable for taxes and the purchase of the national properties (Trask, 2020). In character, they were like English exchequer bills or American bills of credit. Supporters argued that the assignats would provide payments to the state creditors, offer a means for the individuals to purchase lands and properties, draw specie out of hiding, and stimulate trade and industry (Trask, 2020). As such, this opened the way to uncontrollable issues like the creation of unsound money. In the summer of 1791, France doubled its assignats to 800 million, which led to currency depreciation, rising prices, speculation, money shortages, and declining savings.

The government decided to address the problems created by inflation with more inflation. Rather than destroying the assignats received from its state properties, it reissued them in the form of smaller notes. In June 1791, the state issued another 600 million assignats and another 300 million in December. Consequently, the market value of the assignats fell by over 60% in 1792, mandating the state to issue another 600 million assignats (*France: Inflation and Revolution,* 2016). In April 1792, France declared war against Austria. Here, the government deficit increased drastically due to military spending, and repayment of debt was suspended. In 1793, France sought to finance these expenditures by floating two loans, but this initiative yielded little success (Velde & Weir, 1992). As a result, the state printed more assignats to cover its deficit, ushering in high inflation. The government also attempted to terrorize the citizens into accepting the depreciating assignat. In June 1793, the government passed the Forced Loan, which severely impacted ordinary citizens.

When inflation started getting out of control, the state put price control measures from June 1793 to December 1794. The first price controls affected grain but failed to achieve the desired results. Their failure led to the enactment of a new law in September 1793 that reduced the prices of some essential commodities. These price controls made farmers refuse to sell their produce at fixed prices, leading to a severe food shortage (*France: Inflation and Revolution,* 2016). The government reacted by forcing its officials to seize what was available and punish farmers who tried to hoard. However, the assignat still fell by 30% against gold (*France: Inflation and Revolution,* 2016).

Figure 2. *France money supply 1789-1797.*

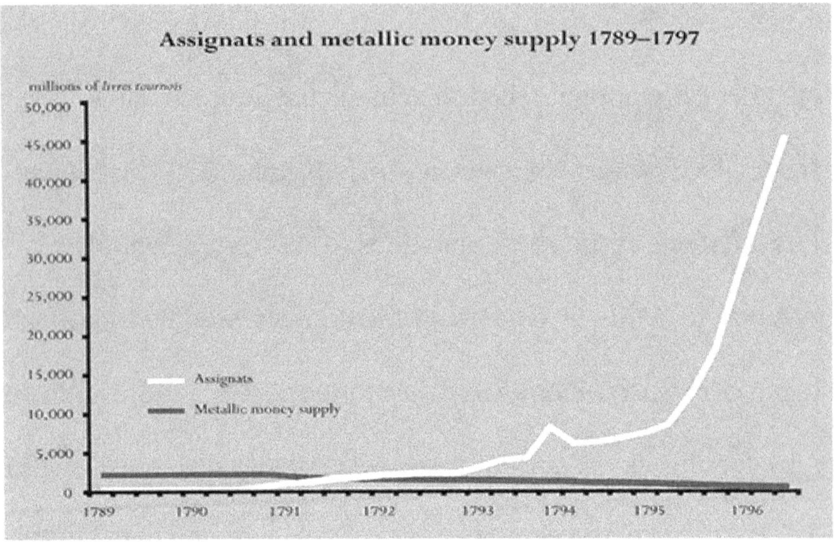

Source: (American Numismatic Society, 2016)

Figure 2 summarizes the pathway to hyperinflation. The state introduced 800 million assignats by mid-1790 despite facing a deficit. By the end of 1791, 1.5 billion assignats circulated the economy, and the purchasing power reduced by 14%. In mid-1793, there were 4.1 billion assignats in circulation, and their value declined by 60% (Trask, 2020). By the end of 1795, 19.7 billion assignats were in circulation, and the purchasing power had depreciated by 99% since the currency was introduced (Trask, 2020). Within five years, the assignats had become worth less than the paper it was printed on.

Impact to Consumers

The impacts of the monetary collapse during this period were enormous. The hyperinflation created many debtors who wanted the inflation because a depreciating assignat meant they repaid in worthless currency. On the other hand, some speculated on land, primarily former Church properties that the state had seized and sold, since their wealth rose with the inflationary increase in land value (Sargent & Velde, 1995). As money became worthless, short term fixes took precedence over long-term thinking. There was a shortage of commodities as sellers hoarded them in anticipation of higher prices in the future.

Figure 3. *Food prices during the French Revolution.*

Prices of Food during the French Revolution.

year	Prices: in Livres					Price increase %				
	Wheat Château-Goutier [1]	Rye Château-Goutier [2]	Wheat Buis [3]	Rye Romans [4]	Wheat Nat. mean [5]	Wheat Château Goutier [1]	Rye Château Goutier [2]	Wheat Buis [3]	Rye Romans [4]	Wheat Nat. mean [5]
1788	120	81	77	52	1609					
1789	126	102	109	55	2192	5.00	25.93	41.56	5.77	36.23
1790	140	112	118	45	1945	11.11	9.80	8.26	-18.18	-11.27
1791	125	103	105	63	1622	-10.71	-8.04	-11.02	40.00	-16.61
1792	156	111	122	92	2209	24.80	7.77	16.19	46.03	36.19
1793	168	112	150	108		7.69	0.90	22.95	17.39	
1794	233	187				38.69	66.96			
1795										
1796	120	139								
1797		95			1948					

Source: (American Numismatic Society, 2016)

The price increases are illustrated in Figure 3 above. Soap became so rare that Parisian washerwomen demanded that any vendor who declined to sell their items be executed. In February 1793, crowds in the capital raided around 200 shops, stealing everything from bread to sugar and clothes (Sargent, & Velde, 1995).

The most affected group by the hyperinflation was the poor. Financiers, merchants, and commodity speculators who took part in international trade could safeguard themselves (Ebeling, 2007). They amassed gold and silver, sent it overseas for safety, and invested in other durable commodities, such as art and precious jewelry. Their theoretical knowledge allowed most of them to take advantage of the hyperinflation and profit from the currency fluctuations. Since the working class and the poor have little to no knowledge of protecting themselves, they ended up holding billions of worthless assignats.

Deleveraging

As inflation worsened, there was an appeal by the people to stop the drastic rise in prices. As a result, in May 1793, the National Assembly imposed price controls on grain and stipulated that it could only be sold in public markets under the watch of state officials. They had the power to break into sellers` homes and confiscate hoarded grain and flour (Ebeling, 2007). Similarly, the destruction of goods under state control became a capital offense. In September, they extended the price controls to all essential commodities. It was to escalate prices by more than a third. They also regulated wages. Goods became scarce because farmers declined to sell their produce to cities, leading to a severe food shortage.

During the Jacobin Republic of 1792–1794, numerous regulators moved across the country, imposing price limits and interfering in every aspect of the citizens` lives (Trask, 2020). They enforced death sentences, seized wealth and property, and sent individuals to jail and slave labor. After the revolutionary war, all sectors connected to national defense or foreign trade were put under state control, including production, prices, and distributing of all commodities by private merchants (Trask, 2020). Consequently, an enormous bureaucracy materialized, swallowing up vast portions of the country`s wealth. The state`s rationale was that it had a duty to impose a collective arm for the country's sake. As such, the individual was nothing, and the government was everything.

However, in 1794, an anti-Jacobin government came to power and advocated for a free market. Farmers, manufacturers, and merchants would now enjoy complete control of their property, production, and industry. In December 1794, the Government abolished wage and price controls, and the economy was allowed to function as a free market. Although agricultural output increased in 1795, industrial output decreased in some parts. Inflation surged upwards to reach 3500%, which erased a significant portion of the public debt (Trask, 2020).

In December 1795, the state stopped the printing of the assignats, allowing the flow of goods and restoring a degree of prosperity.

Additionally, gold and silver transactions were permitted and were legally binding. The state tried a new paper currency called the Mandats Territoriaux to substitute the assignat. By August, the state issued more than 2,500 million Mandats (Ebeling, 2007). People could exchange the currency for land, but it failed to stop inflation. The exchange rate of the assignats to the Mandats was too high, and they had many problems. Within six months, the Mandats Territoriaux had depreciated as much as the assignats had done in six years (Ebeling, 2007). By December 1796, France had returned to specie. It withdrew the Mandat as the legal tender.

However, it took Napoleon to restore hard money in France and to stop the hyperinflation. Napoleon introduced the 20 Franc gold piece and stipulated that all government workers and merchants would be paid only in gold or its equivalent, effectively ending the paper blizzard (Trask, 2020).

It was not an accident that the first modern hyperinflation took place in the 1790s. The French Revolution significantly changed how Europeans thought about money. The French government envisioned the assignat as a way for people to conduct business without requiring the transfer of land titles. The move away from older and more physical manifestations of wealth only became prevalent in the 19th century. Although previous generations had been deeply suspicious of paper money, it became appealing because it was easier to ship paper currency over long distances than to transport gold or goods to businesses operating far away (Trask, 2020).

Hence, the development of paper currency is fundamental to comprehending the political, social, and economic outcomes of hyperinflation throughout civilization. The currencies utilized by Europeans before the 1700s had value outside their function as a medium of exchange. Thus, they did not inflate like paper money.

The move towards paper currency significantly altered individuals` relationships with their wealth. Similarly, in our current society, we are witnessing an identical shift in the way we relate to our money. Today, one can use their phone to pay for almost anything without the need for paper money. As we embrace digital currencies like Bitcoin and Cardano, it is fundamental to examine the history of money to gain insight into the connection between innovation in financial technologies and the types of economic crises we face today.

The Great Chinese Inflation

Inflations have destabilized the cultural and commercial fabric of society, ushering in social disorder and revolt. An excellent example of such an inflation is the Great Chinese Inflation in the 1930s and 1940s. The destruction of the Chinese monetary system in this era facilitated Mao Zedong's communist movement to succeed in China. Between 1935 and 1949, China witnessed a great hyperinflation in which prices increased by more than 1000% in one year (Hewitt, 2007). The primary cause of the hyperinflation was the policies of the Nationalist government, as it repeatedly introduced enormous sums of fiat currency into the Chinese economy. After World War II, the monetary expansion undertaken by the state was so severe that the Nationalist printing presses could not keep up. As a result, the government printed Chinese currency in England and flew them over the Himalayas.

Background

Before 1935, the Chinese had a restricted free banking system. Privately-owned banks were located across the country, though the leading Chinese banks were in Shanghai. Some provincial governments regulated their banks but had to ensure quality to compete with private banks. These private banks were incredibly competitive and operated largely without government regulation. Although coins were made of copper, silver was used as the primary medium of exchange, and the Chinese economy operated on an informal silver standard. Most banks issued distinct notes which were exchangeable with silver. These notes circulated freely with other banks' notes.

When the Nationalist government assumed power in 1927, it began an extensive process to get rid of free banking in the country, and by 1935, it had accomplished this objective. Instead of complete confiscation, the government followed an incremental strategy to control the currency (Habegger, 1988). The initial measures obtained the political and financial support of the biggest banks in the country. The state was to place Chinese banks under the direct authority of the

Nationalists, eliminating any restrictions due to currency regulation. Ultimately, all banks would rely on the state.

In 1927, the process started when banks got involved in the political conflict between the Nationalists and the Communists (Hewitt, 2007). As a result, violent walkouts headed by Communist leaders crippled the economy in Shanghai. And when bankers ask the state for help, the Nationalists government took this chance to strengthen its financial position. It made an agreement with bankers to subdue the strikes in exchange for loans to the state. Banks thought that the Nationalist government would be more supportive of their operations than a Communist regime.

Consequently, they became a fast source of money for the Nationalist regime and firm supporters even though the banks were losing their autonomy. Gradually, banks became worried about the state's capacity to repays its growing debt. Bankers declined to lend the government more money, and the state reacted by employing the same approach against bankers it had applied against the strikes. Bankers who refused to supply loans were arrested, and their properties confiscated.

In 1928, the Nationalist government established the Central Bank of China as an extension of the Treasury. The Central Bank started providing private banks with vast quantities of bonds secured by the state revenue from custom taxes with high interest rates. However, these bonds only made the financial crisis worse. In 1931, Japanese troops captured Manchuria and formed the puppet government Manchukuo. The capture of Manchuria was a devastating blow to the Nationalists because the area had a massive prospect for industrial development. As a result, government bonds went for around 50% of their face value. In 1932, Chinese banks in Shanghai held between 50% to 80% of outstanding government bonds (Ebeling, 2010). To improve public perception, the state appointed numerous directors of private banks to work alongside Central Bank directors. However, they had little or no authority.

Between 1929 and 1932, China battered a global financial and economic hurricane and witnessed an export explosion. Domestic prices increased while the rest of the planet underwent a profound price deflation. In September 1931, Great Britain got rid of the gold standard. Many nations embarked on currency depreciation, which undesirably impacted the worth of the Chinese silver dollar in the financial markets.

However, the disastrous shock came in 1933 and 1934 when the United States` president remonetized silver under the New Deal. Here, the US embarked on a silver-purchasing extravaganza at higher prices in an effort to drive a price high in the US (Hewitt, 2007). As a result, silver flowed out from Shanghai, and exports of silver from China to the US increased drastically. This led to a disastrous price deflation that affected China's agriculture and industry. The appreciation of the Chinese currency during the deflationary era increased the government's debt. Consequently, the Nationalist government implemented foreign exchange regulations on silver exports in late 1934.

Figure 1. *Money Supply in China between 1937-1948*

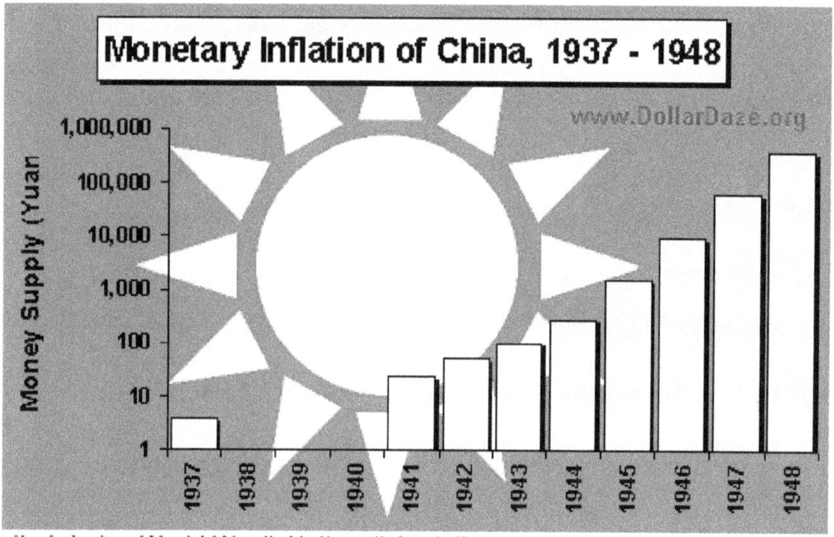

Source (Hewitt, 2007)

First Signs of Inflation

The state gave the Central Bank special rights like an exception from silver export regulations. As a result, the Central Bank became the nation's most lucrative financial establishment in 1937. As the government's finances worsened, it issued the Savings Bank Law, which mandated every private bank purchase government bonds equal to one-fourth of its total deposits (Habegger, 1988). The state started propaganda against the bankers to avert a prevalent bond market collapse. The propaganda blamed the country's economic issues on private bankers. In March 1935, the state clutched control of the two biggest banks in China, the Bank of China and the Bank of Communications. Soon, it utilized the funds from these banks to takeover smaller private banks (Ebeling, 2014). In July 1935, the Nationalist regime had eliminated private banking in the country as it became the majority shareholder in every bank. Despite the enormity of China's biggest banks, the state could not sustain itself. Businesses continued to shut down as more silver was smuggled out of the country.

The end of private banking meant that the resources of the Chinese banks were available to the government which held a majority share in every bank. As a result, the state immediately used these resources to finance its activities. Banks were mandated to buy state securities and to advance loans. Nonetheless, the banking coup had no impact on the deflation as companies shut down, and more silver was trafficked out of the country. Hence, the state imposed a death or life imprisonment on anyone smuggling silver out of the nation. However, deflation persisted.

With the elimination of private banking, the Nationalist government proposed introducing a controlled currency secured by nothing but state promise assurances. The move to a paper currency was supposed to benefit the state in two ways. First, the state would have control of all silver, which would enable the deflation to stop. Second, the state would have a monopoly over the money supply to make it possible to monetize its debt.

In November 1935, the Central Bank of China issued the Currency Decree, took China off the silver standard, and introduced a fiat currency. The Nationalist government has an absolute monopoly over the money supply, meaning that it could monetize its debt. Only the notes issued by the most prominent government banks were regarded as legal tender. The Central Bank regulated the new fiat currency, called the fai-pai. All institutions and people in possession of silver were mandated to exchange it for the new currency within six months.

To maintain confidence in the new currency, the Currency Decree contained provisions to create a Currency Stabilization Fund, which would purchase and sell foreign exchange to keep the rate fixed relative to specific foreign currencies. The Decree also comprised provisions that changed the operations of the Central Bank. Rather than being an extension of the Treasury, the Central Bank became a banker's bank, different from the Treasury. However, the Decree was a state's effort to suppress fears of inflation. Chinese media produced articles aimed at assuring the people that the government was looking at their best interests. Additionally, the international community endorsed the shift towards a fiat currency as a step towards a modern banking system. Nonetheless, the state never removed the Central Bank from the Treasury's control.

Hyperinflation Years

The currency reform of 1935 destroyed the private banking system, which had backed the Chinese economy effectively for decades. Moreover, with an incompetent and corrupt regime in control of the Chinese economy, inflation happened immediately. The monetary authority over the currency was a disastrous blow to China's economy. Massive monetary inflation occurred from July 1937 to 1945 to fund the war with Japan (Ebeling, 2010). As a result, about 70% of China's yearly expenditures were covered by newly printed currency. As a result of the severe financial expansions during World War II, Nationalist printing presses could not keep up, and the country had to outsource from Great Britain. Ultimately, inflation worsened and facilitated the collapse of the Nationalist administration.

The war between China and Japan persisted for eight years, from July 1937 to September 1945. Japanese troops occupied about one-third of China, including all the nation's main port cities and industrial hubs. During the war, over ten million Chinese died fighting.

In 1945, a longstanding civil war broke out between Chiang Kai-shek's Nationalist government and the large communist forces led by Mao Zedong. The conflict continued for four years until the communists emerged victorious and the Nationalist troops retreated to Taiwan in 1949.

During the war with Japan, the Nationalist government decided to print more money to fund its expenditures, covering around 70% of its annual spending via money creation. Between 1946 and 1949, monetary expansion accounted for close to 60% of the state's spending. At the start of the war in 1937, the total amount of money in circulation was 36 billion Yuan. By 1941, the money supply had expanded to 22.8 billion Yuan. This trend continued throughout the war era to 1,506 billion Yuan in 1945.

The civil war worsened inflation. In December 1946, the money supply increased to 9,181 billion Yuan, and by late 1947, it had grown to 60,965 billion Yuan. In July 1948, the money in circulation had risen to 399,091 billion Yuan. Consequently, the government introduced a new currency to replace the old depreciated one at a conversion rate of three million old Yuan for one new currency. The new Yuan was secured by gold. In August 1948, the government stipulated that it would redeem paper Yuan for gold to restore public confidence in the fiat currency (Ebeling, 2014).

As a result, thousands of individuals lined up in front of the Bank of China carrying huge bags filled with paper currency to exchange their paper currency for gold. However, the state seized selling gold the following day. It stipulated that gold, silver, and foreign exchange ownership were prohibited, and individuals had to accept the new fiat currency for the old. The new converted money supply was 296.82 billion Yuan in August 1948, and by April 1949, the supply of the new currency had increased to 5,161,249 billion Yuan.

Consumer Impact

Between 1937 and 1949, prices increased drastically but at varying degrees across various parts of the country because of war-associated scarcities, destructions, and the disastrous effects of the monetary expansion. By December 1941, the Shanghai wholesale price index was 15.98. In late 1945, this index had reached 177,088 and by April 1949 it stood at 151,733,000,000,000 (Ebeling, 2010). The value of the Chinese currency on the foreign exchange market depreciated considerably. Before the start of the China-Japan war in 1937, 3.41 Yuan traded for one USD. In 1945, the Yuan traded at 1,222 to the dollar, increasing to 23,280,000 Yuan in May 1949 (Inflation and CPI Consumer Price Index 1940-1949, n.d.)

During and after the war, the Nationalist regime enacted unworkable price and wage controls to curb inflation. However, this created more distortions and dislocations in the entire Chinese economy, causing shortages, black markets, and increased corruption. The state's policies created social and commercial unrest that helped the communists since Mao's government promised to eliminate corruption and the violations of the Nationalist regime (Ebeling, 2014). The hyperinflation destroyed the wealth and savings of the ordinary Chinese people and ushered chaos across the economy because of the loss of a reliable and stable medium of exchange. Moreover, inflation and its impacts caused a significant portion of the rural population enter severe poverty. As a result, any support the Nationalist regime had in rural areas diminished significantly.

A notable aspect of Chinese hyperinflation is use of currency as a means of payment. This was different from other hyperinflations throughout history (Ebeling, 2014). For instance, during the German hyperinflation after World War II, extensive price controls made barter an attractive way to trade regardless of its many demerits. The Chinese government did not place effective price controls except for rents and a few commodities rationed and distributed by state agencies in big cities. Since prices could increase freely, financial transactions were not penalized. Hence, consumers used the Chinesc currency as the primary medium of exchange throughout the hyperinflation.

The Deleveraging

Saying that the Great Chinese Inflation was the sole cause for the defeat of the Nationalist regime and the triumph of the Communist party would be an exaggeration (Habegger, 1988). The Nationalist government was an authoritarian government, infamous for its corruption and misuse of authority, and relentless in its usage of military power. However, it is evident that whatever support the Nationalist government had gained against the Communist party, particularly among China's middle class, was extensively damaged by the inflation.

The Chinese experience from 1935 to 1949 revealed that individuals might retain currency as a medium of exchange under inflation but discard it as a store of value and unit of account (Ebeling, 2010). Numerous scholars have thought that under such conditions, the usage of currency would have seized entirely. However, the Chinese hyperinflation had the opposite impact. Rather than facilitating the collapse, it led to adjustments that lessened the effects of inflation.

Depreciation considerably increased the cost of using currency. Still, the Chinese were willing to pay a high price to avert the drawbacks of barter and price regulations that might have made barter more lucrative than monetary exchange.

Venezuelan Hyperinflation

The most recent instance of hyperinflation is in Venezuela. The suffering of millions of Venezuelans has been broadcast across the world to demonstrate the raw devastation that hyperinflation can cause. Venezuela used to be one of the richest countries in the world in the 1960's. It had a GDP per capita better than Norway at that time. Failure to diversify their economy away from oil and lackluster governance and embrace of extreme socialist programs has seen a slow decline over the decades, eventually resulting in a modern-day catastrophe.

While the seeds of destruction were sown for decades, the actual trees started growing in the early 2010s. In 2013, prices increased by 41%, and by 2018, inflation was at 65,000%. Between 2014 and 2016, the poverty rate increased from 50% to over 80%. In response to the inflation, the state increased the money supply by 14% in 2017 (Caraballo, Madrid & Barrios, 2018). The people responded by utilizing eggs as currency. In January 2017, a carton of eggs was valued at 6,740 bolivars, and unemployment increase by over 20%. This unemployment was similar to the United States during the Great Depression (Caraballo, Madrid & Barrios, 2018). It got so bad that the populace could no longer afford most essential commodities, as shown in Figure 1.

Figure 1. *The changing Venezuelan diet*

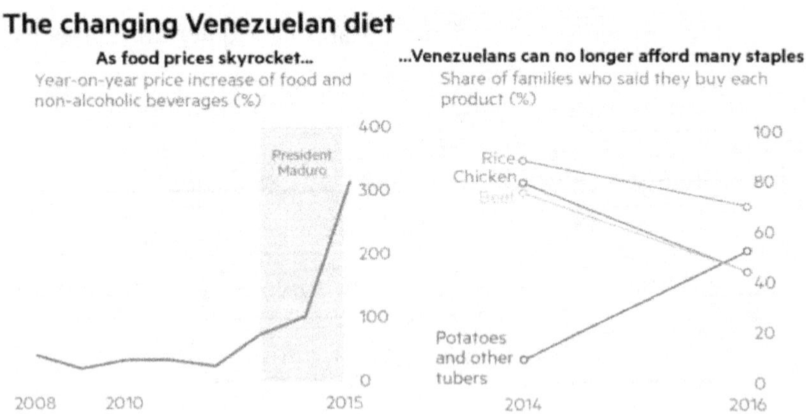

Source: (Population Pyramid, 2019)

What caused the hyperinflation?

Former President Hugo Chavez had implemented price regulations for essential commodities such as food and medicine. However, these prices were low and mandated domestic firms to close shop. In reaction, the state paid for imports. In 2016, oil prices declined drastically, eroding revenue from state-run oil firms.

Consequently, the government went broke and began printing more currency. By 2019, the country`s foreign debt had accumulated to around $100 billion, and in 2020, the yearly inflation rate for consumer prices was about 150,000% (Multimore, 2021). Currently, the Venezuelan government is promoting a new cryptocurrency to offset inflation since the Bolivar has lost most of its value against international currencies. The country cannot afford to continue printing money. As the nation`s economy continues to collapse, the country faces an enormous debt repayment problem. The exchange rate has been skyrocketing since 2015, as shown in Figure 2 below. Today, Venezuela is the only nation on the planet suffering from hyperinflation.

Figure 2. *Money Supply, exchange rate, and consumer prices.*

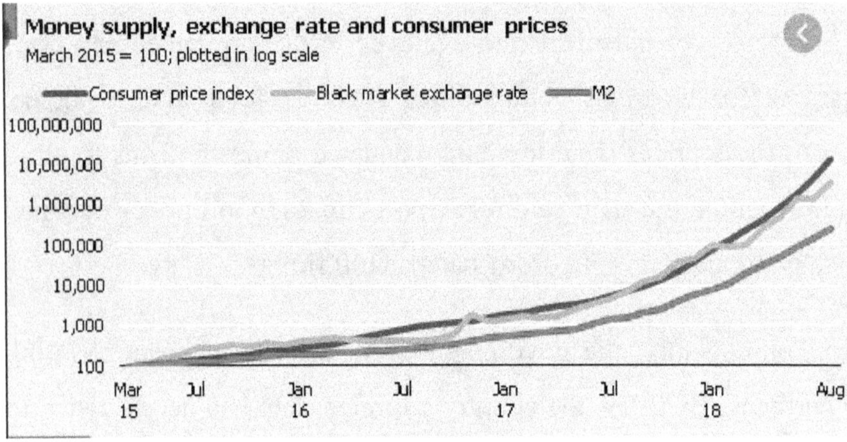

Source: (Venezuela Money Supply, 2021)

The Lead Up to Hyperinflation

To understand Venezuela`s path to hyperinflation, it is essential to analyze the country`s economic, social, and political environment. There was a collapse of the economy, a scarcity of essential goods and services, and lack of public transportation.

First, we look at Venezuela`s natural resource 'curse' to understand the current hyperinflation. The nation is an excellent example of an oil-reliant economy that failed with its trade policy since it is heavily dependent on its oil deposits as a trading product. Venezuela`s oil economy started in 1914 when the Caribbean Oil Company discovered substantial oil reserves (Koech, 2016). Soon, the nation began exporting oil, and the commodity quickly became Venezuela's primary export. Today, the oil reserves are estimated to be around 38,291 billion barrels and are the largest oil deposits in the world (Koech, 2016). Its primary trading partners are the US, China, and Russia. However, the relationship between Venezuela and the US is strained ever since President Maduro accused the US of plotting to overthrow his administration and undermine Venezuela`s economy. The US imposed sanctions against Venezuela between 2014 and 2018. They imposed a ban on using oil from Venezuela, which greatly damaged the economy. Venezuela now has limited customers for its large oil reserves. China is the second-largest oil trading partner of Venezuela.

Venezuela`s oil exports account for approximately 96% of its total exports, which is about 30% of its GDP (Koech, 2016). The second global oil crisis took place in 1980, ignited by the first Gulf War. As a result, the Bolivar depreciated drastically, and commodities within Venezuela become more expensive. For instance, benzene prices shot up, and public transport tickets increased in price (Koech, 2016). Consequently, in 1989, a significant part of the population demonstrated, leading to regulations that made Benzene cheaper than water.

Venezuela`s heavy dependence on an oil economy since the 1940s has caused other sectors to suffer enormously. Subsequent socialist governments have concentrated their trade approaches on the export of oil and neglected other sectors. This made Venezuela`s imports cheaper and helped the Bolivar become a strong currency in the global economy. Consequently, foreign nations couldn't afford local commodities from Venezuela, and the nation's agricultural sector collapsed, destroying the livelihood of most Venezuelan individuals. The nation`s food production system is now completely based on socialism and food rations.

Another factor that is significant to Venezuela`s path to hyperinflation is its weak corporate governance. The era of socialism started in 1998 when President Hugo Chavez was elected. Under his administration, the nation`s name was changed to the Bolivarian Republic of Venezuela (Pittaluga, Seghezza & Morelli, 2021). The president announced that every citizen would benefit from the country`s rich oil deposits. Chavez's administration enjoyed a lucky era, as oil prices surged five-fold during his tenure. At the start of Chavez`s tenure, oil prices were at the lowest in the nation`s history, and at his death, the price had increased ten times. The increased oil revenues enabled the state to invest in social initiatives, such as healthcare and housing, and reduce poverty and inequality.

However, the government failed to invest in other economic sectors believing that the rich oil deposits could sustain the nation`s economy. Similarly, the state expected oil prices to remain stable. The state subsidized gas prices, which led to smuggling. The state, however, failed to take action and stop this smuggling, weakening the nation`s actual output. Despite Chavez increasing the price of gas, the country still has the cheapest gas prices in the world (Pittaluga, Seghezza & Morelli, 2021). This was the onset of inflation. The cost of goods and services then began to increase within the country, causing high inflation. From then, the value of the Bolivar continued to decline, prompting the government to introduce a fixed dollar exchange rate in an attempt to stabilize the currency. However, this effort proved futile since the Bolivar's value was much less than the state wanted to admit.

Another factor that paved the way for Venezuela`s hyperinflation was the exploitation of private companies. The country nationalized the oil sector in the 1970s, and these corporations controlled the industry and embarked on business with foreign firms (Pittaluga, Seghezza & Morelli, 2021). However, when Chavez became president, he decided to place political appointees as heads of these public companies to control them. Most of the appointed executives had no experience or knowledge in the oil sector, leading to badly run oil companies and significant corruption. As a result, oil workers went on a two-month strike, crippling the oil sector nationally. The government responded by firing more than 18,000 employees, and in the following years, more companies were nationalized. For instance, in 2007, Exxon was forced to hand over its shares to the governments. Between 1998 and 2013, Venezuela`s oil profits increased by 90% (Pittaluga, Seghezza & Morelli, 2021).

By the time the Chavez regime was over, Venezuela was a completely government-controlled state, including the steel, power, and food industries. These economic actions eliminated the foundation of a free economy as the state heavily regulated the job market, prohibiting companies from dismissing workers in crises. When President Nicolas Maduro entered office, his administration continued the ongoing nationalization of private firms, causing many companies to go bankrupt.

Additionally, the oil prices fell from $111 per barrel in 2013 to $57.60 in 2014. A year later, the oil prices fell to $37.60, and in 2016, the prices ranged between $27.10 and $57.69 (Pittaluga, Seghezza & Morelli, 2021).

Figure 3. *Oil production reduction*

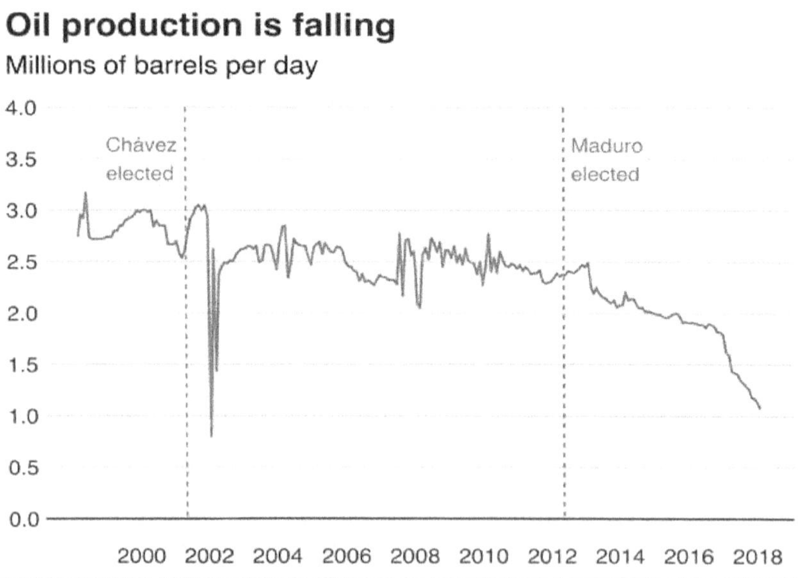

Source: (Trading Economics, 2021).

As a result, the Venezuelan economy declined by 30% from 2013 to 2017, and the dependence on food and consumer goods imports increased immensely. The shrinking economy caused foreign investment to decrease from $30 billion in 2013 to less than $10 billion in 2018. Also, the Trump administration imposed sanctions on the country, forcing the government to print more money.

First Signs of Hyperinflation

Experts stipulate that Venezuela`s economy started to witness hyperinflation during the first year of President Maduro`s regime. The probable causes of hyperinflation include printing more currency and deficit spending. When Maduro took over in 2013, the annual inflation rate was around 30%, and by 2014, it had increased to 61.5%. However, the government did not release the nation`s statistics in an attempt to manipulate public perception. Figure 4 clearly shows the extent of inflation under Maduro. Many international and local agencies, such as the IMF, stipulated those loose macroeconomic policies had created high inflation in Venezuela and drained its foreign reserves. Some experts state that the inflation was around 300% in March 2014 as opposed to the official inflation rate of 60%. In September and October 2014, the Venezuelan government failed to release inflation data.

Also, Venezuelans did not believe that their nation was facing high inflation since there was a lot of money circulating in the economy and few shortages. In 2014, the supply of Bolivar increased by 64%, three times quicker than any other nation in the world.

Figure 4. *Venezuela's Inflation after Maduro's Election.*

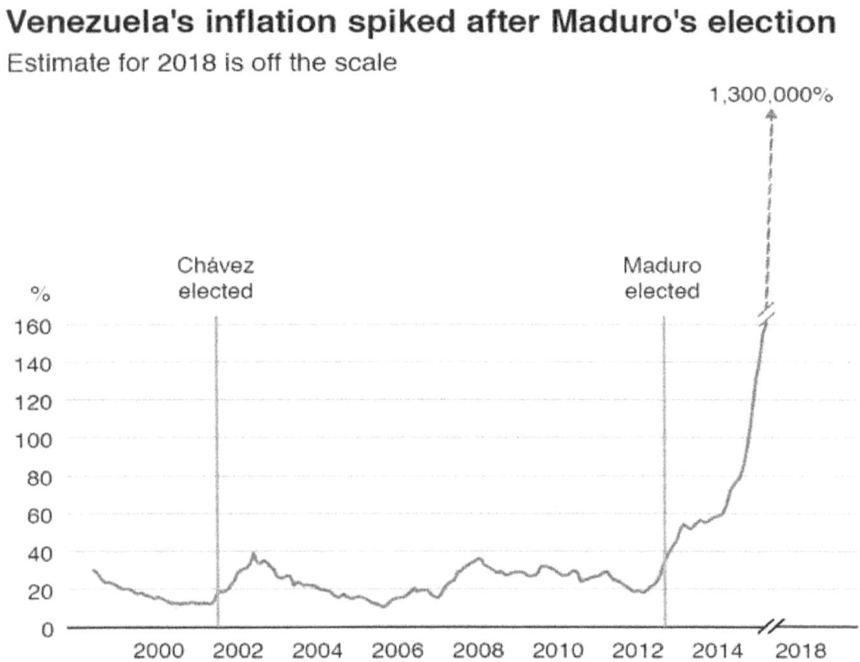

Source: (Trading Economics, 2021).

Maduro`s administration blamed capitalist speculation for hyperinflation and creating widespread shortages of essential goods and services. The state focused on fighting an economic war by implementing new financial measures against political opponents. However, these initiatives were more strategies that tried to hide the extent of the nation`s high inflation. Today, Maduro is criticized for focusing on public opinion rather than addressing real issues regarding hyperinflation.

Hyperinflation Years

As it stands today, Venezuela is close to running out of foreign exchange reserves, and it has lost access to overseas debt markets. Venezuela has also lost support of other governments because of political corruption and its nationalization of multinationals.

The Venezuelan economy declined by 5.8% in the first quarter of 2010, with an inflation rate of 30.5% (Koech, 2016). However, by the time Chavez died in 2013, Venezuela had entered a recession. Consumer prices increased exponentially during this time. By 2010, inflation had reversed any progress in wage increases. Venezuela officially entered hyperinflation in November 2016 after inflation passed the 50% mark. According to the IMF, the country experienced a 500% inflation rate in 2016 and the monthly inflation surpassed 50% (Koech, 2016).

In 2017, the inflation rate reached 4,000%. Consequently, the citizens started a trend of gold farming in cyber games to attain hard currency. During the Christmas season in 2017, most stores did not use price tags due to inflation. According to the Venezuelan government, the inflation rate was 274% in 2017, 863% in 2018, and 130,060% in 2019 (Koech, 2016). However, according to IMF, the inflation rate was 929, 790% in 2018, and over 10,000,000% in 2019 (Koech, 2016).

In 2016, the Bolivar witnessed its largest-ever loss of value. In November, the exchange rate reached 2,000 Bolivar for one USD, and by the 28th of the same month, the currency had lost 60% of its value to reach 3,000 Bolivar per USD (Multimore, 2021). As a result, the state retired the subsidized 10 Bolivar per USD exchange rate in January 2018, making the currency the second least-valued currency in circulation in the world.

Additionally, the minimum wage in the country dropped considerably before and during the hyperinflation period. Between 2012 and 2015, the minimum wage declined from around $360 per month to approximately $31. Following the release of a new currency in 2018, the minimum wage increased from 392,646 Bolivar to 180 million Bolivar per month. In terms of USD, the minimum monthly salary was equivalent to $5 by the end of April 2020 (Multimore, 2021).

During the hyperinflation era, unemployment increased drastically in Venezuela. In 2019, the unemployment rate rose to unprecedented levels; levels not seen since the end of the Bosnia War in 1995. In January 2016, the unemployment rate was 18.1%, and by October 2019, it had reached 35%. By 2020, the rate had increased to 40%, causing many individuals to immigrate to other nations. According to UNHCR, emigration from Venezuela during 2015 is regarded as one of the biggest emigrations in modern history as more than 4.8 million Venezuelans have registered as refugees and migrants (Caraballo, Madrid & Barrios, 2018).

Impact on Individuals

As Venezuela battled inflation, barter and dollars became the new reality. Citizens have been forced to find alternate ways to pay for essential products and services. During hyperinflation, people carry lots of cash around. A shocking example is shown in Figure 4, where the price of a chicken is to the tune of 14m bolivars. However, in Venezuela, the capacity to get hard money has declined significantly. Bolivar notes are increasingly scarce since the government mint no longer works. As a result, the country must source banknotes from abroad. Today, Venezuelans use barter, dollars, and other alternative payment systems since one can go for weeks without touching banknotes (Koech, 2016).

Figure 4. *Money needed to purchase a chicken (14m Bolivars).*

Source: (Partington, 2018)

The Deleveraging

Since the hyperinflation, the Venezuelan government has embarked on several initiatives to tackle inflation and reduce its debts. Despite these measures, Venezuela is still experiencing hyperinflation in 2021. Following the start of the hyperinflation, the state introduced higher denomination banknotes. In December 2016, new notes with higher denominations including 500, 1000, 5000, 10000, and 20000 Bolivars were issued since the 100 Bolivar note was only worth $0.23. In March 2021, the state introduced three new notes to the public, including 200000, 500000, and 1000000 Bolivar notes, with the latest note being worth $0.52 (Huertas, 2019).

Moreover, the government introduced the Petro cryptocurrency in 2017 to try and stabilize the economy. The new cryptocurrency is backed by the nation`s oil, gold, and diamond reserves (Huertas, 2019). Although the cryptocurrency promised to mitigate some of the economic challenges, it has not gathered momentum in Venezuela and the international community.

From the start of 2019, the government embarked on controlling inflation via a combination of fiscal, monetary, and exchange rate policies. Expenditures reduced, VAT increased, bank reserve ratios increased, and the central bank got rid of several regulations on access to foreign currency (Huertas, 2019). Due to increased sanctions in 2019, the state abandoned protectionist policies like price and currency controls, liberating the economy. The extents of these spending cuts are difficult to approximate since most of the information is not released to the public. However, some reports suggest that government expenditures have decreased considerably. Since then, Venezuela has seen its economy rebound from the recession. The fiscal consolidation has yielded some results as hyperinflation fell by close to 200% in 2019 and 2020 (Huertas, 2019).

The state has also modified the exchange rate to offset the crisis. Between August and September 2018, the state temporarily lifted currency controls, allowing individuals and companies to buy and sell foreign exchange (Huertas, 2019). The state also unified and devalued the exchange and announced a new currency that matched the informal price, limiting the black market. In August 2018, the government introduced the Bolivar Soberano with one Bolivar Soberano worth 100,000 Bolivar (Huertas, 2019). The new Bolivar was devalued by close to 96% compared to the old Bolivar against the USD, as shown in Figure 5.

Figure 5.

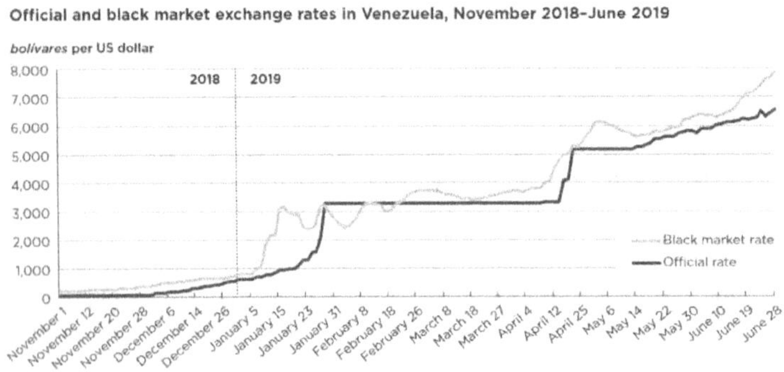

Source: (Hyperinflation in Venezuela: A Stabilization Handbook, 2019).

The introduction of the new currency did not stop inflation. It increased from 48,750% to 65,000% by the end of the month (Huertas, 2019). In January 2019, the state introduced a fixed exchange rate, but by 2020, it has given up on the exchange rate and embraced more of a free-floating exchange rate.

Hyperinflation in Yugoslavia

Introduction

The circumstances leading to hyperinflation are often unique to a particular region. However, most reported cases in history had been influenced by policies that increased money circulation in the economy. When a country experiences an uncontrollable spike in commodity prices followed by devaluing of the national currency against others, it faces the potential for hyperinflation. Excessive money supply creates a scenario where the consumer requires large sums of money to purchase small quantities of commodities in the marketplace. There is an imbalance in the relationship between cash and goods. The consumer's purchasing power reduces due to the inability to buy daily consumables. Such causative factors were witnessed in Yugoslavia during the early 1990s, as Figure 1 shows.

Figure 1. *Yugoslavia Hyperinflation.*

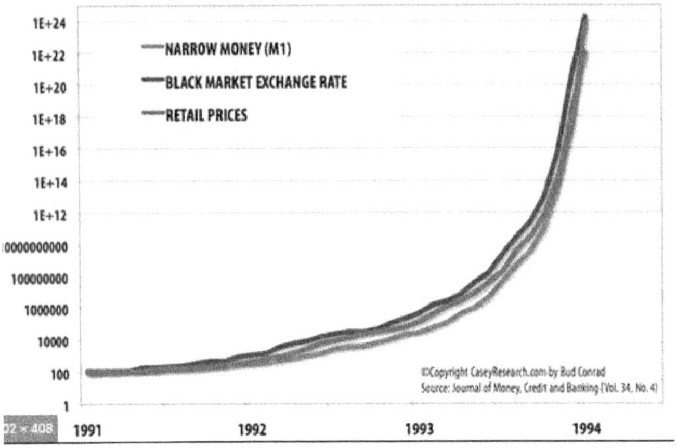

Source: (Watkins, 2010).

The Federal Republic of Yugoslavia (FRY) faced one of the worse financial crises in history. FRY had one of the most extended periods of hyperinflation that lasted from 1992 to 1994. During this 2-year-period, the nation recorded an inflation rate of 313,000,000% each month. The daily inflation was more than 62%, making the situation more dire than in the Weimar Republic (Hanke, 2007). Like other regions that have been unfortunate to experience economic devastation, political instability and poor decision-making on monetary and fiscal policies are often at the center of the crisis. This chapter will reveal an in-depth analysis of the contributing factors, the impact hyperinflation had on society, and the mitigation plans implemented to curb further prices. According to Hanke (2007), the virulent nature of the financial crisis in Yugoslavia in the 1990s made it stand out from other countries that grappled with hyperinflation. The country's highest recorded inflation rate at the peak of the financial crisis was 313 million percent (Watkins, 2010). This made it only second to the Hungarian hyperinflation that occurred in the 1940s.

Background

The causes and origin of the economic problems have been traced back to the Tito regime. When the Tito government embarked on a mission to address budget deficits, it authorized the printing of more money. This marked the beginning of an irrational economic decision that increased the reliance on printing money to finance government operations and boost economic growth. The Communist Party took over the reins of power after the Tito administration adopted the same irrational policies as its predecessors.

The Yugoslav government had depleted most of the currency reserves and imposed restrictions on private citizens. This made it easier for the authorities to access the hard currency reserves of private individuals stored in the commercial banks. The nation's inflation rate increased by almost 25% annually from the 1970s to the years leading up to the hyperinflation. In the early 1990s, it was discovered that the Serbian National Bank, under the instructions of Slobodan Milosevic, had issued more than $1.4 billion credit to his friends (Petrović, Bogetić & Vujošević, 1999). The amount was approximately half of what the National Bank of Yugoslavia intended to pump into the economy. This created deficits for the Markovic regime, making it impossible for the government to support economic growth.

Figure 2. *Aftermath of the of Croatia and Bosnia–Herzegovina war.*

Source: (Taylor, 2012).

Milosevic's heist sabotaged the new regime and escalated the divisive politics in the region. This culminated in Slovenia and Croatia breaking away from the Socialist Federal Republic of Yugoslavia. The disintegration of the former SFRY resulted in political and social unrest in the region. War broke out in Croatia and Bosnia-Herzegovina in 1992, which eventually saw the monthly inflation rate surpass the 50% mark (Taylor, 2012). The newly formed Federal Republic of Yugoslavia (FRY) was on the verge of a severe financial crisis and total destruction as Figure 2 depicts.

The dissolution of the SFRY had far-reaching economic impacts on the region. The political impasse had disrupted regional trade that adversely affected the production level of most industries. The government expense increased due to war and the payment of civil servants. The military and police force of the former SFRY remained in Serbia and Montenegro, which was a smaller territory creating a burden on the region's government expenditure. The administration in SFRY was fighting against all odds to prevent a decline in economic growth, which resulted in the incorporation of irrational policies that escalated the crisis.

The collapse of the stabilization programs implemented by the Yugoslav government also played a vital role in escalating the county's inflation rates. At the beginning of 1989, Markovic's regime had embarked on creating policies aimed at the opening up the nation's economy (Taylor, 2012). This comprised removing economic and political blockades to stimulate economic growth. Although the stabilization programs effectively solved the country's financial problems, they were only short-term solutions that could not address the high inflation rates. The economy was already showing inflation, and any programs to boost the economy failed to bear the desired results.

First signs and the Hyperinflation Years

Since the first signs of inflation were discovered in Yugoslavia, there was an uncontrollable increase in commodity prices. The inflation rate peaked rapidly within the two years, with the highest record being witnessed in 1994 (He, 2017). After the region declared *de facto* trading, activities were adversely affected, with many industries experiencing a decline in total output. The war in Croatia and Bosnia–Herzegovina jeopardized security in the region and made the economic situation worse. The 1990s for Yugoslavia was a period of persistent hardship, creating a slippery slope scenario whereby one problem led to the other (He, 2017). During this time, the United Nations imposed sanctions and trade embargos on international transactions with the Federal Republic of Yugoslavia. The sanctions by the United Nations escalated the decline in output and the productivity of the economy. Following this, the government authorized the printing of more money to boost the purchasing power of the citizens.

Figure 3. *Banknote denomination of RSD 500,000,000,000.*

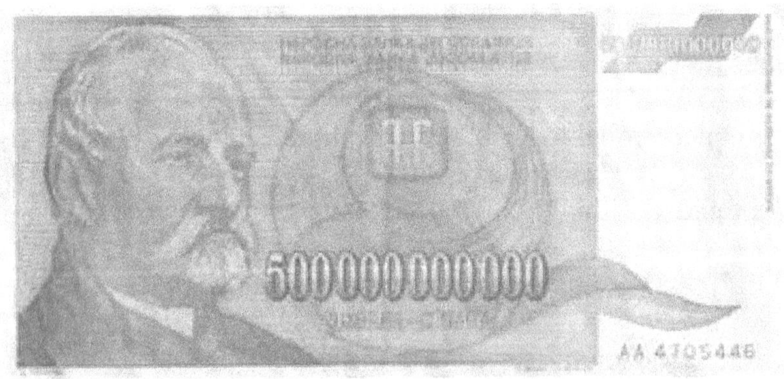

Source: ((Watkins, 2010)

The government mint was working overtime to supply more money in circulation. It is estimated that it was producing nearly nine hundred thousand notes each month. The Topčider mint started making high denomination banknotes such as the RSD 500,000,000,000 as shown in Figure 3. The only problem was that by the time the money was getting in the hands of the citizens, it was already worthless because of the high devaluation of the dinar. This eventually led to the collapse of the national currency forcing the public to adopt the German Mark as the accepted legal tender. The citizens relied on the black-market exchange rate to convert the Dinar to the German Mark. The Yugoslav foreign exchange reserve declined as the value of the dinar dropped against other foreign currencies. The public was starving due to a shortage in commodities, and the high price tags made it difficult for them to afford products in the free market.

Milosevic blamed the country's misfortune on external forces such as the trade embargos initiated by the United Nations (He, 2017). His administration spent most of the printed money to finance the war between Croatia and Bosnia–Herzegovina. Gasoline became a rare commodity in Belgrade, and most people were forced to cease driving (He, 2017). Only government officials and embassy personnel could access the gas from the only station that remained operational.

Sanctions against the FR of Yugoslavia were enforced on 30 May 1992, by the United Nations Security Council on charges of contributing to the conflict in Bosnia and Herzegovina. The UN Security Council goal accommodated a total global financial ban on this country. Affected by worldwide sanctions, there was a significant financial emergency in the country and sparked off hyperinflation, which eventually saw the issuance of a banknote with a record division of RSD 500,000,000,000 (Stojković, 2019).

Starting 1992, the Yugoslav Dinar encountered a hyperinflation that went on for 25 months. Prices rose quickly, taking on practically unfathomable extents. During 1993 prices went up by 116.5 thousand billion percent, and in the initial three weeks of 1994 by 313 million percent (He, 2017). The force of hyperinflation recorded in late 1993 and mid-1994 in the FR Yugoslavia is among the worst (Stojković, 2019) ever recorded in history.

Consumer Behavior

Consumers were the most affected as prices of goods and services skyrocketed overnight. For a long time, essential stores and gas stations remain closed except for one station that served embassies and other foreign personnel. Many people turned to the black market to trade huge amounts of worthless dinars for the US dollar or the German mark note. Between 1991 and 1998, the dinar was devalued more than eighteen times. The country's monetary orgy ended when the Topcider mint became incapacitated because it was converting 500-billion-dinar bills into insignificant change, which caused the machine's ink to dry out.

The Deleveraging and Stabilization

Yugoslavia applied two currency stabilization programs: heterodox and orthodox. The heterodox approach was adopted at the culmination of the socialist federal republic (SFRY) while the orthodox approach was applied at the commencement of the Federal Republic of Yugoslavia (FRY). Both measures were relatively effective in the short-term but remained unsuccessful in the long-term, which led to their collapse. The initial program was implemented in the 1980s as an economic reform program. However, by 1994, another program – monetary reconstruction program and economic recovery (also known as the 'Avramović Program'), was implemented.

This prompted a destruction of the domestic economy, as exports became worthless, and imports were extremely rewarding. Remembering that there has been an advancement of imports, the domestic market is "overpowered" with imported items, which are consumed by expanding domestic interest, only for consumer merchandise powered by quick compensation development (Cunningham et al, 2011). Imports of merchandise became less expensive than domestic ones, so there is a decrease in production because our items are not backed by anything solid. After a few stretches of execution, modern production decreased by 25%, and unemployment expanded by 18% (He, 2017).

The second, long-term stage involved fundamental monetary changes that would prompt the financial recovery of the country. This would guarantee long-term stable financial development. This stage, as the creators of the program have brought up, caused a decline in financial approvals and an increase in "new" capital required for its development. Since this was not accomplished, this subsequent stage got no opportunity for significant achievement, similar to the case with the primary period of the Program (He, 2017).

Hyperinflation in Hungary

Hyperinflation in Hungary after World War II in 1946 remains the most intense ever recorded. Hungary was a part of the Axis powers that allied with Germany during the war. They lost to the Soviet Union forces in 1945. In 1944, Hungary was a battleground that suffered significant losses of over 40000 people, capital, land, and minerals like gold. The Hungarian economy suffered heavy losses, with all sectors falling by over 40% in value. Until this point in time, there have been 56 recorded hyperinflation episodes. Numerous individuals had heard tales of Germany in the mid-1920s, where a loaf of bread cost a barrel loaded with cash. Be that as it may, not many know about the most prominent hyperinflation ever, where, at the pinnacle, prices multiplied every 15.6 hours, and notes were given in divisions of 100 million pengőes and 1 billion pengőes (He, 2017). This chapter explores hyperinflation in Hungary, including the lead-up to hyperinflation, the first signs of hyperinflation, the hyperinflation years, how Hungarians faired during the inflationary period, and the deleveraging period.

The Lead Up to Hyperinflation

In post-WWII, Hungarian policymakers had two issues to deal with: inflation and shortage of products. Grossman and Horváth (2000) investigated the choices policymakers needed to make: either urge inflation or attempt to battle it by raising income and cutting currency flow (Kumar, 2015). Eventually, they decided that inflation was the way to help the economy by energizing production before the new currency was presented. As Valkovszky and Vincze (2012) clarify, expanding the cash supply was considered as an approach to localize utilization. When there is high inflation, cash loses value and, in this way, individuals are forced to purchase products. Nevertheless, an expansion in the cash supply is only helpful if there are goods to purchase. The government tried this approach to animate production, which had devastating impacts.

The First Signs of Hyperinflation

Now, let's investigate the sectors and areas that were negatively affected by World War II. The worst affected were the coal and rail businesses, as their decrease in production and capital killed profitability (Kumar, 2015). The rail line industry was also affected by the war; train lines and rail-related enterprises were obliterated. Without coal, there was little power, and production across all ventures were affected.

The lack of capital for constructing railroads hindered the transportation of products and individuals. All local or domestic travel was restricted, and railroads were only used for factory laborers and emergencies. The year 1945 was an incredibly awful one for agribusiness (Kumar, 2020).

Hungary also encountered a terrible drought, mainly owing to a dry spell: expected wheat production was 3 million tons, while the actual production was just 1 million tons. With lower crop yields, the eating routine of Hungarians changed significantly. All the while, prices of raw materials started to rise due to excessive shortages.

Figure 3. *The cost of living during the onset of hyperinflation*

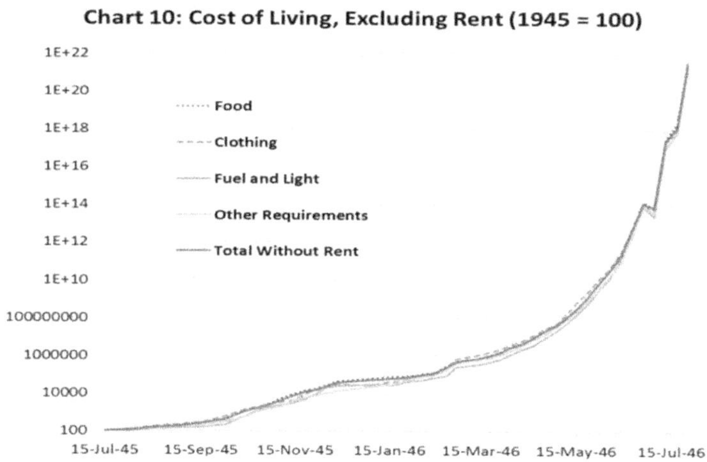

Source: (Kumar, 2020)

Most business activity post WWII in Hungary was nationalized and became state undertakings. The mining businesses and few force plants were nationalized before hyperinflation ended (Valkovszky and Vincze, 2012). During hyperinflation, the government needed to work both openly and secretly to empower businessmen, speculation, and production.

To handle rural issues, a significant land change occurred. Land change split up huge settlements and attempted to give lower class individuals private land. The government offered private loans at interest rates that were not indexed to inflation. This is because the government realized that the installments would become worthless due to hyperinflation (Kumar, 2020). The Hungarian government then urged banks to loan assets to businessmen. Since the national bank's markdown rate was 3%; and the inflation more than 10,000 percent, the real interest rates turned out to be significantly negative.

The Hyperinflation Years and Consumer Behavior

This hyperinflation began in Hungary in August 1945 and halted in July 1946, when the Hungarian pengő was supplanted with the Hungarian forint. There were other endeavors during the period to balance out the currency, most remarkably with an alternative pengő record, where exchange rates were changed each day to represent rising prices (Valkovszky and Vincze, 2012).

Figure 1 below shows how retail and wholesale prices rose during the period.

Figure 1. *Retail and Wholesale prices in Hungary before and during the period*

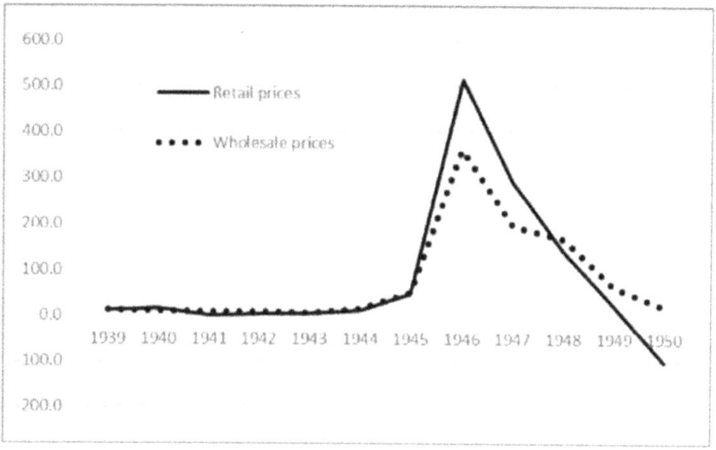

Source: (Kumar, 2020)

Consumer Behavior during the Inflationary Period

Most financial and monetary approaches adopted by the government had a negative influence on consumer behavior. Although stakeholders possessed an essential understanding of hyperinflation, the Government had no experience on dealing with hyperinflation (He, 2017). Both the 1923 and 1946 hyperinflations proved that financial and monetary changes had significant and detrimental effects on consumer behavior.

The prices of consumer goods started rising as the country's production capacity fell. The government took measures to control the sharp rise in prices. Since there was no tax base to rely on, it opted to stimulate its economy by printing more money. Banks were given loans at low rates who then loaned it to citizens and businesses at even lower rates. The government also hired workers directly and gave large amounts of money to people to get its economy running again. The currency in circulation in July 1945 stood at 25 billion Pengö but rose to over 1.6 trillion by the February 1946. By May that year, 65 quadrillion was in circulation and 47 septillions by July 1946 (He, 2017).

Consumers were heavily impacted by the financial measures adopted by government to manage the looming hyperinflation. A commodity that cost 380 Pengö in September 1945 was sold at over 72000 Pengö in January 1946, over 450000 Pengö by February 1946, over 1.8 million Pengö by March, and over 11 trillion billion Pengö by

July that year (He, 2017). By August 1946, the hyperinflation was devastating and challenging to consumers. At the peak of hyperinflation, prices skyrocketed over 150000% daily, making it the worst in world history (He, 2017). Consumers refrained from paying taxes altogether since a day's delay in tax collection wiped out the currency value collected by the government. Prior to the war, 5 Pengö were equivalent to 1 US dollar. However, by June 1944, 1 US dollar was equal to 33 Pengö and over 1300 by August 1945 (He, 2017). The Pengö later collapsed, and 1 US dollar was equal to 10000 Pengo by November that year, over 1.75 million Pengo by March 1946, 59 billion Pengo by April 1946, and over 460 septillions by July that year (He, 2017). 1 septillion is 1 followed by 24 zeroes!!!

The Hungarian government undertook failed measures to counter hyperinflation. In December 1945, it imposed a capital levy of 75% by forcing consumers to return 400 Pengö and receive 100 Pengo as legal tender (He, 2017). Nevertheless, it did not stop printing money. The government was forced to introduce the Adopengö as an inflation indexed currency. However, the Adopengö succumbed to the pressures of hyperinflation and was valued at 2 million trillion to a single Pengö (He, 2017).

The situation in Hungary was so critical that the government had to embrace various unique currencies. Printing new currencies was one of the solutions adopted by the government to stabilize the economy and mitigate the effects of the hyperinflation. It started by reducing wages by over 80%, which pushed many people into poverty (He, 2017). Many creditors were wiped out because production and manufacturing failed to recover. This helped the government to achieve its goal of stimulating and reviving production and raising the country's industrial capacity. Most stagnant industries like railroads and factories started working again and replenished the lost capital stock. The main losers were consumers and workers who lost over three-quarters of their wages and lacked credit services since all creditors had been wiped out (Stojković, 2019).

The Deleveraging

The solution adopted by the government was to change the currency name. The Pengö was replaced with the Milpengö, which was equivalent to 1 million Pengö. The Milpengö was replaced by the Bilpengö which was equivalent to 1000000000000 Pengö (He, 2017). The situation became so dire that consumers identified notes by their color and not value. Cashiers would say to consumers that a product cost one blue and two greens instead of stating the currency value, which they found confusing. By August 1946, the Forint had replaced the devalued Pengö and was valued at 400000 Quadrillion Pengö (Stojković, 2019). 1 Quadrillion is 1 followed by 12 zeroes. However, later measures relatively stabilized prices and by 1960, all Pengös had been discarded because they were worthless.

Politically, the fate of Hungary was sealed by the communist regime in 1949, which seized power after the war and changed the Republic of Hungary into the People's Republic of Hungary. The new republic modeled and adopted financial, monetary, and constitutional models similar to those of the Soviet Union.

Did Hungary Recover? A Historical Perspective

From 1938-1948, annualized change in GDP per capita was better in Hungary than in Germany, Greece, or Romania. I picked 1948 as the endpoint since it was a couple of years after WWII, giving the affected nations time to recuperate. Nonetheless, both Yugoslavia and Italy performed better than compared Hungary in this period. The annualized change in GDP per capita for Hungary between 1938 and 1946 was higher than in Germany and Greece, however, lower than in Italy (Kumar, 2015). From information on production across sectors, it is obvious that Hungary's economy, regardless of hyperinflation, was able to recuperate from WWII.

Figure 4. *100 quintillion (1020) pengő, the largest denomination bill ever issued, Hungary,*

Source - Wikipedia

By 1948, GDP per capita was 83% of pre-war levels. Sectors like coal and railway had recuperated to around comparative levels. Examinations of GDP per capita to close nations show that Hungary had a better recovery than most of her neighbors. This, notwithstanding, doesn't permit us to decide the degree to which hyperinflation influenced their economy. (Kumar, 2015).

Conclusion

Hyperinflation is a rarity in an economy. As discussed in the different cases of extreme inflation in this book, hyperinflation is detrimental to countries. While hyperinflation has become an increasingly popular topic today, few people around the globe understand the toll it has on the common man and the future of generations to come. The subject has become popular because similar situations that later lead to hyperinflation are being witnessed today. Hyperinflation presents governments with circumstances that render them helpless. The various instances of hyperinflation discussed in this book open the lid to a comparable pattern of government becoming desperate and introducing policies that worsen the inflation problem. Most hyperinflations have a catalyst. The catalyst can be an external shock, such as war, famine, or a pandemic, or internal mismanagement of resources. The trigger causes mild to moderate inflation that starts damaging the economy. The Government panics and starts printing money to fix economic problems.

This creates more inflation and further craters the economy, making the Government print even more. This cycle continues till hyperinflation. It's comparable to a person addicted to heroin. The person needs a little heroine at first to feel good and forget about the problems in life. Once the high wears off, he feels terrible at having to return to everyday life. He again takes the same amount of the drug. Since his body has adapted to that amount of the drug, he needs even more heroin to get the same high. And this cycle continues till the person dies or goes into rehab. (Credit: George Gammon Youtube Channel)

Governments that have independent central banks rarely experience extreme cases of hyperinflation, as they are quick to remove the fiscal stimulus. In retrospect, enhancing the independence of a country's central bank helps a country evade the menace of hyperinflation.

The end... almost!

Reviews are not easy to come by.

As an independent author with a tiny marketing budget, I rely on readers, like you, to leave a short review on Amazon.

Even if it's just a sentence or two!

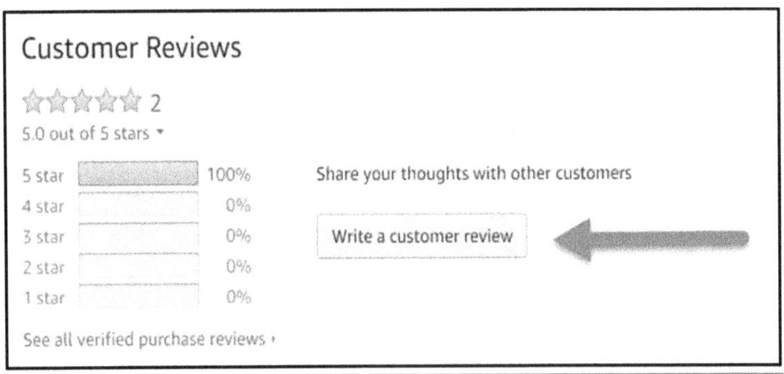

I am very appreciative for your review as it truly makes a difference.

Thank you from the bottom of my heart for purchasing this book and reading it to the end.

Bonus

As you are probably used to not getting enough for your money in an inflationary environment, we've decided to buck the trend and actually give you an extra example of Hyperinflation – The recent Hyperinflation in Zimbabwe under Robert Mugabe.

Hyperinflation in Zimbabwe

Zimbabwe's hyperinflation story is one of the worst in recent history. It's a story of mismanagement and corruption. Zimbabwe had always been plagued by high inflation. Zimbabwe had rates of inflation around 10% in the 1980's and 1990's. It started spiking in 2000 and reached 100% in 2001. That sparked off a period of increasing inflation.

In 2006, the inflation rate rose to over 1500% annually and by September that year, it entered an extended period of hyperinflation. By the year 2009, Zimbabwe was experiencing record hyperinflation of over 80 billion percent every month. By January the same year, the country had experienced a decade of high inflation above 100% every year since 2001 (Matiashe, 2021). As of 2018, inflation in Zimbabwe rose to 10% and jumped dramatically to 622% in 2020 as shown in Figure 1.

Figure 1. *Zimbabwe inflation rate from 1985-2025*

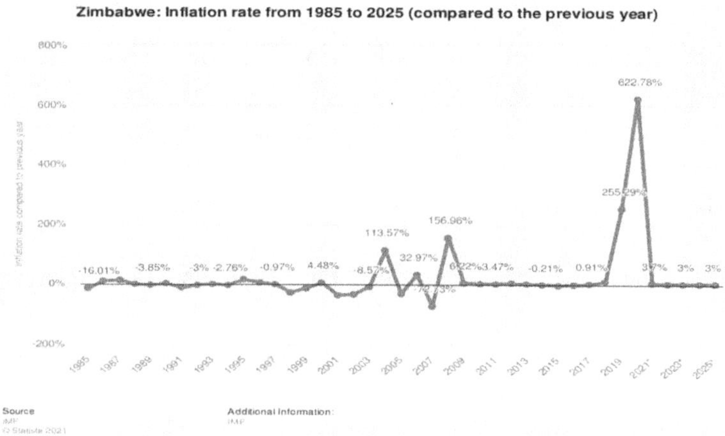

Source: (O'Neill, 2021).

The financial crisis in Zimbabwe was caused by a combination of factors. These causes were linked to poor governance and establishment of inappropriate polices. The Zimbabwean land reforms during Mugabe's regime are an excellent example of poor decision-making that exacerbated the effects of the hyperinflation. In the early 2000s, Mugabe orchestrated a paramilitary mission that involved the seizure of more than 23 million acres from commercial owners and foreigners (Matiashe,

2021). The objective here was to shift ownership of the property rights to the local population. The confiscated land was given to would-be farmers who lacked knowledge on commercial farming. This was a huge blow to the agricultural sector, which was the country's biggest source of revenue. When the new landowners failed to handle commercial production, they went back to subsistence farming causing a shortage in food production. The ripple effect of the land seizure also had a detrimental impact on food processing companies and exporters that eventually shut down their operations.

Background

To understand the reasons behind Zimbabwe's hyperinflation, it is important to have a look at the skewed land reforms, corruption and misguided policies. The initial impetus to Zimbabwe's Road to hyperinflation was from unwise fiscal policies needed to pacify populist groups. This worsened the situation as influential people wanted resources for free (Kairiza, 2012). These resources were being taken from foreign investors with property in the country and handed over to local citizens.

With corruption rife, political and influential figures in the government grabbed majority of the lucrative resources. The move caused investors to exit the country and refrain from trading with the Zimbabwean currency. This resulted in depreciation and cost-push inflation. The subsequent fall in production that accompanied the set land reforms and resultant turbulences in the agricultural sector further worsened the situation. In addition, the central bank was compromised by the ruling party since it was getting funds from state coffers to amass wealth and influence.

Robert Mugabe's rhetoric on confiscating white-owned land was elevated in the 2000s when war veterans assumed prominent seats in the ruling ZANU PF party. As a result, the country's agricultural output fell from 18% of GDP in 2000 to 14% in 2002 (World Bank, 2008).

Tobacco, which is one of Zimbabwe's top foreign exchange earners was also greatly affected, as shown in Figure 2. Export proceeds from tobacco fell from $612 million in 1999 to $321 million in 2003. Failing agricultural output meant that the government could no longer service its debt obligations, which prompted the international financial institutions to suspend further lending to the country.

Figure 2. *Tobacco output (in millions of Dollars) from 1999-2004*

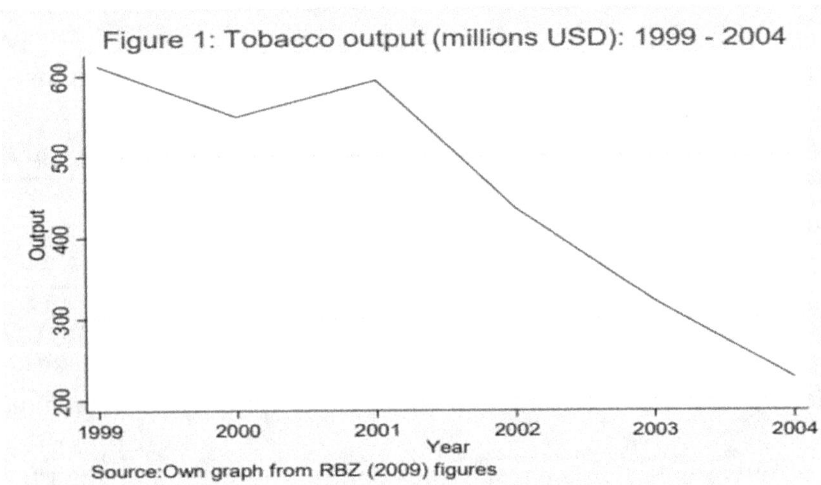

Source: (Reserve Bank of Zimbabwe RBZ, 2021)

By 2008, the country had the second-highest hyperinflation rate in the world which stood at 79 billion percent by November that year. The daily inflation rate was 98%. Prices for all commodities doubled every new day and there was an unemployment rate of 80%. In a bid to save the country from complete ruin, the government became desperate and begun to overprint money in response to the economic shocks.

The First Signs of Hyperinflation

After independence, Zimbabwean authorities launched economic reforms to liberalize the economy and deal with structural barriers to growth. However, there was also an addition of weak fiscal and monetary policies in place. In early 1999, the actions led to a scale-back of assistance from foreign donors and financial institutions (Coomer and Gstraunthaler, 2011). By the start of the new millennium, the country's economy had turned precarious. Inflation began to accelerate after mid-2001 when government borrowing advanced towards the statutory limit set at 20% of the previous year's earnings. Despite this, the government blamed it on avaricious profiteering as opposed to a result of the RBZ's weak monetary policies. Economic deterioration and the road towards hyperinflation began in the first five months of 2005. Annual inflation rates stabilized to 135% in early 2005 and shot up to 164% by June. This mirrored the slackening of monetary policy and decline in foreign exchange. Coomer and Gstraunthaler (2011) state that by 2006, interest rates remained deeply negative with exchange rates against the US dollar sitting at 135,000 Zimbabwean dollars to one US dollar. The money market returns were elevated and the RBZ introduced index-linked, single-yield treasury bills. Figure 3 below shows a 100 trillion-dollar note printed by the Zimbabwean Reserve Bank.

Figure 3. *One hundred trillion dollar note from Zimbabwe*

Source: (Pettinger, 2019)

Zimbabwe officially entered hyperinflation – reaching an annual rate of 2200% and a monthly rate of 50.54% - in March 2007 (Coomber, 2010). Throughout the rest of 2007, Zimbabwe's manufacturing output declined by over 50% (Dewa et al, 2013). Once the inflation rate shot over the threshold of hyperinflation, the erosion of the country's tax base deteriorated. By May 2009, the annual inflation rate surpassed 1000%. Monetary supply figures for that year indicated that the growth rate stood at over 1400%.

By 2008, hyperinflation had begun gaining momentum hitting over 400000% in March. In December the same year, the foreign currency used as a medium of exchange was rendered useless, unofficially. This marked the initial unsanctioned dollarization in Zimbabwe. As of January 2009, the finance minister authorized the legal use of the US dollar and the SA Rand thus affirming official dollarization (Kairiza, 2012). Hyperinflation continued being fueled by weak quasi-fiscal activities that culminated in a swift increase in bank deposits with the reserve bank thereby increasing local currency. As Coomer and Gstraunthaler (2011) illustrate, by the end of 2008, reserve money fell from USD 7 million to an exchange rate of 35 quadrillion Zimbabwean dollars per one US dollar.

The Hyperinflation Years

Towards the end of 2008, Zimbabwe was undergoing one of the worst hyperinflation rates in history. According to the Economic Times (2008), a loaf of bread cost the equivalent of twelve new cars whereas a packet of locally-produced coffee cost 1 billion Zimbabwean dollars. At the peak of hyperinflation, commodity prices doubled daily. Commodities like gasoline had to be traded in US dollars or SA Rands and barter trade became common. Zimbabwean currency became almost worthless as shown in Figure 4 below.

Figure 4. *Zimbabweans out crying over the hyperinflation*

Source: (*mhseconomics*, 2016)

As mentioned earlier, the hyperinflation in Zimbabwe did not occur overnight and was the product of a prolonged decline in the country's economic growth. The unprecedented market forces had adversely affected the economy leading to economic stagnation. Sources revealed that the agricultural and manufacturing sectors were failing long before the outbreak of the financial crisis. The country was also facing an increase in the national debt that became a hefty burden for the taxpayers. With reduced productivity, the economy exhibited a downward spiral that perpetuated the inflationary period. The government, too, played a significant role in exacerbating the situation, by implementing inappropriate policy reforms that caused a decline in economic growth. All the factors that led to hyperinflation seem to be correlated and culminated in severe consequences to the public.

Assessing the level of inflation in Zimbabwe is complex given that the government deliberately failed to post inflation statistics. However, using Cagan's definition of hyperinflation, the conclusion is that the country began to experience hyperinflation in February 2007. The height of the hyperinflation was in November 2008 as shown in Figure 5.

Figure 5. *Zimbabwe's official hyperinflation rate 1980-2008*

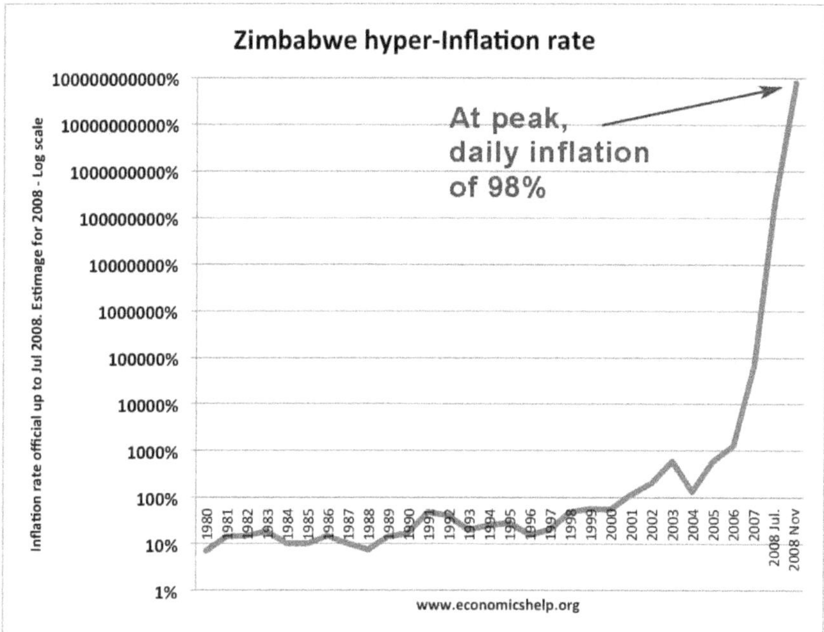

Source: (Pettinger, 2019).

Consumer Behavior during the Inflationary Period

One of the noteworthy effects of hyperinflation in Zimbabwe is that it eroded the consumer's purchasing power. According to the law of demand, an increase in the price of commodities causes a decline in the public's ability to purchase commodities. Hyperinflation is characterized by a prolonged period of more than a 50% monthly rise in the market's cost of goods and services. As a result, it becomes daunting for the consumer to afford basic needs such as food, shelter and clothing. This was the situation in Zimbabwe during the inflationary period. According to Conkling (2010), the price for commodities was increasing at a higher rate than the income and wages of the consumers. Since the income level did not keep pace with the country's inflation, most Zimbabweans couldn't afford basic items such as bread and milk. The cost of living, particularly for those residing in urban areas like Harare, became too much for ordinary people to bear (Conkling, 2010). Urban residents and those who had relocated to the city for employment had to compensate and forego luxuries to thrive and survive the financial crisis. The progression of the challenging economic times culminated in a scenario whereby the citizens experienced prices doubling every day. For instance, a loaf of bread would cost twice as much today as it was yesterday. Such price increases hit the media by storm and cast a spotlight on the country's failing economy.

The government responded by printing more money to offset national debt and cushion the economic shocks the country encountered at the time. This money creation approach adopted by the government aimed to reassure the public and improve people's faith in the government. Consumers lost their confidence in the Zimbabwean dollar, devaluing rapidly against other currencies. For instance, people required millions to purchase essential commodities like bread. According to Baldauf (2008), the average price of a loaf of bread during the inflationary period was approximately 10 million Zimbabwe dollars. The consumers were forced to embrace the use of foreign currencies when purchasing goods and commodities. When the government refrained from further printing money, the people relied on currencies such as the Rand and the American dollar as the accepted medium of exchange.

Inflation was officially declared illegal in 2007 by the government to prevent further increases in prices. This permitted arrests of any businessmen who hiked the prices of goods and services in the Zimbabwean market. Implementing price controls only resulted in more financial problems for the country, instead of stopping inflation. The government's attempts to regulate prices in the economy, coupled with the inability of the agricultural sector to supply food, led to massive shortages. Productivity had dwindled, and business entities had to import foreign commodities to sell to the consumers. The use of foreign currency made it easier for such individuals to import commodities and engage in daily transactions with consumers. For consumers, they needed to switch to other currencies because retaining the Zimbabwe dollar was cumbersome. People were forced to use millions to purchase simple items like bread and milk (Baldauf, 2008).

The government was compelled to adopt the multi-currency system to sustain businesses and other economic activities. Local shops were established in a bid to enable the citizenry to buy foreign currency. However, the demand for foreign currency facilitated by the multi-currency system attracted the attention of the black market. A shadow market existed outside the legal space that provided currency exchange services for citizens who needed to convert their Zimbabwe dollars before it dropped in value. Additionally, the black market provided certain commodities consumed daily by the households in the region. The low productivity in Zimbabwe created a shortage of daily consumables like bread, soap, and in extreme cases, groceries. The people were going through hard times that made life in the country unbearable. The transportation sector was among the industries that were worst affected during the inflationary period. Commuters and bus drivers had to deal with the unprecedented changes in oil prices and currency exchange.

Most of the foreigners living in the region fled the financial crisis. Zimbabwe had received sanctions from the international community that made the region unattractive for foreign investment. The unemployment rate during the economic crisis had reached a record-high of over 70% (Conkling, 2010). With most citizens rendered jobless, the income level couldn't keep up with the inflation. Additionally, the manufacturing and agricultural sectors were underperforming, causing some of the companies to shut down. The high unemployment in the country subjected most of the families in Harare and other areas to abject poverty. The hoarding of perishable commodities was also witnessed among consumers and suppliers. As the money in the economy lost value, people opted for barter trade, where commodities were exchanged for other services and goods. The economy later switched to the American dollar to salvage business activities and prevent further financial problems.

Deleveraging

As mentioned earlier, poor decision-making by the government played a crucial role in exacerbating the inflation. The devaluing of the Zimbabwean dollar had far-reaching consequences. The only feasible solution for the economy was adopting a foreign currency. This led to the demonetization that allowed the switch to the American dollar in 2015 (Conkling, 2010). Since then, most of the transactions in the country were in either American dollars or the South African Rand. The new regime that took the reins of power after Mugabe was ousted, outlawed the use of foreign currency. The decision saw the creation of a new local currency. Despite this, the country is on the verge of another financial crisis, with reports that the price for commodities has increased over the past half-decade. Zimbabwe is yet to fully recover from the 2008 hyperinflation, and citizens face challenges coping with the current economic situation. The International Monetary Fund has ranked Zimbabwe second to Venezuela for having the highest current inflation levels in the world.

References

Intro

Toscano, P. (2014). The Worst Hyperinflation Situations of All Time. Retrieved 31 May 2021, from https://www.cnbc.com/2011/02/14/The-Worst-Hyperinflation-Situations-of-All-Time.html

Civil War HyperInflation

Doyle, B. G. (2001). Hyperinflation and the confederacy: an interdisciplinary lesson in economics and history. *Social Education*, *65*(6), 366-373.

Lerner, E (1955). “Money, Prices, and Wages in the Confederacy: 1861-1865,” *Journal of Political Economy* 63: 20-40.

Library of Congress (n.d). *Confederate flag flying.* https://www.loc.gov/resource/ppmsca.32284/

Rhodes, J. F., & Long, E. B. (1999). *History of the civil war, 1861-1865*. Courier Corporation.

U.S. Department of Commerce (1949). *Historical Statistics of the United States 1789-1945.* [PDF]. https://www2.census.gov/prod2/statcomp/documents/HistoricalStatisticsoftheUnitedStates1789-1945.pdf

Inflation and hyper definition

Amadeo, K. (2020). Could You Survive Hyperinflation?. Retrieved 31 May 2021, from https://www.thebalance.com/what-is-hyperinflation-definition-causes-and-examples-3306097

Salemi, M. (2021). Hyperinflation - Econlib. Retrieved 31 May 2021, from https://www.econlib.org/library/Enc/Hyperinflation.html

Venezuela

Caraballo-Arias, Y., Madrid, J., & Barrios, M. C. (2018). Working in Venezuela: how the crisis has affected the labor conditions. *Annals of global health, 84*(3), 512.

Population Pyramid of World from 1950 – 2100 (2019). *Population Pyramid.* [Image] Retrieved from https://www.populationpyramid.net/

Venezuela Money Supply (2021). *Trading Economics.* [Image]. Retrieved from https://tradingeconomics.com/venezuela/money-supply-m2

Multimore, J. (2021). Reuters: Cash 'Disappearing' in Venezuela despite Hyperinflation. *Foundation for Economic Education.* Retrieved from https://fee.org/articles/reuters-cash-disappearing-in-venezuela-despite-hyperinflation/

Koech, J. (2016). Oil-Rich Venezuela Tips Toward Hyperinflation. *Annual Report, Globalization and Monetary Policy Institute*, 4-11.

Pittaluga, G. B., Seghezza, E., & Morelli, P. (2021). The political economy of hyperinflation in Venezuela. *Public Choice*, *186*(3), 337-350.

Huertas, G. (2019). Hyperinflation in Venezuela: A Stabilization Handbook. Retrieved from https://www.piie.com/sites/default/files/documents/pb19-13.pdf

Zimbabwe

Baldauf, S. (2008, March 25). In Zimbabwe, bread costs Z$10 million. Retrieved from https://www.csmonitor.com/World/Africa/2008/0325/p06s02-woaf.html

Banque internationale pour la reconstruction et le développement. (2008). *Migration and Remittances Factbook.* World Bank

Conkling, T. S. (2010). Analysis of the Zimbabwean Hyperinflation Crisis: A Search for Policy Solutions (Doctoral dissertation, Pennsylvania State University).

Coomer, J., & Gstraunthaler, T. (2011). The Hyperinflation in Zimbabwe. *Quarterly Journal of Austrian economics*, *14*(3).

Dewa, D., Musara, E., & Mupfururi, E. (2013). Industrial decline in Zimbabwe, Gweru post-2000: Which way now. *World Journal of Arts, Commerce, and Sciences*, *1*(1), 1-13.

Kairiza, T. (2012). *Unbundling Zimbabwe's journey to hyperinflation and official dollarization, GRIPS Policy Information Centre* (No. 09-12). Discussion Paper.

Matiashe, F. S. (2021, January 28). Zimbabwe: Can the central bank hold rate as inflation soars? Retrieved from https://www.theafricareport.com/61176/zimbabwe-can-the-central-bank-hold-rate-as-inflation-soars/

Times, T. E. (2008, June 13). Zimbabwe inflation now over 1 million percent. Retrieved from economictimes.indiatimes.com: https://economictimes.indiatimes.com/news/international/zimbabwe-inflation-now-over-1-million-per-cent/articleshow/3126631.cms

Inflation. (2021). *Starving Billionaire*. (2016). MHSECONOMICS. Retrieved from https://mhseco2016.wordpress.com/2016/04/25/starving-billionaire/

Pettinger, T. (2021). *Hyper Inflation in Zimbabwe* [Image]. Retrieved from https://www.economicshelp.org/blog/390/inflation/hyper-inflation-in-zimbabwe/

O'Neill, A. (2021). *Zimbabwe: Inflation rate from 1985 to 2025* [Image]. Retrieved from https://www.statista.com/statistics/455290/inflation-rate-in-zimbabwe/

Mzimkhulu, L. (2019). *A Zimbabwean child carrying large currency bills* [Image]. Retrieved from https://iharare.com/boy-carriying-huge-amounts-of-cash-in-a-sign-of-zimbabwes-hyperinflation-11-years-later/

Hungary

Bomberger, W. A., & Makinen, G. E. (1980). Indexation, inflationary finance, and hyperinflation: the 1945-1946 Hungarian experience. *Journal of Political Economy*, *88*(3), 550-560.

Bomberger, W. A., & Makinen, G. E. (1983). The Hungarian hyperinflation and stabilization of 1945-1946. *Journal of Political Economy*, *91*(5), 801-824.

Boross, E. A. (2015). The Role of the State Issuing Bank in the Course of Inflation in Hungary between 1918 and 1924. In *Die Erfahrung der Inflation im internationalen Zusammenhang und Vergleich/The Experience of Inflation*

International and Comparative Studies (pp. 188-227). De Gruyter.

He, L. (2017). *Hyperinflation: A world history*. Routledge.

Kumar, V. (2015). The Hungarian Hyperinflation–A Look into the Production Side. *Studies in Applied Economics*, *42*.

KUMAR, V. (2020). The Hungarian hyperinflation: A look into the production side. *Journal of Economics Library*, *7*(1), 54-68.

Siklos, P. L. (1989). The end of the Hungarian hyperinflation of 1945-1946. *Journal of Money, Credit and Banking*, *21*(2), 135-147.

Siklos, P. L. (Ed.). (1995). *Great inflations of the 20th century: theories, policies, and evidence*. Edward Elgar Publishing.

Valkovszky, S., & Vincze, J. (2012). Estimates of and problems with core inflation in Hungary. *Central Bank Review*, *1*(1), 69-99.

Weimar Republic

Amadeo, K. (2020). Could You Survive Hyperinflation?. Retrieved 31 May 2021, from https://www.thebalance.com/what-is-hyperinflation-definition-causes-and-examples-3306097

Pettinger, T. (2021). *Hyper Inflation in Zimbabwe* [Image]. Retrieved from https://www.economicshelp.org/blog/634/economics/the-problem-with-printing-money/

Haffert, L., Redeker, N., & Rommel, T. (2019). Misremembering Weimar: Hyperinflation, the Great Depression, and German Collective Economic Memory. *Economics & Politics.*

The Weimar Republic: The Fragility of Democracy (2012). Facing History. Retrieved from https://www.facinghistory.org/weimar-republic-fragility-democracy/economics/inflated-weimar-currency-1923-economics-1919-1924-inflation

Lessons from the Past - Hyperinflation in Weimar Germany (2021). Stewart Investors. Retrieved from https://www.stewartinvestors.com/all/insights/stap/hyperinflation-in-germany.html

Salemi, M. (nd). Hyperinflation. Econlib. Retrieved from https://www.econlib.org/library/Enc/Hyperinflation.html

Hanke, S. (2007). The World's Greatest Unreported Hyperinflation. Cato. Retrieved from https://www.cato.org/commentary/worlds-greatest-unreported-hyperinflation?queryID=5d3023212546a02921dbd9abd48e1922

Goodell, N. (2018). 1920s Hyperinflation in Germany and Banknotes. Retrieved from https://www.spurlock.illinois.edu/blog/p/1920s-hyperinflation-in/283

Pardon, K. (2013). Wheelbarrows of Money. Keripardon Blog. [Image]. Retrieved from https://keripeardon.wordpress.com/2013/06/01/wheelbarrows-of-money-and-the-weimar-republic/

Hyperinflation in Weimar (n.d). Research Online. Retrieved from https://researchonline.jcu.edu.au/21599/3/21599.pdf

France

Brezis, E. S., & Crouzet, F. H. (1995). The role of Assignats during the French Revolution: an evil or a rescuer? *Journal of European economic history*, *24*(1), 7.

Trask, S. (2020). Inflation and the French Revolution: The Story of a Monetary Catastrophe. Mises Daily Articles. Retrieved from https://mises.org/library/inflation-and-french-revolution-story-monetary-catastrophe

Velde, F. R., & Weir, D. R. (1992). The financial market and government debt policy in France, 1746-1793. *Journal of Economic History*, 1-39.

France: Inflation and Revolution. (2016). American Numismatic Society. [Image]. Retrieved from http://numismatics.org/france-inflation-and-revolution/

Sargent, T. J., & Velde, F. R. (1995). Macroeconomic features of the French Revolution. *Journal of Political Economy*, *103*(3), 474-518.

Ebeling, R. (2007). The Great French Inflation. Foundation of Economic Education. Retrieved from https://fee.org/articles/the-great-french-inflation/

North Korea

He, L. (2017). *Hyperinflation: A world history*. Routledge.

Powell, B. (2009). Economic 'Reform' in North Korea: Nuking the Won. *Time*. Retrieved from http://content.time.com/time/world/article/0,8599,1945251,00.html

Eberstadt, N. (2010). North Korean Money Troubles. WSJ. Retrieved from https://www.wsj.com/articles/SB10001424052748704500104574651090133811018

Hanke, S. (2013). North Korea: From Hyperinflation to Dollarization. Globe Asia. Retrieved from http://centerforfinancialstability.org/oped/NorthKoreaJuly13.pdf

Pearson, J. (2015). North Korea's Black Market Becoming the New Norm. Reuters. Retrieved from https://www.reuters.com/article/us-northkorea-change-insight-idUSKCN0SN00320151029

Yugoslavia

Cunningham, R., Desroches, B., & Santor, E. (2010). Inflation expectations and the conduct of monetary policy: A review of recent evidence and experience. Bank of Canada Review, 2010(Spring), 13-25.

Hanke, S. (2007). The World's Greatest Unreported Hyperinflation. Cato. Retrieved from https://www.cato.org/commentary/worlds-greatest-unreported-hyperinflation?queryID=5d3023212546a02921dbd9abd48e1922. USDCrisis. Retrieved from

He, L. (2017). Hyperinflation: A world history. Routledge.

Petrović, P., Bogetić, Ž, & Vujošević, Z. (1999). The Yugoslav hyperinflation of 1992–1994: causes, dynamics, and money supply process. Journal of comparative economics, 27(2), 335-353.

Stojković, M. Hyperinflation in Yugoslavia: An Example in Monetary History. Open Journal for, 43.

Taylor, A. (2012). 20 Years since the Bosnia War. The Atlantic. Retrieved from https://www.theatlantic.com/photo/2012/04/20-years-since-the-bosnian-war/100278/

Watkins, T. (2010). The Danger of printing too much Money. USDCrisis. [Image]. Retrieved from https://usdcrisis.com/history/the-danger-of-printing-too-much-money/

Ancient Rome

Andreu, J., & Blanco-Pérez, A. (2019). Signs of weakness and crisis in the Western cities of the Roman Empire (c. II–III AD). https://d1wqtxts1xzle7.cloudfront.net

Bhardwaj, D. (2020). Unit-4 Crisis of the Roman Empire. Indira Gandhi National Open University, New Delhi. http://www.egyankosh.ac.in/bitstream/123456789/67912/1/Unit-4.pdf

Butcher, K. (2015). Debasement and the decline of Rome. *Studies in ancient coinage in honor of Andrew Burnett. SPINK, London*, 181-205. https://warwick.ac.uk

Dimitrijevic, M., & Golubovic, S. (2017). Monetary System of the Ancient Rome: Implications on Contemporary Monetary Law. *Ius Romanum*, 313. https://heinonline.org

He, L. (2017). *Hyperinflation: A world history*. Routledge. https://doi.org/10.4324/9780203712061

Heather, P. J. (2018). *Rome resurgent: war and empire in the age of Justinian*. Oxford University Press. https://books.google.co.uk

Horesh, N. (2020). 2. From Coinage to Paper Money. In *Chinese Money in Global Context* (pp. 41-8 https://doi.org/10.1515/9780804788540-005

Parsons, T. (2010). *The rule of empires: those who built them, those who endured them, and why they always fall*. Oxford University Press. https://books.google.co.ke

Stange, N. (2021). Politics of Plague: Ancient Epidemics and Their Impact on Society. https://scholarship.claremont.edu/cclura_2021/4

United States

Aizenman, J., & Marion, N. (2011). Using inflation to erode the US public debt. *Journal of Macroeconomics*, *33*(4), 524-541. https://doi.org/10.1016/j.jmacro.2011.09.001

Baack, B. (2008). America's first monetary policy: inflation and seigniorage during the Revolutionary War. *Financial History Review*, *15*(2), 107. DOI:10.1017/S0968565008000127

Berg, E. (2021). Centralizing the Purse: Why a More Centralized National Government Was Crucial for Managing America's Revolutionary War Debt. https://digitalcommons.wku.edu/stu_hon_theses/899

Bezanson, A. (2016). *Prices and Inflation During the American Revolution, Pennsylvania, 1770-1790*. University of Pennsylvania Press. https://doi.org/10.9783/9781512814439

Bredin, D., & Fountas, S. (2018). US inflation and inflation uncertainty over 200 years. https://ruomo.lib.uom.gr

Ferraro, W. M. (2021). Washington's Revolutionary War Generals.

Hamilton, E. J. (1977). The role of war in modern inflation. *Journal of Economic History*, 13-19. https://www.jstor.org/stable/2119441

Hildebrand, D. K. (2018). The Revolutionary War and War of 1812. In *Music and War in the United States* (pp. 20-40). Routledge. ISBN 9781315194981

https://doi.org/10.1093/jahist/jaaa537

Taskinsoy, J. (2020). From Primitive Barter to Inflationary Dollar: A Warless Economic Weapon of Mass Destruction. *Available at SSRN 3542145*. https://dx.doi.org/10.2139/ssrn.3542145

China

Ebeling, R. (2014, March 21). *China's Great Inflation Helped Bring Communists to Power.* The Nassau Institute. https://www.nassauinstitute.org/article1211/

Ebeling, R. M. (2010, July 5). *The Great Chinese Inflation | Richard M. Ebeling.* Fee.org; Foundation for Economic Education. https://fee.org/articles/the-great-chinese-inflation/

Habegger, J. (1988, September). *Origins of the Chinese Hyperinflation | Jay Habegger.* Fee.org; Foundation for Economic Education. https://fee.org/articles/origins-of-the-chinese-hyperinflation/

Hewitt, M. (2007, May 22). *Hyperinflation in China, 1937 - 1949:: The Market Oracle::* www.marketoracle.co.uk. https://www.marketoracle.co.uk/Article1068.html

Inflation and CPI Consumer Price Index 1940-1949. (n.d.). InflationData.com. https://inflationdata.com/articles/inflation-consumer-price-index-decade-commentary/inflation-cpi-consumer-price-index-1940-1949/

www.ingramcontent.com/pod-product-compliance
Lightning Source LLC
LaVergne TN
LVHW052206200926
848481LV00001B/41

9781922659194